LAUGH LINES

Other Books by Alan Zweibel

North

Bunny Bunny: Gilda Radner—A Sort of Love Story

Our Tree Named Steve

The Other Shulman: A Novel

Clothing Optional: And Other Ways to Read These Stories

Lunatics (with Dave Barry)

Benjamin Franklin: Huge Pain in my . . . (with Adam Mansbach)

Benjamin Franklin: You've Got Mail (with Adam Mansbach)

For This We Left Egypt?: A Passover Haggadah for Jews and Those Who Love Them (with Dave Barry and Adam Mansbach)

A Field Guide to the Jewish People: Who They Are, Where They Come From, What to Feed Them . . . and Much More. Maybe Too Much More (with Dave Barry and Adam Mansbach)

LAUGH LINES

MY LIFE HELPING
FUNNY PEOPLE BE FUNNIER

A Cultural Memoir

ALAN ZWEIBEL

ABRAMS PRESS, NEW YORK

Library of Congress Control Number: 2019939897

ISBN: 978-1-4197-3528-8
eISBN: 978-1-68335-683-7

Printed and bound in the United States
10 9 8 7 6 5 4 3 2 1

Abrams books are available at special discounts when purchased in quantity for premiums and promotions as well as fundraising or educational use. Special editions can also be created to specification. For details, contact specialsales@abramsbooks.com or the address below.

Abrams Press® is a registered trademark of Harry N. Abrams, Inc.

ABRAMS The Art of Books
195 Broadway, New York, NY 10007
abramsbooks.com

For my sister

Franny

I loved making her laugh

"To make it in the writing biz, just stay incompetent/unemployable at anything else."

—MARY KARR

CONTENTS

FOREWORD

Billy Crystal

WRITING A FOREWORD to a great friend's memoir is not unlike trying to write a perfect eulogy. The difference, of course, is that Alan Zweibel is very much alive, and whoever will read this is not grieving and hoping that there is going to be good food at the reception at the house after, or, if you're a comedian friend, you're not praying that I don't reference something you have in your eulogy forcing you into a rewrite on the spot . . . so here goes.

I've always been amazed that in this world there is someone who is skilled at something that others can't do. Plumbers plumb, sculptors sculpt, painters paint, weightlifters lift, bronco riders ride broncos, watchmakers make watches, surgeons surge, welders weld . . . Alan Zweibel writes. He writes all kinds of wonderful things. Starting his career with jokes for cummerbunded comics, to sketches and character monologues for the funny people who changed the face of comedy altogether, to wonderfully witty and telling short stories and novels and hundreds, maybe thousands, of after-dinner talks, lectures, television appearances, benefits, tributes, small-claims-court pleas, Bar and Bat Mitzvah speeches, the ones he gave and the ones he wrote for his kids, children's books and grandchildren's birthday cards and humorous tweets—are all attacked with the same fervor and dedication to making it funny, and grammatically correct to boot.

I love working with Alan and watching his focused mania/glee in putting words in the right order. I think that is what makes him the happiest, and that is what this book is about. I watch him scrutinize a word, a verb, a noun, a parenthetical, an exclamation point, even the amount of . . . in-between words that would show a character hesitating to find the right . . . word.

We started out as stand-up comedians in our twenties and have grown older together in many of the shared galaxies in the comedy universe. When we were puppies, I would pick him up at his parents' home in Woodmere, Long Island, in my $2,100 VW bug and we'd make the hour drive into New York City together. We'd hope to get on to do a set at a reasonable time at Catch a Rising Star, which meant by 1:00 A.M., and then we'd drive home together listening to our cassette tapes of our sets and help each other get better.

He is in some ways not your typical Jewish comedy writer. First off, he's over five foot seven . . . he doesn't smoke or drink, looks bad in baseball hats, will buy retail, and is now vegan, but does like his carrots "lean."

He is also a great person, a unique friend, and a loving husband, father, and grandpa. I don't know of anyone who doesn't have a kind thing to say about Alan . . . except Alan.

Sometimes he will joke about his Ice Capades character–size head or his terrible sense of direction. He must have been a direct descendant of the ancient Jews who took forty years to go from Egypt to Israel when WAZE basically said go straight for three days, part the Red Sea, and you've arrived at your destination.

If life were a forties movie, Alan would be called "a big lug." He is a large man with a sensitive persona and a heart of gold. His instincts about people and his humanity are why I asked him to work with me on 700 Sundays. Sharing my life's journey, my joys and sorrows, was the task at hand. I had been thinking about a one-man Broadway show that would confront my complex relationship with my late father, who died when I was just fifteen, and the ensuing time with my grieving mother. I thought if I could discuss my grief and still have it be funny and moving, it could be special. I had a four-page outline for the play, as this was not an evening of stand-up but rather a two-act play that had me reliving funny and painful moments as well as portraying a myriad of relatives and characters, including my late parents. I trusted Alan with them. He will bring you his perspective of the experience in chapter ten, but I will tell you that he became a brother to me. Able to confide in and trust and laugh with Alan as we created not just a Tony Award–winning show but a moving and important healing experience for children of all ages is one of the great highlights of my life.

I was twenty-six when we first met; he was twenty-four. I'm now seventy-one and he's sixty-nine, and I'm writing this in the midst of preproduction on *Here Today*—a film we wrote together that I'm going to not only star in but direct as well, and Alan and I are going to produce . . . so there.

One day, after we had done a big rewrite on the script, fine-tuning character arcs and simply making it better, Alan suddenly blurted out how happy and grateful he was that we were getting the chance to do this. In a time where if you're over twenty-five you're old, we're making a funny and emotional movie about real people who don't have superhuman powers. Exhilarated after our work session, we walked to the parking garage where Alan's Lexus was waiting, as he was going to drop me off at my apartment. We drove off with me hoping he remembered how to get me home. I looked at the big lug and smiled. "You know. Al," I said, "here we are, forty-five years later, and once again we're on our way home after work, and the only difference is, now you're driving!"

PREFACE

O THERE I WAS IN 2015 at the cocktail party hosted by NBC before the *Saturday Night Live* "40th Anniversary Special." This evening was all any of us had been talking about for some time.

The previous fall Billy Crystal and I were sitting in a Manhattan Chinese restaurant when Jason Sudeikis came over to our table, introduced himself, and after a brief chat left, saying, "See you at the Fortieth." A few weeks later, I ran into Paul Simon, who told me that he would be touring in Australia but planned to fly back just for the *SNL* 40th and then fly out again shortly afterwards. And even Lorne Michaels, to whom I'd written an e-mail wishing him good luck at the start of the current *SNL* season, wrote back, signing off with "See you at the 40th."

"See you at the 40th" became a mantra among all of us who'd been associated with *Saturday Night Live* over the previous four decades. It was a fraternity whose members felt a real kinship with one another no matter which era of the show they had been a part of. We had the camaraderie of army vets—even when they hadn't served together.

I looked around the room and saw old friends. Elliott Gould. Candice Bergen. Jane Curtin. Laraine Newman. There was Larry David, who is one of my oldest friends. Keith Richards, who'd looked old when the show launched in 1975 and who'd somehow managed to stay looking just as old. There was Penny Marshall sitting at the edge of a huge flowerpot in the center of the atrium. And there was Sir Paul McCartney sipping a glass of wine and chatting with Martin Short while Senator Al

Franken grabbed an hors d'oeuvre from the same passing tray as Jimmy Fallon. And when I went to the men's room, I saw Peyton Manning at the urinal to my left and his brother Eli at the urinal to my right. It was, to the best of my recollection, the first time I'd ever peed between two All-Pro quarterbacks while I was wearing a tuxedo.

Some nerves accompanied the excitement. To begin with, my weight. As I had done with every one of my high school reunions, I started dieting about six months earlier, but was it enough? Or did I stand the chance of overhearing the notoriously quiet Prince, whom I'd never met, come out of his shell long enough to whisper to the notoriously dour Bill O'Reilly, whom I also didn't know, "Boy, it looks like Zweibel has put back those same thirty-five pounds he's been gaining and losing since his Bar Mitzvah."

But the bigger concern, I'm almost embarrassed to admit, had to do with another kind of insecurity. With how I regarded my status in this room. Whether I was content with what I'd accomplished both professionally and personally to account for my time since I'd left the show. Truth was, this was such a formidable crowd that even the most prominent icons in this gathering were craning to see who else was there.

"Jesus, look at all the celebrities that are here," said a familiar voice behind me.

"It is a little intimidating, isn't it?" responded another familiar voice.

I turned around and couldn't help but raise my own voice when I saw exactly who was speaking

"*You're* intimidated!" I yelled at Steven Spielberg and Whoopi Goldberg. "Then how the hell am I supposed to feel?"

"Invisible?" Whoopi asked before giving me a big hug.

"That's about right," I answered.

Comedy writers learn early on that we have a high degree of anonymity. Our words are spoken publicly by others who often have famous faces. Or by unknown people on their way to having famous faces. So the fact that I was hardly a high-profile figure this particular evening was understandable. Still, in the weeks leading up to this reunion, I had taken inventory, given careful consideration to the hits and the foul tips, and concluded that I was fine. I had somehow weathered the challenges of the previous three and a half decades. And though I was humbled by the giant shadows cast by so many around me, I felt confident that I had enough checks in the plus column to comport myself among this collection of cultural overachievers without embarrassment or the need to make excuses.

"Zweibel, I really liked your last book."

Once again I turned around, and this time saw Dan Aykroyd, whom I'd lost touch with and hadn't seen in a couple of years. I had sent him the novel *Lunatics* that I'd co-authored with Dave Barry, but I'd never heard back from him.

"You read it?" I asked.

"No, but my assistant said the thirty pages she read were good and that I'd enjoy it."

"You're such an asshole," I said, laughing.

"I love you, man," he said before enveloping me in a bear hug. I'd forgotten about Danny's bear hugs. Danny is intense. Whoopi's hug didn't hurt. Danny's hurt a lot.

"See you after the show, Zweibs."

He then ran off.

ϟϟϟ

AS THE LIGHTS STARTED FLASHING to signal that we should begin working our way to Studio 8H, I paused to remember it was here that everything had begun for me. It was the fortieth anniversary of the show for which I was one of the original writers. The show that I'd worked on with the Not Ready for Prime Time Players, in addition to Steve Martin, Lily Tomlin, Eric Idle, and my boyhood hero, Buck Henry. It was also the show where I'd met my wife, Robin, who was now holding my hand as we entered Studio 8H as if it were a shrine.

Robin had been a production assistant who joined the show at the beginning of our third season. We fell in love and dated secretly until a big fight in this very studio, at which point our relationship ceased being a secret to everyone at the network. We got married Thanksgiving weekend of the show's fifth season.

"Excited?" Robin asked as we looked around and saw Martin Scorsese and Tom Hanks and Tina Fey and Jerry Seinfeld and, for some ungodly reason, Donald Trump (yes, the same Donald Trump) and the Reverend Al Sharpton (yes, the same the Rev. Al Sharpton) taking their seats.

As I looked around, I also saw the ones who were missing. The ones who had left us since we had all worked here. Gilda, a can of Tab in her hand, off to one side, making members of the crew laugh. Belushi, dressed as a samurai, raising an eyebrow before slicing a tomato with a sword. Fellow writers like Herb Sargent, Tom Davis, and Michael O'Donoghue showing pages with rewritten lines to the actors. Director Dave Wilson blocking a scene while eating a jelly donut. I not only felt their presence but could see them as they were back then. Frozen in time. Forever the same age. Wearing the same clothes. Unaware of what the future had in store for them.

"Yeah, really excited," I answered Robin, emerging from the daze. "Look at what we were so lucky to be a part of."

Like everyone who attended that evening, I was celebrating the longest-running staple in television comedy I had been fortunate to be with, that had provided enormous opportunities for me as a result. The doors it opened. The people I got to work and become friends with. And the life I've been privileged to lead. Tonight would be both a celebration as well as a milestone on a journey that had begun for me some forty-two years earlier. Long before I ever dreamed of peeing between two All-Pro quarterbacks while wearing a tuxedo.

CHAPTER **1**

THE CATSKILLS COMICS

(Writing for the Wrong People)

PLEASE DON'T FUCK the joke up. I beg of you. Say it the way I wrote it.
It was September 1972, and I was seated at a back table in the nightclub of a Catskill Mountains hotel called Kutsher's, nervously waiting to see how the comic onstage was going to deliver one of the jokes I'd written for him. It was a joke about a sperm bank. If it got a laugh, he would pay me $7.00.

> *They have a new thing now called sperm banks. It's like an ordinary bank except here, after you make a deposit, you* lose *interest.*

That was the joke I was waiting for him to deliver. I was twenty-two years old, living at home with my parents after college, and had scribbled that line on a napkin in the delicatessen on Hillside Avenue in Queens, New York, where I was slicing every kind of meat imaginable.

This comic and I were not a great fit. I had long hair, had been to Woodstock (okay, I'd bought the album), and this guy up onstage was wearing a tuxedo that was almost as ill-fitting as his dentures, which looked stunningly like oversize bathroom tiles. But this was a first step into the world of comedy. The real world. Where the objective was to put words into the mouths of comedians who would deliver them to elicit laughs from audiences of strangers.

Ironically, it was not my choice to become a comedy writer at this point in my life. It was actually a decision that was made for me about six months earlier by just about every law school in the United States.

I did well as an undergraduate at the University of Buffalo, but the law boards were another story. Back then the LSATs were graded from 200 to 800. If you could write your name, you got a 200. If you were a Supreme Court justice, you got an 800. If you were Alan Zweibel, you got a 390, which pretty much reclassified me as a mineral. Shortly afterward, I returned home and told my Long Island Jewish parents that I got a 390 on the law boards, and about a week later (after they uncovered the mirrors) my father gave me $1,000, which I then handed to a man named Stanley Kaplan, who had schools all over the country where they taught you how to take standardized tests. So I studied for six months—wearing headphones, using #2 pencils, memorizing flash cards—and retook the law boards and my score catapulted up to a 401. So, figuring that at that rate I'd be about ninety-seven before I got into an English-speaking law school, I decided to take the plunge into the unknown and pursue my real dream.

My Bar Mitzvah. Currently dieting so I can fit back into that snazzy iridescent gray suit.

I'd wanted to be a comedy writer since watching *The Dick Van Dyke Show* on television as a young boy. I was twelve years old when that series first came on the air, and when I saw that Rob Petrie, a TV writer, had a very pretty wife named Laura, lived in a nice house in New Rochelle with their son, Ritchie, and spent his days at the office lying on a couch cracking jokes with Buddy and Sally, I turned to my parents and said, "I want to do that."

My father manufactured fine jewelry. He was a craftsman who took great pride in the rings, bracelets, brooches, and necklaces that he designed and sold to stores like Tiffany and Cartier. My mother was a homemaker back in those days when most mothers were just moms, and they raised us to be Conservative Long Island Jews who were strictly kosher, until a Chinese restaurant called Ming Dynasty opened up about two miles away from our house. It was at that point that she single-handedly modified the rules of Judaism and the structure of human anatomy by declaring that we now had two stomachs—one that was kosher in our home, the other that you took outdoors where all hell could break loose. This worked fine until my mom discovered that Ming Dynasty delivered. So once again, the time-honored dietary laws of our ancestors were altered to allow us to order in from Ming Dynasty as long as we ate their delicious food in our garage, because that technically wasn't part of the house—that's where our car lived, so we were simply eating out using that second stomach.

I was the oldest of four children. After me came Franny, Barbara, and David. Perhaps because she was just two years younger, I was closest with Franny. We shared a bedroom when we were very young and, when we got to high school age, we hung out in the same crowd and even dated each other's friends. She was my pal. A slightly younger sister who seemed slightly older than me and loved to laugh. And I loved making her laugh.

So, it was in junior high, back in those days before anyone even thought of putting the words middle and school together, that I started seeking out those who could make *me* laugh. It was a newfound desire fueled by television shows and an after-school diet of comedy albums like Mel Brooks and Carl Reiner's *The 2000 Year Old Man*, Allan Sherman's *My Son, the Folk Singer*, Vaughn Meader's *The First Family*, *The Button-Down Mind of Bob Newhart*, and, when my parents weren't home, Redd Foxx's *You Gotta Wash Your Ass*.

Paul Reiser tells me he had a similar experience. "When I was fifteen, I was introduced to *The 2000 Year Old Man*—the original. It was like the Rosetta stone for me. The world shifted. Suddenly I was in a whole other thing, a whole other level of comedy and depth of fun." (For the record, as hard as I tried, I couldn't find anyone who said the same thing about *You Gotta Wash Your Ass*.)

Later, television shows like *Rowan & Martin's Laugh-In* and *The Smothers Brothers Comedy Hour* came along, and I was further intrigued. So my senior year in high school I started writing. Jokes. Song parodies. A poem to an English teacher explaining why I hadn't studied for an exam on the seventeenth century poets.

> It's useless, Mrs. Marmor,
> There's nothing I can do,
> But last night I had fever,
> And other symptoms of flu.
>
> I'll make it up on Monday,
> But not today, I fear,
> That I'll fail and then I'll go
> To Vietnam next year.

If memory serves me well, Mrs. Marmor laughed at my poem, let me take the test on Monday, and I still failed in spectacular fashion.

However, writing things that made your parents, friends, and teachers—people who knew and liked you—laugh was one thing. But total strangers? It was reminiscent of an old joke that was on a comedy album titled *You Don't Have to Be Jewish* that my parents listened to when I was growing up in the early 1960s. The joke started with a man wearing a recently purchased captain's hat, captain's shirt, and captain's watch telling his elderly parents after they boarded his recently purchased boat, "You see, Mom and Dad, your son's a real captain." To which his father replied, "Sonny, to me you're a captain, to Momma you're a captain, but to a captain you're no captain!" Okay, I thought, now is the time to see if I can become a captain.

So I kept writing, and when I got to college, something happened that kicked everything into a different gear. I discovered Woody Allen. First on *The Ed Sullivan Show*, when he did the famous moose routine. And then his movie *Take the Money and Run*. Then *Bananas*. I actually found myself laughing aloud at this little Jewish guy with reddish hair whose self-deprecating character was easy for me (a large Jewish guy with reddish hair) to relate to. The ingenuity of the heightened reality he claimed to exist in was something I marveled at. Like when Woody said, "I was thrown out of NYU for cheating on my metaphysics final. I looked within the soul of the boy sitting next to me."

So while still an undergraduate at the University of Buffalo, as a hobby I began writing topical jokes and mailing them to *The Tonight Show* and *The Dick Cavett Show* and my efforts were rewarded with a three-inch stack of form rejection letters. Still, when I watched those shows, I noted that my jokes about a big blizzard or Watergate or the long lines of cars at Exxon stations during the gas shortage were close enough to the ones the professionals on staff were writing to be encouraged.

The same thing happened with my submissions to *MAD Magazine* and *National Lampoon* and the dozens of television variety shows that were on the air in the early seventies. I still have their rejection letters, which were, for the most part, personal and complimentary with requests to see more material. Looking for positive feedback from wherever I could find it, I wondered if perhaps I did have something to offer.

But how did one go about becoming a professional comedy writer? It wasn't like you could major in comedy writing, fly to Los Angeles, plop your degree on Norman Lear's desk, and say, "Your troubles are over."

The prospect of attempting to do such a thing was scary. Especially that September, after graduation, when my college friends went

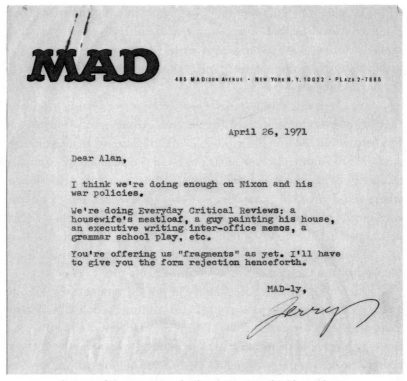

April 26, 1971

Dear Alan,

I think we're doing enough on Nixon and his war policies.

We're doing Everyday Critical Reviews: a housewife's meatloaf, a guy painting his house, an executive writing inter-office memos, a grammar school play, etc.

You're offering us "fragments" as yet. I'll have to give you the form rejection henceforth.

MAD-ly,

Jerry

Just one of about seventy rejections letters I received from this guy.

off to medical, dental, law, and all sorts of other postgraduate schools, where, after completing the prescribed curricula, they would emerge as professionals, while I was moving back into my old bedroom, where my younger brother, David, had now graduated to my old bed and charged me ten dollars to have it back. Driving my parents' Chrysler New Yorker to my job as a cashier in a luncheonette in Far Rockaway. And then, after being fired from the luncheonette for my inability, despite graduating cum laude, to master the art of consistently giving the correct amount of change, driving it to my new job at that deli in Queens.

"You want to be a deli man?" asked my boss, Sid Leinwand.

"I want to be a comedy writer."

"This place is great training for that. You know Mel Brooks?"

"Mel Brooks worked in this deli?

"No, but his old dentist has been in here a few times. Now watch how I chop this liver."

⚡⚡⚡

AND THEN THINGS TOOK a turn during that summer of 1972, when my parents went on vacation to Lake Tahoe and saw a nightclub performance by the singer Engelbert Humperdinck. (Really. That was his name.) The next morning, my mom ran into his opening act, a Catskill comic named Morty Gunty (really, that was his name) in the hotel's coffee shop and told him that her son wanted to be a comedy writer. He gave her his address; I mailed him a few jokes that he liked, and I started writing for him.

My grandfather has an electronic pacemaker in his heart. Works great. Except every time he sneezes, the garage door goes up.

And when other comics who played the Borscht Belt circuit asked Morty Gunty, a former speech teacher at Midwood High School in Brooklyn, who wrote that pacemaker joke, he gave them my parents' phone number, and then I started writing for them, too.

Can't remember how many jokes I wrote to earn that check.

7

ƒƒ

IT WAS A THRILL. Writing jokes and hearing them get laughs in nightclubs I used to sneak into when my parents took us to the mountains on holiday weekends. Just a few years earlier, the Catskills had been thriving, and writing jokes for the comedians who performed there would have been a viable first step in my quest to become a television comedy writer. In those bygone years it was a rite of passage that so many other fledgling scribes had taken back in the 1950s and '60s by furnishing material for funny people with names like Jerry Lewis, Alan King, Phil Silvers, Red Buttons, Totie Fields, Shecky Greene, Jackie Mason, and Buddy Hackett. The fabled Borscht Belt had been the spawning ground for so many comedians, who honed their craft by doing their acts two, sometimes even three, times a night, driving to and from family-owned establishments with names like Nevele, Grossinger's, the Raleigh, Brown's, the Homowack Lodge, and the Concord, not to mention bungalow colonies like the one portrayed in *Dirty Dancing.*

These comics delivered Yiddish punch lines to an audience whose parents had left Europe in search of the lives that their children were now enjoying in postwar America, who would give birth to a generation that would come to be known as the baby boomers. It was an America where a war hero named General Eisenhower would become President Eisenhower. A time when young veterans could become homeowners thanks to low-cost mortgages they could obtain through the G.I. Bill. This new era had arrived with a vocabulary just begging to be made fun of. Suburbia. Car pools. Crabgrass. Air-conditioning. Little League. Dr. Spock. Television. Jackie Kennedy. Rock 'n' roll.

This was a generation that suddenly had leisure time on its hands and found diversion at these upstate resorts, laughing about a wife whose credit cards were stolen but her husband didn't report it because the thief spent less than she did. Or laughing at mothers-in-law who were so fat, they had their own zip codes. Or car mechanics who said, "I couldn't fix your brakes, so I made your horn louder."

Comedy material here was delivered in plush nightclubs where "hell" and "damn" and certainly "shit" were considered too "blue" for prime-time audiences. These words were only heard in the lounges, where late shows started at 1:00 A.M., a time when the kids were allegedly asleep. Then a comedian like Shecky Greene could tell the audience, "My brother-in-law is a proctologist. Should have been a gynecologist. The shmuck missed having a good time by [holds two fingers an inch apart] this much." Or where just about every Catskill lounge comic who ever lived said, "A young man was wondering if his new bride was a virgin, so, on their wedding night, he snuck out and bought a can of red paint, a can of blue paint and a shovel. When they got to their hotel, he went into the bathroom, painted one of his balls red, his other ball blue, and when his bride said, 'That's the strangest pair of balls I've ever seen,' he hit her over the head with the shovel."

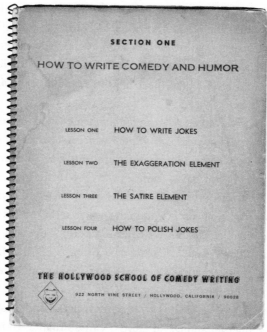

A correspondence course that was a glorious waste of
my parents' money.

Because the comics who played the Catskills were also on television a lot, they needed a steady flow of new material so as not to repeat themselves when they appeared on Ed Sullivan, Merv Griffin, Mike Douglas, or *The Tonight Show*. As a result, their writers were constantly working, and, if any of those comics got a television series, they were apt to ask their writers—the same ones who had furnished them with the material that got the interest of TV producers in the first place—to come along with them and write for those shows.

"They all wrote for me," Morty Gunty said in 1972 while opening a desk drawer, then pulling out manila folders that had names on them like Neil Simon, his brother Danny Simon, Larry Gelbart, Garry Marshall, and Arnie Kogen. "They'd come here and sit in that chair you're in right now and learn how to write."

"Back then the first New York television job you'd hope to get was a staff job writing Johnny Carson's monologues on *The Tonight Show*," says Arnie Kogen today. I first became familiar with Arnie from the pieces he'd written for *MAD Magazine*. I always thought his were the funniest—whether they were parodies of popular movies or a feature he created where he looked into the wallets of celebrities like Ringo Starr. *"Note to self: 'Love Me Do.' Hit the drum three times, then look to John for further instructions."*

Arnie started out by writing for the same Catskills comics about fifteen years before I got there and then went on to write for Carson. He tells me, "Then you'd graduate to writing some of the longer pieces like Aunt Blabby and become proficient in sketch writing," which is exactly what Arnie did before joining the staffs of many variety shows, including *The Carol Burnett Show*, for which he won a closetful of Emmy Awards, and then sitcoms like *The Bob Newhart Show*. Most of the writers Arnie worked with at *The Tonight Show* from 1966 to 1968, like David Lloyd, Ed. Weinberger, and Marshall Brickman, participated in both monologue and sketch writing for Carson.

Afterward they all moved on to other arenas. In addition to Kogen's successes, Weinberger and David Lloyd became situation-comedy legends

(*The Mary Tyler Moore Show, Taxi*), while Brickman won an Oscar for co-writing *Annie Hall* and also wrote the book (with Rick Elice) for the 2006 Tony Award–winning musical *Jersey Boys*. Says Brickman, "Johnny's daily monologue was written by an unofficial group of three to five writers who scoured newspapers and other periodicals for material and delivered to him by 3:15 on the day of the show, about three pages or twelve jokes, plus an opener like: 'Sure, you like me now—but will you call me in the city?'"

This was the career path I aspired to take. And Morty Gunty seemed like a good start, just as he had been for the writers he'd mentioned. I vaguely remembered him from my childhood, when he hosted a local children's program called *The Funny Company*. I later learned that he had appeared in a CBS television pilot written by Carl Reiner called "Head of the Family." The pilot was subsequently reshot after Gunty was replaced by Morey Amsterdam—in the classic television series that was renamed *The Dick Van Dyke Show*.

"I've done a few things in this business, Alan. So, stick with me; I might be able to help you, too."

"Sure."

"Hey, we just had our driveway repaved."

"Uh-huh . . ."

"Think there's a song in that?"

"A song about paving a driveway?"

"Funny idea, isn't it?"

"Well . . ."

"Look at all the words I wrote down that rhyme with 'tar.'"

At that point Gunty, then forty-four years old, was still a working comic, but his television appearances had dwindled. The exceptions were those times when a friend of his like Steve Lawrence guest hosted *The Tonight Show* or when he served as a co-host of a United Cerebral Palsy telethon. I wrote him jokes for the telethon, and I accompanied him there, where he introduced me to Virginia Graham, a rather proper-looking woman with a rather lofty voice who hosted a daytime talk show. Thinking that if I got on her good side she might consider me for a job on her writing staff, I reluctantly agreed when she asked that I walk her miniature poodle, Soufflé.

Whatever it takes, I figured. But when I took Soufflé outside, it started to rain, so I carried the dog back inside the studio and lied when I told Virginia that Soufflé had relieved himself—this was about thirty seconds before tiny Soufflé took an actual dump the size of a Baked Alaska on Virginia's dressing room floor, which pretty much dashed my chances of her hiring me.

✦✦✦

GUNTY, LIKE A NUMBER of Catskill comics, lived in the suburban Rockland County town of New City because of its equidistance between Manhattan, where their agents had offices, and the Borscht Belt hotels, where they made their livings. Freddie Roman lived New City. So did Dick Lord. As did Myron Cohen. Vic Arnell was in nearby Suffern.

My routine was simple. I'd write the jokes on small #2-size bags— the kind they used to sell single packs of cigarettes in—during my breaks at the deli, read them to my sister Fran over the phone to see if she laughed, then go home, type them up on my parents' portable Olivetti, wash the ink from the typewriter ribbon off of my fingers, mail the jokes to these comics, and then wait for them to call back with their verdicts.

"I like the line about the IRS, Alan," I remember one comic saying.

"Great."

I had written a joke about the economy being so bad that I'd just received a refund for my tax return: a check for $48 with a note asking if I could please hold it until Monday.

"I changed it to forty-nine dollars," he said.

"Okay. Just curious . . . How come?" I asked.

"It's a funnier number."

"It is?"

"Don't you think?"

"Uh, sure."

"I tell you, I tried it with your forty-eight, and it got a few laughs . . ."

"Uh-huh . . ."

"Then the next show I changed it to forty-nine dollars, and it got screams."

"Really . . . ?"

"Some people laughed so hard, I actually got worried they'd choke from lack of oxygen."

"Just from hearing the number forty-nine?"

"Yeah, but don't worry. I'm going to pay you the full amount, even though I wrote half of that joke."

". . . Thank you."

While I understand that some sounds land on the ear as being funnier than others, like hard "c's" and "k's," and that as a species we've become rhythmically programmed to expect a punch line to be the last thing mentioned in a series of three, I had come across this fascination with "funny numbers" many times through the years. Even these days when I'm writing, there's an innate instinct to choose one number over another for reasons that are, well, inexplicable.

But I have to say that the most extreme example of this occurred years later, in 1986, when Garry Shandling and I were in New York City and stopped into a comedy club while casting for our show. We ran into David Brenner—a very funny comedian who was always extremely supportive of me—who told us, with no provocation whatsoever, that he had figured out the funniest number.

"You what?" said Shandling.

"You know what it is?" Brenner asked.

"Ah, no," I answered.

"Guess," he said.

"Guess the funniest number?" said Shandling.

"David, there are a lot of numbers," I added. "We don't have that kind of time."

Brenner looked around and made sure no one was within earshot, lest his secret be overheard and fall into the wrong hands, turned back to us, placed a single finger up to his lips, and whispered.

"Two hundred sixty-seven."

I remember being speechless as I studied Brenner's face in search of a smile or a wink or any indication whatsoever that would convey he was kidding or, at the very least, not insane.

While Brenner was a renowned practical joker, at this particular moment Shandling and I both wondered if we should pray for his soul.

"I tested it out," Brenner assured us.

"You tested all of the numbers?" a stunned Garry asked.

"Trust me, it's two hundred sixty-seven," Brenner said conclusively.

I remember Garry and I thanking him for sharing this secret with us before we walked away slowly and silently, as if we'd just visited an old friend who'd gotten hit on the head by a falling anvil. We said nothing more about it—except, on occasion, when Garry and I were doing our show and one of us would say that a particular script would be funnier if we had a character say the number 267.

⚡⚡⚡

OKAY, SO NOW BACK TO writing for the Catskill comics.

On many occasions I'd go to their homes on a Friday afternoon and work on material in their study. Invariably the walls were adorned with pictures of them posing with headliners like Tom Jones, Steve Lawrence, Eydie Gormé, Tony Orlando, Frankie Valli, and Totie Fields, for whom they had been the opening act when those celebrities played Las Vegas, Lake Tahoe, theaters-in-the-round, and any of the bigger rooms in the country. Then, after dinner with them and their families, we'd drive to the mountain hotels to see how the new material worked.

And while they were performing, I'd sit there and listen to the jokes that made my parents' generation roar with laughter.

My wife wants to have her breasts enlarged. I said, "Why go through all that expense? All you have to do is take some toilet paper, crumple it up like this, and rub it on your breasts once a day."

"And that will make my breasts bigger?" she asked.

I said, "Sure, look what it's done for your ass."

After the show, we'd drive back to their houses, where I'd pick up my parents' Chrysler New Yorker and get home to Long Island at about 4:30 in the morning. On more than one occasion my father would be waiting up, and he'd make me breakfast while asking how my jokes had played.

"I'm getting a little discouraged," I'd tell him.

"Don't worry about the money, Alan. That will come."

"No," I'd say, shaking my head. "It has nothing to do with all that money I'm not making."

By now, my price had soared to ten dollars a joke, or, if I wrote a full-fledged routine, they paid me a hundred dollars a minute. That is, the delivered minute. That is, the number of minutes it took for them to tell the jokes. And since these guys were not storytellers and tended to make a mad dash from one punch line to another, my pleas to talk more slowly usually fell on deaf ears.

"Or, if you'd like, I'll pay you a hundred fifty dollars for a pound of jokes," a comic named Billy Baxter told me.

"A pound of jokes?"

"Assorted jokes about any subjects you want."

"How many jokes are in a pound?" I asked.

"Sixteen."

"Oh, so each joke is, like, an ounce?"

"Funny idea . . ."

"But if you're paying me ten dollars a joke, and you pay me a hundred fifty for sixteen, didn't my price just go down?"

"Well . . ."

"What if we compromised, and you pay me the same amount for, let's say, a baker's dozen of jokes?"

"How many jokes are in a baker's dozen?"

"Thirteen."

". . . Fine."

As you can see, it wasn't about the money, I explained to my dad. It had more to do with the work.

"It's just getting harder for me to write for these guys," I told him. "It's weird. They make me laugh, but it's not really my sense of humor."

It wasn't just me.

"I wrote for several Catskill comedians—miserably," says Richard Lewis. "Morty Gunty was the best of the lot and often did TV shots. I think out of the two million jokes I wrote, one was used, and I got eleven dollars."

⚡⚡⚡

I WAS OF A DIFFERENT GENERATION. The same age as the sons and daughters of the Jackies and Mortys and Dickies and Lees I was writing for. The same age as the children these comics were doing jokes about—and I much preferred to speak the language of my peers. The world was changing, but it seemed that the Catskills hadn't been informed, and, sadly, its days as a breeding ground for new talent were pretty much over. Says Freddie Roman, who had been playing the Catskills since the mid-sixties, "When I started playing in the Borscht Belt, there were about thirty-five big hotels, one hundred smaller ones, and about one hundred bungalow colonies."

By 1973 the number of Catskills stages had dwindled considerably: Hotel after hotel was shuttering due to the growing preference to travel ninety minutes in the other direction to Atlantic City, New Jersey, where plush venues featured gambling casinos and Las Vegas–caliber entertainment. And the handful of hotels that still existed in the early seventies, even while operating at a loss, did so by hanging on to the hope that gambling would come to the area and revitalize the region. It never happened.

So by the time I arrived on the scene, I found myself writing for the comics who had been left behind, destined to toil before shrinking audiences. They were the Willy Lomans of stand-up comedy, men with little hope that they'd be seen by anyone in a position to offer them a television series. Which pretty much dashed any possibility that I might get my big break there.

By now, most talk shows had moved to the West Coast, and the relevance of the Borsht Belt sensibility was diminishing with the emergence of a younger audience who preferred to hear what George Carlin and Richard Pryor were talking about. That also meant that the Catskill comedians had less need for new material, as its exposure was limited. These comedians were only appearing in nightclubs, and as they traveled from one to the next, they saw little harm in repeating the same material time and again. It was as if they were on automatic pilot. For years.

An example? Fast forward to the year 2000. Robin and I were living in Los Angeles and went to see a show called *Catskills on Broadway*, which consisted of four Borscht Belt comics doing their stand-up acts onstage. Conceived and produced by one of the best commercial comedians in the country at that time, Freddie Roman, its cast this particular evening included Freddie, Dick Capri, Mal Z. Lawrence, and Marilyn Michaels. As we sat there listening and laughing, I started to lean over and whisper a few of their punch lines to Robin, who asked how I knew them.

"I wrote these jokes in 1973," I told her.

"Did you really?"

It was a routine I'd written about the comic's family tree.

. . . And then there was my Middle Eastern ancestor who was at the Last Supper. You can't see him in that painting because he wasn't at the dais. He was at Table Six. He won the centerpiece.

And though I was surprised to hear material that I'd written almost three decades before, I was flattered that the comic—a lovable man named Dick Capri who was the personal favorite of many of the Catskill audiences because of a heart-transplant routine he mimed while the drummer provided the heart's beats—was still using it and that it was still getting laughs.

What I hadn't bargained for, however, was another incident that took place that same year with another comic (who shall remain nameless, lest we embarrass his family who loves him) who was still using some of the more topical material I had written back then.

"Any notes for me?" he asked backstage afterward.

"Well, as long as you asked," I told him, "that joke I wrote for you in 1973 about the secretary of state . . . ?"

"Yes?"

"Well, it seems to me that it would sound more current if you took out Henry Kissinger's name and replaced it with Madeleine Albright."

Since he just stared at me, I took the liberty of continuing.

"Because unless you do that joke in the past tense, it will sound more topical if you use the name of the person who is *now* the secretary of state."

". . . Let me think about it," he said.

Think about it! What in God's name was there to think about?

Whatever the reason, he apparently gave it some thought, because about six months later, when I walked into a crowded New York City restaurant that he also happened to be eating in, when he spotted me, he stood up and shouted, "Alan! Madeleine Albright!" before flashing me a thumbs-up gesture and then sitting back down.

I swear.

"Alan," Morty Gunty said to me one Friday afternoon at his home, "here's a joke Arnie Kogen wrote for me that's not playing as well as it used to." Arnie had written a joke based on two books that were very popular a few years earlier, saying, "My wife and I are both into reading. Last week she was reading *The Joy of Cooking*. I was reading *The Joy of Sex*. That night we brought a brisket to climax." I remember Morty saying that he wanted to update the joke. Naturally, I thought he meant naming more current books. But I was wrong—Morty said he wanted a more topical meat. He said that brisket was old-fashioned, that he wanted to replace brisket with a hipper part of the cow. You read that correctly—he asked about a hipper part of the cow! But when I off-handedly suggested pot roast, Morty started laughing. A lot. And then told me I have a good future in this business.

♪♪♪

I CONTINUED TO SERVE MY apprenticeship to these comics in the early 1970s. They were great to me, and I found them as intriguing a breed as I had ever come in contact with before and—dare I say?—since. There's even a large part of me that believes their comedic DNA was a unique strain that is now extinct.

No greater example of this was when they began taking me to the Friars Club—that legendary fraternity for nightclub comics, entertainers, athletes, and writers. At its peak, the Friars Club was considered to be the mecca of comedy, to the point that when my dad first heard I was being taken there, he was certain that I'd arrived.

Founded in 1904 by composers Irving Berlin, George M. Cohan, and Victor Herbert as a private club where celebrities could casually gather with no fear of the distraction or interruptions of autograph-seeking fans, the Friars began as a quiet haven. An unassuming retreat in contrast to the otherwise public profiles of its members.

Through the years, however, its luster grew with the advent of their roasts of major stars such as Frank Sinatra, Johnny Carson, Milton Berle, heavyweight champ Rocky Marciano, Humphrey Bogart, and George Burns. As a result, the Friars Club became the preeminent show business haunt whose unique distinction from the other prominent private clubs in New York City was aptly described by the great playwright George S. Kaufman, who said, "The Players are gentlemen trying to be actors, the Lambs are actors trying to be gentlemen, and the Friars are neither trying to be both."

It was at the downstairs bar of the Friars' five-story English Renaissance "monastery" on East Fifty-Fifth Street in Manhattan where I would often meet with the comics to show them the jokes I'd written, with hopes that one would be rewarded with a seven-dollar check as well as introductions to other comics I could possibly write for.

It was there that I was exposed to an intriguing array of characters who simply amazed me. Gene Baylos was an older, slightly hunched comedian with a sad-sack expression punctuated by bags under his eyes so big that you could store a change of clothes in them. Upon my introduction to Gene by another comic named Corbett Monica, whom I had written a number of jokes for, Baylos said, "Corbett tells me you have a great sense of humor. You know who also has a great sense of humor? My dentist." At which time he opened his mouth wide and allowed about twenty white Chiclets to spill into his hand as if they were his teeth. And, to this very day, I have no idea whether he saw that he was about to be introduced to me and surreptitiously snuck a handful of Chiclets into his mouth, or whether he always *walked around with a mouthful of white Chiclets praying that he would be introduced to someone.* Either way he, among so many others of his generation, was hardwired to go for the joke, for a laugh, no matter the situation or size of the audience.

Perhaps the ultimate example of this almost pathological need to be funny occurred a number of years later, after I became a Friar myself. One day I was walking toward the club, located between Madison and Park Avenues, and at that particular time, for whatever reason, there was no one else on the street. Now, this is an important part of this story, because when Henny Youngman, the comic affectionately known as the "King of the One-Liners" exited a building in front of me, he thought he was alone. He didn't know I was behind him when he crossed the street. He didn't know I was behind him when, as he was about to step onto the curb in front of the club, a pigeon fluttered down and landed a few feet away. Henny didn't know I was there when, without a moment's hesitation, he looked down at the pigeon and asked, "Any mail for me?" Again, *he thought he was alone!* And he *was talking to a bird!*

As I sit here, I wonder, now that their generation is all but gone, who takes their place? Which young comedian (younger than dead, I mean) is so conditioned to have such a knee-jerk reaction? Who is funny for the mere sake of being funny, without forethought or calculation, or without an audience beyond a pigeon?

ƒ ƒ ƒ

YES, THEY WERE HILARIOUS. Unfortunately, the culture outside the Friars Club's marble walls and the upstate nightclubs was changing. It was getting grittier. Comedy was growing socially and politically more purposeful than what was being offered by these wonderful performers who merely wanted to entertain. In effect, they were, in a way, all the same person. Even the ones with signature pieces, like Jerry Shane, who did a very funny rope trick, or a comic named Larry Best, who did a hilarious bit where he pretended to eat an imaginary apple that was legendary throughout the mountain hotels because it was so realistic that, "If you closed your eyes, you'd swear that the apple's juice was running down his chin and wetting the front of his shirt," says Dick Capri. However, just as Mel Brooks told me years later, "Sure, people might remember that in the late 1800s there was a guy who had such control of his anal sphincter muscles that he was able to fart the French national anthem onstage while the audience sang along. But very few people know that this talented flatulist's name was Le Pétomane." At which point, Mel would pause, shake his head, and lament, "A crying shame."

That was the problem with the great majority of these comics. Yes, they were funny, but they were also interchangeable. They were joke tellers as opposed to characters. Without specific voices or individual points of view, they were showmen: setup, punch line, setup, punch line. A predictable rhythm that generated laughter without the benefit of nuance. As a result, they were effective, but they were not memorable.

Years later, when I wrote for comedians like Rodney Dangerfield, it was easier. Rodney, for example, had that catchphrase "I don't get no respect." He looked and acted the part. So it was easy for me to have him say, "Even as an infant I got no respect. My mother wouldn't breastfeed me. She said she liked me as a friend." Or "No one in my family ever got any respect. During the Civil War I had an uncle who fought for the West."

That kind of writing was fun. The comedians who made me laugh the most did so because of their distinct personalities, not through the manufactured cadence of setups and punch lines. And because my goal was to write scripts one day, and I didn't want all the characters to sound alike, I devised a method that would, I hoped, train my ear. Every week I would pick a subject to write about. For example, one week I chose the topic "buying a car." On Monday, I wrote a monologue as if Bob Newhart was talking about buying a car. On Tuesday, it was Joan Rivers. Wednesday, Richard Pryor. Thursday, George Carlin. Friday, maybe David Steinberg. So, by the end of the week, I had five different monologues about the same topic but written for the sensibilities and speech patterns of five distinct voices.

I knew that character was what endured. There is probably no more profound example of this than when you consider legend has it that the longest laugh in the history of radio was born out of silence. That when Jack Benny, whose characteristic stinginess was so ingrained in the public's consciousness, was approached by a thief who stuck a gun in his back and said, "Your money or your life," the longer that Benny was silent, the louder the laughs grew, because the audience knew he was mulling over the choices. And when the laugh crested and started to ebb, the thief finally said, "Well?" and Benny replied, "I'm thinking!" and the laughter spiked again. Or years later, when Archie Bunker's bigotry was so well known, audiences would start to laugh when he approached his front door in anticipation of his reaction when he'd see his African-American neighbor, Jefferson, sitting in his favorite chair upon entering. Or how *The Honeymooners* characters were so well defined that it only took five words ("the Kramdens get a phone") to form the shortest episode description in the history of *TV Guide*.

Real. Organic. Nothing manufactured, like the catchphrase of a comic named Bob Melvin, who lived with his long-suffering wife one town away from my parents in Cedarhurst, Long Island.

A tall, handsome man in his mid-fifties when I met him, Bob had an inflated—no, make that wildly overblown—opinion of his place in the pantheon of comedy due to the years he spent as the opening act for Sammy Davis Jr. and his catchphrase, "You got a minute?" Onstage, when he was about to start telling a story or elongate one he was already telling, he would look to the audience and ask, "You got a minute?"

"It's a classic line," he told me.

"Uh-huh . . ."

"I'm telling you, I walk down streets and people roll down their car windows when they spot me and shout, "You got a minute?"

"Uh-huh . . ."

"Shopkeepers also say it when I walk into their stores."

"Uh-huh . . ."

For the record, I walked down a number of streets and stopped into a number of stores with Bob Melvin, and not once did I ever hear another living person say, "You got a minute?"

"So, you think you could write for me?"

"I can try . . ."

"It's tricky, Alan."

"Uh-huh . . ."

"I'm not easy to capture, because I'm handsome."

"Uh-huh . . ."

"I'm not fat or have a big nose or one leg shorter than the other . . ."

"Uh-huh . . ."

"So the material has to be sharp and classy, because I look dapper in a three-piece suit."

If this dialogue looks similar to the scene in *Annie Hall* in which a comedian explains to a writer, Woody Allen, why he's hard to capture, it's because this has actually happened to a number of young writers who were furnishing material for comics. In the movie, that actor was a comedian named Johnny Haymer, and when I saw *Annie Hall* for the first time, it stunned me, because I had actually lived through that scene with Johnny Haymer. And Jackie Miles. And Lee Stanley. And Pat Henry. And Mickey Marvin. And Burt Leigh. And now Bob Melvin.

"So, what would you, like, write about?" he asked.

"Watergate," I said.

"No."

"Why?"

"No one knows about it."

"Who doesn't know about Watergate?"

"My audience."

It's in every newspaper! I said to myself. It's all over television! It's all anyone anywhere is talking about!

"How's it possible that *anyone* doesn't know about Watergate?"

"My audience likes to laugh at things they can relate to. Like farting and leaving a stain."

"Uh-huh . . ."

"It's a funny idea, isn't it?"

"I guess so, but . . ."

"What's the problem?"

"No problem. But you just got done telling me how classy you are, so that seems to be a tad at odds with you having skid marks under your dapper three-piece suit."

⚡⚡⚡

DESPITE THEIR INABILITY to do anything that might really distinguish themselves from their peers, I loved these old guys. Appreciated them, their humor, and the memories it evoked of my parents and even grandparents laughing when they heard the great storyteller Myron Cohen say in a thick Yiddish dialect, "A woman walks into a butcher shop and asks the butcher how much the lamb chops are, and he says $2.39 a pound. And she says, 'The butcher down the street charges only $1.95 a pound.' So the butcher says, 'Then why don't you buy the lamb chops from him?' and the woman says, 'I went there, but he's out of them.' And the butcher says, 'If I was out of them, I'd also charge $1.95 a pound.'" Or Freddie Roman, a former ladies' shoe store salesman who liked to tell his audience, "My wife is on a new diet. Every day she eats six cloves of garlic and a wedge of Limburger cheese, doesn't brush her teeth, and, from a distance, she looks thinner."

Or the comic I was now watching from a back table in the Kutsher's nightclub, waiting for him to deliver my sperm-bank joke. In my heart I knew this was a dead end and wondered what other road I should take to achieve my goal.

"Boy, Alan, that sperm-bank joke really went into the toilet," the comic said in his dressing room after his show.

"Well, I wish you would've told it the way I wrote it," I said.

"How did you write it?"

"That it's like an ordinary bank except here, after you make a deposit, you *lose* interest."

"What did I say?"

"That after you make a *withdrawal,* you lose interest."

"Well, it's true, isn't it? That after you pull out, all you want to do is leave and get a slice of pizza?"

"I think you may have missed my point."

"Tell you what, I'll give you four dollars, okay?"

For the record, it wasn't okay with me. I didn't accept the four dollars. Instead, I wrote another sperm-bank joke ("They're starting to freeze sperm, which I think can be a big problem in the future. I mean, it's hard enough telling a child he's adopted, how do you tell him he's been defrosted?") and sold the two of them to Freddie Roman for fifty dollars. I then extended the routine to four minutes, for which Freddie paid me five hundred dollars. It was the most money I had ever earned to that point. Freddie was always a generous man. He recently told me that he's still using those jokes.

CHAPTER 2

THE CLUB YEAR

(A Large Jew Sweating)

"ARE YOU KIDDING ME, ZWEIBEL?"

The speaker was a talent manager named Dave Jonas.

"You're a terrific joke writer. There's no one else around like you. Why the hell would you want to become a comic?"

"I don't want to be a comic."

"You just said you want to go onstage and tell jokes. What do you call that? An electrician?"

Dave Jonas was a very nice, rather slight, sixty-four-year-old man who mispronounced relatively easy words, wore synthetic blends that relaxed out of shape within minutes of his putting them on, sported a hairpiece that shifted about an inch to the left in a breeze, and was an inspiration for Woody Allen's character Broadway Danny Rose. And though he didn't represent any piano playing birds or blind xylophonists, his stable consisted of most of the Catskill guys I was writing for. And because I was in his presence a lot, I naturally gravitated to him with every hope that having someone rep me would give me validation. That it would be a step in the right direction if someone who wasn't me would actually take the time to pick up the phone and speak to other human beings on my behalf. Despite the fact that he referred to my favorite singers as Simon and Garfinkel and once almost threw his back out trying to pronounce the eastern Long Island town of Amagansett.

"I think I should go onstage to advertise my writing. To let people my age know who I am and how I think."

"You sure about this . . . ?"

Dave was good to me. Devoted as he was to all of his comic clients whom I had written for, like Freddie Roman, Dick Capri, Billy Baxter, Dick Lord, and a singer named Errol Dante, Dave even gave me a key to his 101 West Fifty-Seventh Street office so I could let myself in when he wasn't there so I would have a place to write. He introduced me to even more comics when he took me to a West Fifty-Fourth Street restaurant called Al and Dick's, where a lot of the Catskill entertainers hung out on Wednesday nights. Because that was when Phil Greenwald, the social director at the Concord Hotel, held court, and the comics gathered with hopes that Phil would book them for a club date in his lounge or to open for a big-named singer on a holiday weekend in the Imperial Room, which, at the time, was the biggest nightclub in the country, seating more than three thousand people.

He also told me about another legendary hangout called Hanson's. According to Kliph Nesteroff, a comedy historian who wrote what many consider to be the definitive book on the subject, *The Comedians: Drunks, Thieves, Scoundrels, and the History of American Comedy,* who told me, "Hanson's was a drugstore with a long rectangular lunch counter that took up the majority of the space. There were shelves near the lunch counter with small items for sale—dime-store paperbacks, compacts, lipstick, aspirin—that kind of stuff. Despite the name, I don't think they actually filled prescriptions. There were four or five booths in the back, a phone booth against the back wall, and a door that led into the lobby of 1650 Broadway. The upstairs was notable because of the many booking agents—and one in particular. The Rapp Agency was a family enterprise, father and son working in tandem, as they booked comedians for the major Catskills hotels. This was one of the reasons comedians hung around at 1650. If there was a last-minute cancellation, there was a good chance they could pick up a well-paying gig."

Still, on the other hand, Jonas knew that I had loftier goals for myself and was encouraging. He told me about a few other successful writers he had handled and intrigued me with stories about Tamiment, a Catskills-like resort in the nearby Poconos where, in the early 1950s, a weekly live revue was written by Mel Tolkin and Lucille Kallen consisting of sketches and novelty songs. Again, according to Nesteroff, producer Max Liebman gave the group a lot of freedom, and because Tamiment was way hipper, way younger, and way more left-wing than the famous Catskills hotels, they wrote stuff that was atypically cerebral and experimental. This is precisely what they brought to television when they started writing *Your Show of Shows*. Mel Tolkin ran the writers' room on *Your Show of Shows*, while Kallen worked closely with Imogene Coca to ensure an accurate and ample female point of view. Of course, that writers' room also included Carl Reiner, Mel Brooks, Neil and Danny Simon, and Larry Gelbart. For obvious reasons, this excited me more. "Getting the job at Tamiment was my first exposure to writing for the stage," Neil Simon said, "and I knew as soon as I did that, it was what I wanted to do for the rest of my life."

"So you're serious about going onstage?" Jonas asked again, hoping that my answer would be different this time.

In that moment, I remember hearing my sister Franny's voice repeating what she'd been saying to me a lot lately: "Alan, your funniest material are the jokes those older comics are rejecting."

"Dave, I'm twenty-three years old, and I work in a deli and live at home with my parents and my brother just raised the price to twenty dollars for me to sleep in my old bed. With all due respect to your comics, I just can't write any more jokes about my wife's varicose veins looking like a road map of Connecticut. I can't. I just can't."

⚡⚡⚡

SO HERE WAS THE PLAN. I would take the jokes that the Catskills guys wouldn't buy from me, get up onstage, and deliver them myself with hopes that I could insinuate myself into the comedy community of my peers with shared sensibilities.

But where?

In the early 1970s, at the same time as I was struggling as a writer–deli man, two new showcase clubs called the Improvisation and

Catch a Rising Star were becoming popular in Manhattan. These were rooms where the careers of such comics as Richard Pryor, Robert Klein, Stiller and Meara, impressionist David Frye, David Brenner, and Bette Midler were born, and the careers of newcomers like Larry David, Freddie Prinze, Richard Lewis, Elayne Boosler, Andy Kaufman, and Billy Crystal were just beginning to be launched.

Founded in 1963 by thirty-year-old Budd Friedman, who was working for a Boston advertising firm but had aspirations to become a theatrical producer, the Improvisation on West Forty-Fourth Street was originally an after-hours coffeehouse for Broadway actors. As Tripp Whetsell, author of *The Improv: An Oral History of the Comedy Club That Revolutionized Stand-Up*, told me, "At first singers provided the entertainment, but about six months after it opened, a comedian named Dave Astor asked if he could get up and perform some material. Shortly afterward, he brought in friends like Richard Pryor, Jerry Stiller, Anne Meara, and this new breeding ground for young comics came into being."

Rick Newman's Catch a Rising Star came along a few years later; it opened on December 18, 1972, with a fiftieth-birthday party for the former middleweight champion of the world Rocky Graziano. "And though Graziano had nothing to do with the club's format," Newman says, "he brought another former champ, Jake LaMotta, and comedian Jackie Kannon, who rose to fame in the Rat Fink Room in the early 1960s, to the party for publicity, and the next day Catch a Rising Star was in all of the New York newspaper columns."

With wooden chairs and wobbly tables, both venues were rickety in comparison to the crushed-velvet booths and plush rugs of the Vegas, Atlantic City, and Catskills nightclubs. There was nothing slick about these rooms. That was part of their charm. The comics and their audience wore jeans, flannel shirts, and sneakers. Their kitchens served greasy burgers and even greasier fries. The décor was minimal apart from photos on the walls of those comics who had started there who now had their own TV series or, at the very least, were now successful enough to be able to afford to have framed photos of themselves on those walls.

Included in this scene were the managers, agents, and talent scouts looking to represent or book new comics. They came to watch the acts perform for free in front of a young audience who laughed raucously at routines about pot, Nixon, premarital sex, and Howdy Doody. On occasion, these performers also said "shit." Robert Klein told me, "Back then I used to bring one of those huge Wollensak reel-to-reel tape recorders onstage so I could record my act and listen to it when I got home."

These clubs were vibrant, exciting. The comics vied for better time slots so they could perform for free in front of more receptive crowds.

"I did thousands of shows developing my monologues. My act. New material. Every set," says Richard Lewis. "Mostly, the Improv was a sandlot where I gained supreme confidence in who I was onstage."

The audience loved seeing these young performers who were developing their own stage identities and felt invested when a regular like Gabe Kaplan went on to star in *Welcome Back, Kotter* or when one of the club's vets, like David Brenner, would return to try out new material for his next *Tonight Show* appearance or Robert Klein would do the same for his next album.

Dave Jonas provided help with this experiment. Freddie Roman had recently seen Freddie Prinze perform at Catch and urged Jonas to come watch him perform. Jonas was impressed and signed him immediately. Since Prinze was now (especially after his first *Tonight Show* appearance) the current sensation at the showcases, Dave had some clout and used it by calling Rick Newman and asking if I could have an early spot one night that week because he wanted to see me perform. Rick said yes.

ϟϟϟ

WHO WAS I GOING TO be onstage? Whom would I be writing for? Wayne Kline, a comic and great writer who later wrote for Jay Leno's *Tonight Show* said I looked like Woody Allen with a glandular condition. I remember disagreeing with him. I remember him suggesting I try the line onstage to see if the audience agreed with him. I tried the line. The audience laughed. A lot. And then applauded. A lot. If anything, too much. It hurt my feelings.

Even so, what did someone who looked like Woody Allen with a glandular condition sound like? What was his point of view?

To my mind, the most natural thing for me was to talk about being the product of that generation I had been, and still was, writing material for. Observations and complaints about the world we were handed. As if a son of comedian Alan King was given a chance to have his say.

Growing up on Long Island, Alan King railed about the same subjects that just about everyone's father did, except he got to say it on *The Ed Sullivan Show.* Whether it was marriage, the airlines, or suburbia in his hilarious book *Anyone Who Owns His Own Home Deserves It.* Alan King (née Irwin Alan Kniberg) was the son of immigrant parents and quite successfully rose from the streets of Brooklyn to become the spokesman for those who achieved the American Dream. He was very wealthy and politically connected. Alan presented the image of an angry executive in a tuxedo with a big cigar who occasionally took a sip of scotch while his audiences were laughing at his rants about insurance companies or his routine called "Survived By His Wife," in which he read the obituaries from that day's newspapers and noted that every man who died, no matter his age, was survived by his wife. Even when a distraught woman attempted suicide by throwing herself out of a third-story window upon being told that her husband was leaving her only sustained minor injuries when she happened to land on her husband, who died instantly and was survived by his wife. Yes, he was extremely funny.

But now it was our turn to talk. About our life experiences. And the politics and social mores reflective of the rebellion that was ongoing in the country at the time.

So I took the jokes the Catskills guys wouldn't buy from me and structured them into what I believed were six coherent minutes. My parents drove me into Manhattan and dropped me off at Catch a Rising Star. Dave Jonas introduced me to Rick Newman, I got onstage, and I managed to get some laughs. So now, in addition to being a writer and a deli clerk, I was a comic.

⚡⚡⚡

I STARTED TO HANG OUT at the clubs and quickly became friends with Larry David, Richard Lewis, and Billy Crystal. Billy had just split from a trio he was performing with that called themselves 3's Company and was embarking on a career as a solo performer. Since I was still living on Long Island with my parents in Woodmere, Billy—who lived a few towns away in Long Beach—used to pick me up every night in his powder-blue Volkswagen and drive us to Manhattan. Then, at the end of each evening, after we were done with our respective sets (which we recorded), we'd listen to the cassettes and critique each other during the drive home.

"That new joke you did about the confessional?" he once asked.

I had written a line about a church in my neighborhood whose confessional had an express line—for people who had ten sins or less.

"What about it?"

"Isn't that Dick Lord's joke?"

I had written that joke for Catskills comic Dick Lord, and it was cited in a recent review he'd gotten.

"I'm not sure," I said. "He still hasn't paid me for it."

"It's a funny joke."

"I know. I'm hoping he never pays me so I can keep on using it."

Billy, already married to Janice and the father of one-year old Jenny, rose through the ranks at a meteoric pace that had him leapfrogging over more experienced comedians who had been performing at those clubs for years. He was incredibly inventive; for example, when parodying a jungle movie, Billy had an audience member place her hands in a bowl of potato chips and crunch them each time he took a step, so it sounded like he was crushing dry leaves. Before too long Billy got booked into some of the hipper clubs like the Bitter End, My Father's Place on Long

Island, and Larry Magid's Bijou Café in Philadelphia before starting to appear on such popular television shows as *All in the Family* and the Dean Martin Celebrity Roasts.

"Your character's name on *All in the Family* was Alan, right?" I asked him.

"Right."

"Should I just assume that you named him after me?"

"You could assume whatever you want, but, no, the writers gave him that name. It was a coincidence."

"Oh . . . Well, would it be okay with you if I told everyone you named him after me? It might help me with girls."

"Do whatever you have to do."

"You're a real pal."

♪♪♪

AT THAT TIME, Richard Lewis was already a force to deal with onstage: handsome, kinetic, and funny as hell. Armed with pages of notes that he placed on a stool next to him, Richard often referred to them during sets that generally blew audiences away with animated descriptions of his neuroses and inadequacies when it came to relationships. Since then Richard has grown to become the iconic comedian whose act and social insights have often been compared to those of Lenny Bruce. Yet, even back then, one could feel how the air in the room was electrically charged after one of Richard's performances.

As for Larry David, well, as much of a cliché as it sounds, Larry was the ultimate comedians' comedian. He was the one all the comics watched from the back of the room and marveled at how he operated on a different plane than everyone else. With wire-rimmed glasses, hair reminiscent of Larry Fine of the Three Stooges, and a green army jacket, Larry provided a unique comedic perspective, whether he talked about having driven still another woman to lesbianism or belted out a song he claimed that thirteen-year-old boys sang at their Bar Mitzvahs on Staten Island.

On a few occasions, the lineup had me following him. Normally, each act was allotted about twenty minutes. But if Larry was scheduled to go on at, let's say, 9:00, I would make sure that I got there at the same time, because there was no telling what time I would actually get on.

"I feel very comfortable with you people tonight," Larry would tell the audience. "In fact, I feel so comfortable that I'm thinking of using the *tú* form of the verb instead of *usted* . . ."

I remember watching my new friend and laughing hysterically for two excellent reasons. First, I thought it was a hilarious joke that I could never have thought of. Second, the audience, comprised mostly of Long Island and New Jersey suburbanites—the women sporting blue bouffant hairdos, the men, visions in pastels—just sat there staring at Larry, offering no evidence whatsoever that they were even alive. Usually when a comedian hits a roadblock like that, especially right out of the gate, he shifts gears and goes another way. But not Larry.

"I think a lot of people misuse the *tú* form of the verb. Like when Brutus stabbed Caesar, Caesar said, "*Et tu, Brute?*" and even Brutus said, "Caesar, I just stabbed you. If there was ever a time for *usted*, it's now!"

Again, the audience would sit there stunned, he'd leave the stage with a wave of his hand conveying they weren't worth his time, and I'd get on at 9:01.

Larry always thought differently. He had the ability to see the same things the rest of the world did but in a way that no one else in the world could. Larry would take a morsel and make a banquet out of it. Most comedians and comedy writers I know carry a small pad in their pocket, and whenever something strikes them as funny, they take it out and scribble the idea down for future reference. Back then and even today, I've been with Larry and other comics in a restaurant when something obvious presented itself—like a waitress who looked exactly like Lee Harvey Oswald—and everyone at the table quickly took out their pads, made note of it, returned their pads to their pockets, and continued with their meals. But on more than one occasion, we'd all be eating, when only Larry took out his pen and wrote something down, leaving the rest of us wondering, "What just happened?" or, "What did we miss?" and we wouldn't find out until it appeared in Larry's act or years later in an episode of *Seinfeld* or *Curb Your Enthusiasm*.

Perhaps the greatest example of this was when, on a Sunday afternoon before either of us was making anything that even resembled a living, Larry and I attended a free recital given by a pianist named Claude Frank that took place in someone's Upper West Side apartment. It was close quarters, with chairs for approximately thirty people. And for reasons that to this day are unclear to me, Larry and I sat in the first two seats of the front row, maybe two feet from the piano bench Claude Frank, formally dressed in white bow tie and tails, was sitting upon while playing something quite classical. Stirring. With great flourish. And massively discrepant in spirit to the PEZ dispenser we spotted on the floor next to my seat, after which we dispatched nearly every muscle in our bodies to our mouths in an attempt to suppress mounting laughter in this proper setting. Pretty much the same way in that classic *Mary Tyler Moore Show* episode written by David Lloyd when Mary, seated in a back pew, tried her best to stifle her laughter at the funeral of Chuckles the Clown—upon hearing in the eulogy that he died in a parade from

Larry and I dressing alike—as old friends born in Brooklyn often do.

being crushed to death by an elephant's trunk that was reaching for Chuckles, who was dressed as a peanut. Or very much the same way that Larry had Elaine laugh when she saw a PEZ dispenser at a piano recital decades later on *Seinfeld*.

Larry, probably the most ethical person I've ever met when it comes to respect for the authorship of material, called me about it at the time.

"It's okay that I do that, right?"

"Larry, it was a shared experience. Of course you have every right." Shared experiences are fair game for all involved.

"It's not like I was by myself when I saw that PEZ dispenser, told you about it, and you used it," I assured him. "I'm just kicking myself for never having written anything that involved a PEZ dispenser."

"Okay, thanks."

"If you want to use it in an episode, go for it."

"I appreciate it."

It was at this point that I heard Julia's voice in the background, saying, "PEZ dispenser." At first, I thought she had merely overheard Larry say the word and was laughing at the reminiscence. But when she repeated it with the same inflection a second time, and I heard what I thought sounded like an audience laughing, and then a third time, when I heard what I was now certain was an audience laughing, it crossed my mind that Larry was calling me from an editing room, and then I started laughing.

"You already shot the episode, didn't you?"

And then Larry started laughing and said, "Yeah, I forgot to tell you."

"And what if I'd said you shouldn't use our PEZ dispenser story? Would you have erased the tape?"

ϟϟϟ

ROUNDING OUT THE SCENE at the clubs in 1974 were some pretty terrific performers, like Elayne Boosler. She was funny, bold, politically astute. A pioneer. Elayne was feministic in her attitude about the changing culture and aggressive in her point of view about guys and dating—as opposed to the older generation of female comics who played the part of the shrinking violet waiting for the phone to ring or bemoaning their timidity in bed. "Elayne was the first to break away from the 'Am I right, ladies?' approach that the female comedians before her had," says writer-comedian Carol Leifer. "At a time when the clubs never had two female comics following each other for fear that people would lose interest, Elayne slayed audiences by delivering material that could've been done by a guy."

"I know what men want," said Elayne. "Men want to be really really close to someone who will leave them alone."

Then there was the brilliant Andy Kaufman. Though also from Long Island, Andy and I may as well have been from different planets, as he mimed singing along with a scratchy recording of the theme to *Mighty Mouse*, and read *The Great Gatsby* onstage as he manipulated audiences into loving, then hating, then back to loving him again better than anyone I've ever seen. Jay Leno was such an audience favorite at the Improvisation that its owner, Budd Friedman, had a Leno Burger on the menu. Ed Bluestone not only delivered terrific jokes in a droll monotone but also possessed the wonderfully twisted mind behind the famous *National Lampoon* cover that showed a hand holding a gun to the head of a black-and-white mutt with the caption "If You Don't Buy This Magazine, We'll Kill This Dog."

The rest of the scene included John DeBellis, who was a very funny joke writer; Bob Shaw, who became a successful television and screenwriter; and Mike Preminger, who once got a big laugh on *The Tonight Show* with the punch line "Your vegetables went to Connecticut." I grew to have a big-brother relationship with a very funny nineteen-year-old girl from Canada named Marjorie Gross, whom Larry David and Jerry Seinfeld later hired as a writer on *Seinfeld* and put a bed in her office when she had cancer. The Untouchables were a musical/comedy trio, and Lenny Schultz was a gym teacher by day whose wife always entered the clubs a few steps behind him holding a large box containing his props, which included a webbed lounge chair that he opened and closed to music onstage as if it were an accordion. Also in that carton was a huge rubber penis on which he played "Turkey in the Straw" with a violin bow.

And I suppose it's a supreme tribute to a comic named Ronnie Shakes who is now deceased that I remember, some forty-five years later, him telling one of the best jokes I'd ever heard. "I've been going to the same shrink for seven years," said Shakes. "I've poured my heart out to him and told him every secret I have. And today he said three words that literally brought tears to my eyes. He said, *"No hablo ingles."*

♪♪♪

ME AS A PERFORMER? In a word, dreadful. Unless you enjoyed watching a large, nervous Jew sweat and stammer.

Catch a Rising Star owner Rick Newman says, "My first impression of you was, here is a pleasant-looking, nice young man who has some very funny material but needs to develop his own identity, style, and stage presence."

Rick is being kind. Extremely so. In fact, of the three comics from that era whom I asked to describe me onstage for this chapter, two of them diplomatically ignored that question in the e-mails I sent them, while the third one told me outright that he didn't want to come off as being cruel in print.

No, I was not a comedian and had little desire to become one. Once again, going onstage was a means to an end. The emcee, usually Richard Belzer, introduced me as a writer, and I presented myself as such. So if people laughed at what I was saying, great. If they didn't, well, what did they expect? I was only a writer.

> *I've written for comics, singers, a few Exxon attendants. Ever pull into a station and the attendant says, "Fill her up?" I wrote that line.*

I'd go onstage with weak knees, recite my routines, and if the audience laughed, I went with the flow and had a good time. But if they didn't enjoy what I was telling them or, God forbid, heckled, that part of the brain responsible for snappy retorts went AWOL. Case in point, the night I was onstage at Catch a Rising Star and said that I was from Long Island, and someone (who I later I learned was Bill Murray) called out from a back table, "Me, too. Can you give me a ride home?" After regaining some of the blood that had drained from my limbs, the best I could muster was a barely audible "I can't. I took the train to the city tonight." Upon which Bill replied, "Damn you to hell!" and got the laugh that any comedian who wasn't me would have gotten.

Still, as inept as I was as a performer, I did actually get a few paying gigs. Starting with the thirty-five dollars comics got when they performed at a club called Pips in the Sheepshead Bay section of Brooklyn. The club's owner, George Schultz, was encouraging and had me appear there a handful of times, opening for singer-songwriter Josh White Jr., Elayne Boosler, and an older comic named Uncle Dirty, who was a close friend of George Carlin.

An astute comedy man with a million facial tics, Schultz knew a comic with potential when he saw one. Although not exactly blessed with the gift of eloquence, he wisely told a young Richard Lewis at the start of his career, "You got it. And you have to eat, shit, suck, and fuck this career if you want to be a star." Needless to say, Richard heeded George's advice and went on to reach the heights he's achieved.

George was also instrumental in the revival of the career of Jack Roy after he had had enough of the aluminum-siding business and changed his name to Rodney Dangerfield. "I think my dad found that name in a phone book," says Melanie Roy, Rodney's daughter. "My mother told him, with a name like Rodney Dangerfield, 'You'd better be funny.'"

I also appeared at a Playboy Club in Baltimore, where I did eight shows over a weekend and must've bored the shit out of the staff, who heard me say the same words verbatim to the point that the Hispanic busboys were saying punch lines along with me in Spanish during my last show on Sunday night. And Dave Jonas actually booked me at two places in the Poconos. Host Farms, which was basically a gentile version of the Catskill hotels, and the Downingtown Inn, where, in the heart of Amish country, two things stand out for me about this appearance. First was the phone call from the Downingtown Inn's social director, who wanted to know what my "act" was like and, just before we hung up, asked if I had a stage name. Giving him the benefit of the doubt by assuming he was joking, I joked back by giving him the name of my hero. "Sure, it's Carl Reiner," I said. Little did I expect, after he picked me up at the train station and we approached the hotel, to see a marquis on the front of the property welcoming the comic appearing that weekend, whose name was "Carl Ryner."

The other surprise that night was, I found out that I was the opening act at a stag convention of insurance agents who were less interested in hearing jokes about my hilarious college test-taking adventures than in seeing the private body parts of the stripper who was following me. Attempting to be as professional as possible, I soldiered on but ended up leaving the stage after telling every joke in my act (and just about every joke that I'd ever heard in my life) in about six minutes, at which time I relinquished the stage to the stripper. The stripper with whom, by the way, I spent time afterward. The stripper who, by the way, called my parents' house a few weeks later, where my grandmother answered the phone and then came back to the Seder table asking in her still-thick Yiddish accent, "Alan, do you know a Boom Boom Trussels?"

§§

TRYING MY BEST NOT TO get discouraged, I continued to slice all kinds of meats and cheeses in a delicatessen and write jokes on small bags during the day, then delivered the ones I had a feeling the Catskills guys wouldn't buy from me onstage at night. No, let me revise that. Truth is that at this point I became conflicted about the fate of the material I was writing. Do I sell the better lines to the comics, which would not only augment my meager salary as a deli man but would also satisfy the

Me at the deli before *SNL*. You name it, I
sliced it for about two years.

comedians who showed faith by giving me down payments to write material? Or do I hold on to those jokes so I could put my best foot forward
by delivering them in front of people who could potentially further the
career I was hoping to have? In some situations, there was no dilemma.
If Vic Arnell wanted a routine about his mother-in-law's weekly canasta
game, odds were, I would never have been tempted to keep any lines
about the inedible snacks Blossom put out when she hosted the game in
her Forest Hills apartment. On the other hand, if Roger Riddle (that's
right, I actually wrote for a comic named Roger Riddle) wanted a pound
of jokes on any subject of my own liking, I'd be lying if I said I didn't
keep the better ones for myself—rationalizing that chances were that the
six-year-old children at the birthday parties he performed at as a clown
wouldn't understand them.

How long would this last? I wondered. Looking back, it had only
been about seven months since I'd embarked on this experiment. But
while you're going through something with no end in sight, the prospect
of being there for years and becoming embittered, like some of the others who had seen younger comics who came along later bypass them,

was daunting. One night at the Improvisation the great manager, Jack Rollins, brought Woody Allen in to see Andy Kaufman perform. At this stage in Woody's career, he had just made *Play It Again, Sam* and was well on his way to becoming an iconic filmmaker. After seeing Andy, Woody was leaving the club, when an old comic friend of his intercepted him at the door and asked if Woody could stay to see a new routine he'd be doing when he went onstage at 1:00 A.M.

Just as disturbing to me was a young comedian who was seen performing at Catch a Rising Star by a producer who cast him to star in a new television series. The comedian signed a contract for a lot of money, moved to Los Angeles, bought an expensive sports car, and basked in all the adulation of TV stardom for six weeks before the show was canceled and he was back at the club competing for good time slots to perform for free again.

♪♪♪

My grandparents live in Miami in a condominium called The Wrinkled Arms. It's got a kidney-shaped pool. And to make things a little more realistic, every morning someone goes outside and puts little stones in it.

As for my fate, well, there came a night in May 1975 that I had particularly rough time at Catch a Rising Star, when I just couldn't make six drunks from Des Moines laugh about the Chassidic orgy I said I'd gone to. ("It was really unusual—the men were on one side of the room, the women on the other.") It was about 1:00 in the morning, and after my set was mercifully over, I went to the bar to wait for Billy Crystal, because he was my ride home. As I sat there hanging my head, a young man with long-ish hair came over, sat down on the stool next to mine, started staring at me, and wouldn't stop. Finally, when I asked him what he wanted, he proceeded to tell me that I was one of the worst comics he'd ever seen. Exactly what I needed to hear at that moment.

"But your material isn't bad," he added. "Did you write it?"

"Yes, I did."

"Well, can I see more?"

"You bet."

I had no idea who this guy was, but, at this point, I would've shown my stuff to a gardener. It turned out that this young man with longish hair was a producer named Lorne Michaels who was combing the clubs looking at talent for a new show to replace Johnny Carson reruns. That show, which was going to premiere in the fall, was going to be called *Saturday Night Live*.

The next day I called Jonas, and he had a William Morris agent named Leon Memoli schedule a meeting for me. Meanwhile, I knew that this could be the break I was hoping for, so I did my best to prepare by staying up for two days straight at my parents' kitchen table and typing what I believed to be 1,100 of my best jokes. Ones that I had written for the Catskills comics, for myself, and even a lot of the practice monologues I'd written in the voices of comedians I had never met.

I put the pages into a binder and, after taking one of the most thorough showers in the history of my body, couldn't decide what to wear to my big interview. I thought to myself: young, hip producer of a young, hip show. So I figured I'd dress young, and I'd dress hip. I put on my father's maroon polyester leisure suit. A sartorial miscalculation if there ever was one, as I looked like a big blood clot sitting on the Long Island Rail Road barreling toward Manhattan.

I arrived at Lorne's hotel early enough to find a pay phone and call Billy, who'd had a number of meetings with Lorne. I told him where I was and asked if there was anything he could tell me that might give me a leg up in my interview. He said that Lorne had worked with Richard Pryor, had produced a Monty Python special, and that he hated mimes. I thanked Billy and, armed with this info, went upstairs, knocked on Lorne's door, and entered. I remember taking a seat on the edge of the bed across from the chair he was sitting on and, after a few ice-breaking pleasantries, handing him the thick volume of jokes.

He opened the binder and read the first joke. One that I had strategically placed on top of the first page because I had confidence in it.

The post office is about to issue a stamp commemorating
prostitution in the United States. It's a ten-cent stamp. If
you want to lick it, it's a quarter.

"Good," said Lorne before nodding and then closing the book.

It was a joke that took me about a week to write. That year (1975) the post office announced that it was going to issue a number of stamps commemorating the upcoming bicentennial. So the premise of the joke was easy: What else would be funny to pay special tribute to? Okay, prostitution. That could be funny. The punch line was a different story, though. I had a feeling that licking it could come into play, but the first wave of potential endings was the stamp responding with an array of sounds including sighs, moans, cries of "Oh, God, more!" and "Smaller circles!" but none of them seemed just right. Neither did any of the other ones that are too graphic to mention in a book that has my children's names in it. So I switched the setup to the cost of the stamp, which, at the time, was ten cents. Again, this took a while, as the candidates for the line after "If you want to lick it" ranged from the stamp wanting to be taken to dinner first, to some convoluted phraseology that involved the health department. So when I finally hit upon the word "quarter," I felt the line was concise, and I was ecstatic that I could finally move on to writing another joke about something else.

"How much money do you need to live on?" Lorne asked.

Now feeling relaxed after seeing the reception of that one joke, I took a stab at levity by telling him, "Well, I make $2.75 an hour at a deli. Match it."

Thank God he smiled before saying, "Tell me a little more about yourself," which I took to mean that before he committed to this kind of cash, he wanted to know what he was buying. So I took a deep breath, remembered what Billy had said to me on the phone, and told Lorne that I was a huge fan of Richard Pryor and that I loved Monty Python but prayed to all that's holy there wouldn't be any mimes on the show. The meeting was over. We shook hands, I left the binder with the 1,100 jokes with him, and he thanked me for coming in.

On the train back to Long Island I replayed the meeting. Like after a first date you have with someone you really want to see again, I analyzed everything that was said and what my alternate choice of answers could have been to maybe elicit better responses. Did I put the right jokes under the stamp joke on that first page? Did I put strong enough jokes on the last page in the event the NBC executives Lorne was going to share my binder with went straight from the first page to the last one without reading anything in the middle? Did I smile enough when I said that I didn't need a lot of money because I wanted to live at home with my parents for the rest of my life so he knew I was kidding? Did this fucking leisure suit kill any chance I had of getting a job on this cool show?

When I got home, I changed my clothes, drove my parents' Chrysler New Yorker to work at the deli, and for the next few days replayed that interview over and over again.

ϟϟϟ

I WAS WITH RICHARD LEWIS when the call came. We were working on a spec pilot script for Robert Klein called "Boiling Points" in a house that Richard was renting in Hasbrouck Heights, New Jersey. No, referring to it as a house is being overly generous. In actuality it was a free-standing converted garage that, upon seeing it for the first time, David Brenner told Richard that when he died, they were simply going to lower it into the ground with him inside.

"It's Jonas," said Richard, who was now a Dave Jonas client himself, handing me the phone. I envied Lewis. He had a phone. With his own phone number. Like a grown-up. "He wants to speak to you."

The script we were working on had Robert playing an investigative reporter for a *Village Voice*–type newspaper. We liked writing together. This was our third spec script, and because we were on a roll at this moment, we both considered Jonas's call a bit intrusive, so I assured Richard I'd only be second when I took the receiver from him.

"Hi, Dave. What's up?'

"You got it!!" Jonas was yelling. "We just heard from Lorne Michaels. You got the job on *Saturday Night Live!*"

"When that call came," says Richard, "I was proud of you. You lacked the demonic need to lead a tortured life as a full-time comic. Lucky bastard!"

ϟϟϟ

CELEBRATIONS ENSUED. My parents took me out to dinner. My bosses at the deli made me an overstuffed sandwich. And a man named Howard Hinderstein told me I was making the biggest mistake of my life for turning down a job he'd just gotten me writing the questions and bluff answers for Paul Lynde on *Hollywood Squares*.

Allow me to explain. While I was writing for those Catskills comics, I had traveled with them when they appeared in larger venues like theaters-in-the-round as the opening acts for Totie Fields. As a result, I was often in the company of her manager, Howard Hinderstein, a very nice, Los Angeles–based man who also not only represented Arnie Kogen but also a game-show host named Bert Convy. And because Totie and Bert often appeared on *Hollywood Squares*, Howard had sway with the show's producers and a few weeks earlier had arranged for me to have an audition—writing a dozen sample questions for host Peter Marshall to ask Paul Lynde ("Paul, according to the National Wildlife Foundation, what creature has a coat of the longest, most colorful feathers?") and for Paul Lynde to answer ("Elton John") that they apparently liked enough to want to hire me.

And though it seems like an absurd consideration so many years later, at the time Hinderstein's argument was not without merit—*Hollywood Squares* was a proven hit entering its ninth season. It was prime time, which was a higher pay scale. It was on the West Coast, where the entire industry was located. And in the boxes were all of these celebrities who starred in their own television series and had Las Vegas acts whom I could develop relationships with. In effect, this would be the perfect entrée into the business.

Whereas this *Saturday Night Live* was going to be on at the ungodly hour of 11:30 P.M. And East Coast, late-night television had a pay scale tantamount to what I was making at the deli. And who the hell were John Belushi and Gilda Radner when compared to the likes of Florence Henderson, Wally Cox and Charles Nelson Riley, who were regulars on *Hollywood Squares?*

Out of respect for Howard, I thought about it. For maybe three seconds before coming to the conclusion that this crazy new show with a left-of-center sensibility whose agenda would be to satirize the world we lived in sounded like everything I was dreaming about.

CHAPTER 3

SATURDAY NIGHT LIVE

(The Early Part of the Early Years)

"LET'S JUST MAKE each other laugh. And if we do, we'll put it on television."

Those were the first words I remember Lorne Michaels saying in the very first meeting of *Saturday Night Live*. The actors and writers had piled into his office on the seventeenth floor of what was then called the RCA Building to discuss this new show. And to this very day, so many years later, I can still say that reporting for my first day of work as a television comedy writer was the most exciting professional moment I've ever had.

When I was growing up, I often came into Manhattan during days off from school to run errands for my dad. Alfran Jewelry, named after me and my sister, was on East Fifty-Second Street between Fifth and Madison Avenues, but no matter where my destination was, I made sure that I went by way of Rockefeller Center . . . 30 Rock, to be exact. I would walk through the great art deco lobby and slow down when I reached the studio elevators with hopes that I'd catch a glimpse of any one of my heroes. Upstairs Johnny Carson was doing *The Tonight Show*, and in the mid-sixties there was a comedy news series called *That Was the Week That Was* produced by a man named Herb Sargent that starred, among others, Buck Henry. It excited me. There were people in that building who were doing what I wanted to do someday.

On July 7, 1975, that someday had come.

I entered that same lobby, showed my temporary NBC pass to a uniformed security guy, and rode the elevator up to the seventeenth floor for the first meeting of this new show. As he had told me during my interview, Lorne repeated that there was an audience out there that TV was not playing to—a younger generation with shared political views and social experiences who grew up on television but wanted something more relevant than what was being offered. To achieve this, Lorne had scoured the country (make that two countries, when you include Canada) for a cast and a staff of writers whose individual and collective sensibilities would bring a different voice to the medium. He said that this would be a variety show—then elaborated by saying that that meant it would be a variety of different kinds of comedy.

This was made immediately clear to me about ten minutes before our first meeting began that day. When I entered Lorne's office, I saw Michael O'Donoghue—the brilliant satirist who had founded the *National Lampoon* magazine, written for the *Paris Review*, and was going to be a staff writer on this new show—standing at the window that overlooked the Rockefeller Center skating rink and wrapping the cord from one of the venetian blinds around Big Bird's neck and then raising the blinds as if hanging this yellow stuffed character to show his disdain for the fact that the Muppets were going to have a recurring spot on this new show.

"You like the Muppets?" he asked me.

I did like the Muppets. A lot. In fact, I thought they were adorable. But looking at Michael glaring back at me through wire-rimmed sunglasses while Big Bird hung behind him looking even more inanimate than it did a few seconds before, I couldn't help but feel that I might not want to let on.

"I hate the Muppets. Those furry little bastards make me sick to my stomach," I told him.

O'Donoghue held his glare. For quite a while. And I got worried that he knew I was lying. I remember telling myself to hold our locked look for as long as Michael found necessary, for fear that to turn away could be interpreted as insincerity.

"Good," said Michael, nodding. "Very good," he said as if I had passed some kind of nihilistic comedy litmus test.

"I'm Michael."

"I'm Alan," I said while shaking his outstretched hand. He held his stare. Even when the handshaking part was over.

"You may want to rethink that shirt," he eventually said.

I was wearing a plaid Brooks Brothers shirt. A brand-new one that I'd bought about an hour before downstairs in a Rockefeller Center men's shop for my first day of work. For the record, Michael was wearing what I later learned was vintage clothing. A loose-fitting off-white shirt. Loose-fitting, pleated, off-white pants. Oh, and a Panama hat that was, if memory serves, off-white.

"Yeah, this shirt sucks," I agreed while trying my damnedest to duplicate the same conviction I'd faked when I told him how much I hated the Muppets. "I just threw this piece of shit on, but, trust me, you won't see it again."

O'Donoghue stared at me some more before putting what I later learned was a hand-rolled cigarette into his mouth and walking away.

I had never met another person like him before, and I was now a little nervous.

ϟϟϟ

SHORTLY AFTERWARD, the room started to fill with the likes of John Belushi, Dan Aykroyd, Laraine Newman, Chevy Chase, and Al Franken—none of whom I knew, but I saw how funny they were by the improvs they were performing with one another right there in the room. They were creating short scenes in front of us, and I had never witnessed anything quite like it. Remember, I was little more than a slightly overweight Jewish gag writer from Long Island wearing a plaid Brooks Brothers shirt who now found himself in the same room with people who had arrived here via Second City, The Groundlings, *The National Lampoon Radio Hour,* and an "underground" comedy show that had played downtown called *Lemmings.*

So sitting there listening to Lorne describe what was going to be an off-Broadway version of what was ordinarily seen on television and looking at the extraordinary comic minds I would be working with, I became so consumed by the fear that, if called upon, I could never measure up, I sought refuge in a corner of the office behind a potted plant. That's right, I was at the first meeting of the biggest day of my life, and I was squatting behind a plant. Moments later, another unknown actor by the name of Gilda Radner spotted me and started talking to me through the leaves.

"Can you help me be a parakeet?" she asked.

"What?"

"I think it would be really funny if I stood on a perch, scrunched up my face, and started talking like a parakeet. But I need a writer to help me figure out what the parakeet should say. Are you a good parakeet writer?"

And though I had no idea what she was talking about, I assured her that I was.

"Why are you squatting behind that tree?" she asked. "Nervous?"

"A little."

"First TV show, Alan?"

"Yes. How did you know my name's Alan?"

"You're the only one wearing a name tag."

Yep, I was. I had found one lying on the receptionist's desk and, well, let's just call this a gross miscalculation and move on to the part where Gilda asked if there was room behind the potted plant for her to also crouch. Because this was also her first TV show and she was also a little nervous.

So I scooted over, and she came behind the plant and squatted next to me. We got to talking and made each other laugh, and it was there, during that very first meeting of this new show, that Gilda and I decided that we should write together. Actually, it was Gilda who decided that she and I should write together. I was thrilled. And it was also then that she said that we would be platonic friends forever. That I was less thrilled about, because I was already in love.

ƒƒƒ

MY LIFE CHANGED IMMEDIATELY. As an apprentice writer making $350 per show, I could now afford to move out of my parents' house on Long Island and get a small studio apartment in a brownstone on Manhattan's extreme West Side about a mile short of Kansas. Still, I was living in New York City, which, in the mid-1970s, seemed incredibly provincial despite being the biggest city in the country. The baby boomers were now out of college, and many settled in Manhattan, where they entered the workforce, and back then it was unusual to walk down city streets and not bump into someone you knew. It was a post-Woodstock, pre-AIDS era when sex was still casual and some of the boomers' newly disposable income was spent on comedy albums and concert tickets. For the most part, they did not watch television at 11:30 on Saturday nights. They were out getting laid. Or, if they were home, they were pissed off that they weren't out getting laid.

Still, I was indescribably excited. I had a job. A place to go to every day. For at least seven episodes, that is. That was NBC's commitment to the show they were going to now call *NBC's Saturday Night*, because ABC had a prime-time show called *Saturday Night Live with Howard Cosell* that was going to premiere before we did . . . before we did—so it wasn't until 1977 that the show was officially called *Saturday Night Live*. Lorne said that he had insisted on a multi-show order as opposed to doing a pilot because he felt it would take a number of shows for the series to find itself.

I was given a desk that had a push-button phone on it. The desk was not in an office but in an open area behind Tom Schiller, who was a writer and filmmaker whose sensibilities could not possibly be further from mine. Tom (whose father, Bob, wrote dozens of episodes of *I Love Lucy* and *All in the Family*) knew everything about Eastern philosophy and nothing about sports and ultimately made some of the most memorable stylized short films on *SNL*, including "La Dolce Gilda" and "Don't Look Back in Anger," in which Belushi played an older version of himself visiting the cemetery where all the other cast members were buried. And when our country was considering going metric to be in step with the rest of the world, Tom had Dan Aykroyd describe the Decibet—the new ten-letter alphabet.

Lorne later said he purposely put my desk behind Tom's, thinking that we would get along, and he was right. Tom and I became good friends, well aware that we both observed each other with the same intrigue as one would a member of another species.

"You know, that binder was on Henry Miller's pool table," he said about the book with the 1,100 jokes that had served as my audition for getting the job on the show. Apparently Lorne had shown the book to Tom, who had just so happened to have it with him when he was at some guy named Henry's Miller's home.

"Henry Miller?" I asked.

"He wrote *Tropic of Cancer.*"

"Oh, of course," I lied. "I thought you said Henry Aaron."

"Henry Aaron?"

"Last season he broke Babe Ruth's lifetime home-run record."

"Oh, of course," he lied.

⚡⚡⚡

AFTER PUSHING "9" ON MY phone dozens of times to call everyone I'd ever met to tell them I had a job, I got to work. Started writing. As an apprentice trying to prove that I belonged, I practically chained myself to my desk, writing commercial parodies, sketches, and anything I thought might make the others laugh. Lorne, Chevy, and O'Donoghue were my triumvirate, and it was they I worked hard to please and learn from. Chevy's comedy was silly and physical. Not only falling down impersonating President Ford, but I remember a commercial parody of a drug called "Triopenin," which was just a close-up of Chevy's hands unsuccessfully trying to remove the childproof cap of a prescription pill bottle; it was hilarious. O'Donoghue was dark. Death was a favorite theme. Like the joke he wrote about the murder of a vaudevillian comic named Professor Backwards, whose act consisted of him spelling and saying words backward, and O'Donoghue reporting that after Backwards was shot, no one responded to his cries of "Pleh! Pleh!" I soon realized that O'Donoghue was a total original, unlike anyone I could ever have imagined existed on this planet. Says original *SNL* writer Anne Beatts, "Michael was considered to be a tastemaker. Even at the National Lampoon, he was the one that everybody wanted to please. To make Michael take that cigarette out of his mouth and say, 'That's funny' before putting the cigarette back into his mouth and walking away. You felt validated."

As for Lorne, he could not have been more encouraging and receptive of what I was writing. I was treated like an equal. Which included being made fun of when it came to my work ethic—with Chevy dubbing me "1,000 Monkeys," paraphrasing the theory that, given an infinite amount of time and an infinite amount of paper, a thousand chimpanzees typing at random would almost assuredly write one of Shakespeare's plays.

But I put in my time because sketch writing was a new frontier for me that I forced myself to learn. Prior to *SNL*, I wrote jokes that played to the ear. Setups and punch lines that sounded funny. Even if the joke painted a mental picture, its delivery by a man dressed in a tuxedo facing his audience was relatively one-dimensional.

But writing for actors who spoke to one another, had wardrobes that helped define their characters, and could get a laugh by merely raising an eyebrow was a new world for me.

It was fun. A lot of fun. As it was when I first started writing jokes for those Catskills guys to tell on a nightclub stage, I was now writing whatever I thought was funny but knowing that what I was doing could very well end up on television. I was even in one of the first pieces ever filmed for *SNL*. It was a commercial parody written by Al Franken and his partner, Tom Davis, for a product they called Spud—the beer made from potatoes. In it, I was cast to portray a hospital patient who'd just had electroshock therapy, as the tagline for Spud was "For people who don't know the difference." So as I was led back to my bed, I tried my best to act like someone who'd just been zapped with God knows how many volts—stunned and zoned out. But after each take, the director

Dave Wilson said, "Cut," and asked that we do it again. After about seven of these unsuccessful attempts, Dave took me aside and gave me the note to not act the part. To just be natural and look the same dazed way I always did. The next take I did exactly what he said and walked into the room the exact way I walked through life. Everyone laughed, Dave yelled, "Print!" and we broke for lunch.

In total, during my five years with SNL, I appeared as an extra in about fifty shows. Whenever they needed a large Semite to be dead, drunk, in the shower, or to play a donkey that the Virgin Mary rode into Bethlehem on, it was me. The scariest thing was how terrified I'd get when appearing on live television. I'd actually lose sleep the night before. Afraid that I'd faint. Forget how to read my lines off the cue cards. Or suddenly develop a case of Tourette's syndrome, and involuntarily start shouting dirty words or confessing to crimes committed before I was born. As a hedge against such possibilities, Gilda usually gave me a shot of vodka to calm my nerves before the scene started, and, for the most part, it worked. Although there was one piece where I played a corpse lying in a coffin in a funeral sketch, and, if you look closely, the corpse's hands are shaking.

$$\xi\xi\xi$$

SINCE JOKE WRITING was my strong suit, I initially gravitated toward "Weekend Update" and supplied Chevy with a lot of material. That prostitution stamp joke was actually on the "Weekend Update" of our opening show, and it was a thrill to hear something I had written said on television and getting laughs from a studio audience. It was during this time that I met and got to be friends with Herb Sargent, who produced the segment.

Herb, fifty-four years old when we started the show, was the grown-up of the writing staff and Lorne's trusted consigliore. Herb was a veteran radio and television writer-producer whose name I used to see on the credits of shows like *That Was the Week That Was*, and it was he who came up with the phrase "Not Ready for Prime Time Players" to describe our cast.

A great-looking man who at one time or another was married to just about every beautiful woman who ever lived, Herb was a throwback to a romantic New York that took place in black-and-white. Late nights, cabarets, and the infancy of a new medium called television. Steve Allen. Jack Parr. Mort Sahl. To know Herb was to be two degrees of separation from just about anybody on the planet. Art Buchwald. Herb Gardner. Ben Bradlee. Mayor John Lindsay. Mayor Ed Koch. Paddy Chayefsky. Gloria Steinem. I met them all in Herb's office. He knew everybody and had their respect, because they knew that Herb, a soft-spoken, discreet man, would never betray a confidence, which once prompted Larry Gelbart to say, "If Herb Sargent could talk, can you imagine the stories he'd tell?"

At first I was afraid to approach Herb, because I was I awed and felt, well, a tad unworthy. In the days when I used to run errands for my father's jewelry business, I would sometimes think I saw him. I'd figure that the guy coming off the elevators with the cast of *That Was the Week That Was* might very well be the show's producer, Herb Sargent. And I now knew it *was*. And I was actually working with him. But, as shy as he was, he ended up introducing himself to me.

One day I came to work, and on my desk was a framed cartoon. A drawing—no caption—of a drunken rabbi staggering home late and holding a wine bottle. And waiting for him on the other side of the door was his angry wife, getting ready to hit him with a Torah instead of a rolling pin. I had no idea who'd put it there. I started looking around, and out of the corner of my eye I saw a white-haired man in his office, laughing. He had put it there. That was the first communication I had with Herb Sargent—funny that someone who didn't speak gave me a cartoon that had no caption.

So I found my way into his office to thank him for the picture and before too long, I found myself spending untold hours there as we would go through the newspapers together and write jokes for "Update." We made each other laugh. Even our silences were comfortable. And over time, the relationship grew deeper.

I believe that you choose people to fulfill roles in your life. And I cast Herb in the role, not only of mentor but—there's a Jewish expression

My friend and mentor, Herb Sargent
© Courtesy NBCUniversal

called tzaddik. If someone's a tzaddik, it means that they're "just." They're righteous. That they embody wisdom and integrity. I cast Herb in that role. He was the oldest person I knew, and I treated him with the kind of respect afforded people who symbolize a person's private definition of truth, to the point that he was the one guy I knew I couldn't lie to. And as the show became more successful and I started making a little money, he was the only one I didn't do drugs in front of. Still later on, when I was having problems with a woman I was going out with, I went to Herb, who was married something like thirty-four times, for advice.

More than anything, I found myself observing Herb. My guru, who wore his reading glasses toward the top of his forehead, wrote speeches for presidents. His comedy had a conscience. And he was mindful of its power to influence. From the silly "Franco is still dead!" jokes to softer ones about global warming, Herb taught us about the equal weight they carried. "Even if they don't laugh, if the audience sees we bothered to make a joke about a subject, we will have made our point," he used to say.

Again, when Lorne founded the show, he said that our generation was not being spoken to on television. But here was Herb, a charter member of the older generation, who validated us. And encouraged us. And quite often led the way. What a curious hybrid he was—a man older than my father, at the same time spiritually younger than my younger Republican brother, who wasn't trying to be preachy or controversial. Herb Sargent wrote about those things that he genuinely felt. So when he wrote, he wrote from within.

↯↯↯

IN THOSE EARLY DAYS, *SNL* was a mom-and-pop store. The staff was so small that we occupied maybe a quarter of the space the show currently occupies on the seventeenth floor. Lorne's door was always open. And I quickly learned that his method was to throw you into the deep end of the pool, and it was up to you to figure out how to survive. Sure, Al Franken, Tom Davis, and I were apprentice writers, but we were welcomed in all meetings—during which I sat quietly while strategizing when would be the right moment for me to speak. And I learned to never say no when asked to do something, no matter how challenging it was.

For example, it was Tom Schiller who wrote the first samurai sketch. It was a character that John Belushi brought to the show, and Tom wrote "Samurai Hotel" for the seventh show, which was hosted by Richard Pryor. In the sketch, Chevy played a traveler checking into a hotel whose proprietor was a samurai warrior.

"John's audition consisted of waving a stick around, and just when you thought he was going to be violent, he gently mimed playing pool, with little samurai grunts and flourishes," says Schiller now. "It was quite charming and funny. I immediately spotted Belushi's genius at acting that character and knew it could be applied to endless situations. The first one I wrote was 'Samurai Hotelier.' I don't know why, but imagining a samurai greeting you when you are simply trying to check into a hotel seemed funny and unexpected. Lorne thought 'Hotelier' was too sophisticated a word, so it was changed to 'Hotel.' I made a list of about thirty-five samurai situations, from Film Editor to Gift Return Counter, and gave it to Zweibel, but I don't think he used any."

Schiller 1-2-76

SAMURAI

★ SAMURAI HOSPITAL
SAMURAI LAUNDRY. DRY CLEANERS
DUCK SHOOT
SAMURAI TAX TAILORING
→ SAMURAI GIFT RETURN COUNTER
SAMURAI SHIPPING CLERK
SAMURAI NEWSCASTER
★ SAMURAI ROAST
★ SAMURAI SAUNA
SAMURAI SWAP MEET
SAMURAI PLUMBER
SAMURAI DOG SHOW
SAMURAI POST OFFICE
SAMURAI CUSTOMS OFFICIAL
SAMURAI CANDY FACTORY
★ SAMURAI HAT CHECK GIRL
SAMURAI ROCK LEAD SINGER
SAMURAI BABYSITTER SERVICE
★ SAMURAI CHEF COOK SHOW
SAMURAI CRIME DESK
SAMURAI LIBRARIAN
SAMURAI PILOT
SAMURAI SKIER
★ SAMURAI DATA KEY PUNCH OPERATOR
SAMURAI XEROX COPY CENTER
SAMURAI CASINO

Samurai Pastry Chef
Samurai Supreme Court JUSTICE OF THE
The Last Samurai Movie
Samurai Cabaret
Samurai Drag Strip
Samurai Tailor
Samurai Film Editor

"Samurai Hotel" was a big hit, and everyone felt that the character should be seen again. So, when Buck Henry was scheduled to host our eleventh show, Lorne said to me, "Before you got this job, you worked in a deli, right?" I told him that I had. He then asked, "So you think that you could write 'Samurai Delicatessen'?" I assured him that I could with no idea how to do what I'd just enthusiastically agreed to do.

It ended up being easy. Buck, on the eve of the Super Bowl, would enter the deli and request a lean corned beef sandwich that he could eat the next day while watching the game. It was then a matter of giving Buck enough dialogue to cover all of the sandwich-making moves that I suggested the samurai make, like:

> [Buck enters and tells the samurai he wants a sandwich.
> Although the store is empty, John grunts that Buck
> should take a number. Buck does so without question.
> John starts grunting as if he's calling out numbers.
> When he gets to the third grunt . . .]
>   BUCK
>   *That's me.*

Or:

> [John throws a tomato into the air, grunts, and slices
> it on its way down.]

I wrote the next nine samurai sketches that we did. We would first decide who the samurai would be that week, and I'd write a draft. In my office. John would then come by to take a look at it, say something along the lines of, "Looks like I'm gonna have to save your ass again," wink, and leave. One time, however, I didn't show John the first draft in my office. Instead I took a cab to Tenth Street and I entered a place called the Schvitz, took my clothes off, and showed John the pages stark naked in a steam bath while he was sweating out whatever naughtiness he had put into his system.

In order for the samurai series to grow, we tried to expand the visuals in terms of what we could get away with. In "Samurai Tailor," Buck was being measured for a tuxedo, and when John was checking out the inseam, we had him grunt a one-syllable question, to which Buck responded, "To the left." This did not present a problem for the censor—a very nice man named Jay Otley. I always felt that left to his own devices,

Jay would let us say or do just about anything we wanted. But since he had a boss that he had to answer to, a man named Herminio Traviesas, Jay often asked us to soften something a bit so he could push it through.

One such occasion had to do with an episode in which I had Buck say something that the samurai didn't believe, so I wrote the stage direction, "John raises and lowers his sword into the sheath three times," the way guys make a fist and move it up and down when they think something is bullshit. Okay, it's a jerk-off motion. And Otley thought that three up-and-down movements made the masturbation gesture too blatant. I remember the talk degenerating into how many up and downs were needed to get the point across. Just know that I purposely put in three because I anticipated a problem and figured we could negotiate it down to two. This is done a lot. A writer padding a joke with multiple options so it appears that he's showing good faith when he cuts one and ultimately settles for the choice he really wanted in the first place. Otley, however, was well aware of this trick and insisted that one up and down would get the laugh we wanted. I remember smiling when I said, "Fine, Jay. If all it takes for you is one stroke . . ." And I remember him smiling when he said, "Alan, how many strokes I personally need is none of your goddamn business. But Belushi's only getting one." So on air, Belushi did it once, it got a huge laugh, and all was well with the world.

Although it seems so tame given what is said and seen on television today, you have to remember that we were doing the show at a time when there was no original cable programming. There wasn't even a FOX network at this point. ABC, CBS, and NBC. That was television. So at times concessions had to be made in order to get what we'd written on the air. When I wanted Emily Litella, Gilda Radner's little old lady character who was hard of hearing and often came on "Update" to rail about an issue that she had misheard, to give an editorial reply about "presidential erections," we were told that we could do it if her rant spoke about monuments and buildings, as opposed to tumescent chief executives. Or when socialite Gloria Vanderbilt came out with a line of designer jeans, I wrote a joke for Roseanne Roseannadanna saying that Vanderbilt had besmirched her family's good name by putting it on every ass in America. The censor at that time, a very nice man named Bill Clotworthy (he was the *SNL* censor from 1979 to 1991), would only allow us to do the line by saying she had put her family's good name on every ass who would buy them. Clotworthy, who is now ninety-three years old and still loves referring to himself as Doctor No, says, "The first thing I did when I got a script was read it and laugh. And then I went to work."

The censors would get all drafts of the script as it evolved during the course of the week and alert us along the way if they saw any potential problems. But during the dress rehearsal they sat in the control room with the script in front of them and followed line by line, as it was their last chance to raise an objection before we went on the air live and it would be too late to do anything about it. That said, any new material that was written between dress rehearsal and air would have to be shown to them first before incorporating it into the broadcast script or committing it to cue cards.

Lorne let us fight our own battles with the censors but always came to the aid of the cause if we needed his clout. One that I handled by myself was an absurd encounter with a nice but rather staunch censor named Jane Crowley—over a pun in "Weekend Update."

One night after I took over producing that segment of the show, Michael O'Donoghue called me at home and asked if "Update" could be sponsored by a product that we made up. I thought it was a great idea and told him to go for it. So the next show, O'Donoghue had Don Pardo, the show's legendary announcer, announce, "And now Weekend Update. Brought to you by Pussy Whip—the dessert topping for cats." It worked great. In fact, it worked so beautifully that I wanted to create a fictional sponsor of my own. So during dress rehearsal of the following show, I had Don Pardo say, "And now Weekend Update. Brought to you by Bleu Balls—the cheese snack from France." It played perfectly. The audience, our staff, everyone loved it, except for one person. Jane Crowley, who left the control room and waddled over to tell me that we couldn't say blue balls on the air.

"Why?" I asked.

"Because it has to do with the male genitalia," she explained.

"Wait a second, Jane. Last week you let us say pussy whip, which was clearly the female genitalia, but now this week . . . what kind of sexist organization are you running here?"

After looking at me the way the actress Margaret Dumont did in the Marx Brothers movies whenever she didn't quite understand that Groucho was trying to put one over on her, she said, "Give me a minute." She then returned to the control room, picked up a phone, and called God, I guess. After about ten minutes she found me in the studio.

"Alan, I've given this a lot of thought and have come to the conclusion that because I gave you pussy whip last week, I would be more than happy to give you blue balls this week."

I looked into the face of this very sweet, jumbo-size woman and said, "That's not necessary. Just let us say it on TV and we'll call it even."

Franken recalls another run-in with the same censor. "Tom and I put the word 'horny' into a sketch, and Jane Crowley wanted us to change it to 'sexy,'" he says. "I told her that a dog humping your leg is horny, not sexy."

$$\frac{f}{f}\frac{f}{f}$$

MOSTLY I WROTE WITH GILDA. I was shy and needed someone to speak through. Gilda, after a childhood in Detroit and her years in

Constant reminder not to take things too seriously.

Toronto with Second City, was overwhelmed by New York and in want of a huge Long Island Jew to lean on. Our chemistry was magical. We brought out the silly in each other. At any given moment she would walk into my office and out of nowhere announce, "I'd like to play Howdy Doody's wife, Debby Doody," and I would follow her lead. She would improvise the impersonation while I did my best to watch her and suggest dialogue and physical movements she could make.

We wrote everywhere. At the office, during walks in Central Park, late at night on the phone after dates with other people. That first year we were on a subway one night, heading toward Queens College, where we were scheduled to give a talk. Gilda mentioned a commercial for a cold medicine that was on TV at the time in which a completely bald man in a T-shirt, looking straight into camera, coughed and pointed to his throat while a voice-over said, "This is your cough center." The man then turned to be in profile, sneezed, and pointed to his nose as the voice-over said, "And this is your sinus center." Gilda, who liked to remind me that God had given me a much bigger head than was necessary, suggested we parody that commercial by having me dress as that guy and after coughing and sneezing, point to some buildings on my face, which would be my Lincoln Center, and then I thought it would be a nice idea to have a skating rink for my Rockefeller Center, and the two of us got so excited about the different things we could build on my

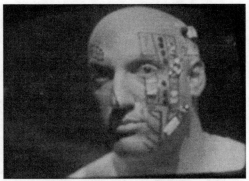

Sometimes, on special occasions, I put those buildings back onto my face.

head (one passenger who overheard us suggested they paint germs on my Center For Disease Control) that we missed our subway stop and were an hour late for our presentation.

But mostly we wrote over dinner. In restaurants in or near 30 Rock. Charley O's. The Palm. Gallaghers Steakhouse. A Japanese restaurant called Chin-Ya off the lobby of the Hotel Woodward that stayed open until 4:00 A.M. often fit the hours we were keeping.

When the show first started and neither of us had any money, we would take our legal pads on Friday night to those restaurants and use her brother Michael's credit card to pay for dinner while we were writing. And after we started making money and had our own credit cards, we would still occasionally try to get away with charging our meals to Michael.

"How about Nadia Comăneci?" I'd ask her about the fourteen-year-old Romanian gymnast who had scored perfect tens at the 1976 summer Olympic Games in Montreal and was about to embark on a multi-city tour in the United States. And instantly, as if a switch had been turned on, Gilda looked up from the five desserts she was picking at, stood, did a few spastic gyrations, and then started speaking in some unknown dialect while I jotted down whatever I thought we could use and then augment later.

GILDA

Hi, I'm Nadia Comăneci. Aren't I cute? Please see me when I come to your city, because I won't be cute for long. We Eastern European women don't age gracefully. Pretty soon I'm going to look like mother with big floppy arms and a little moustache above my lip.

Lorne wrote "AZ" at the top of the letter of objection from the Romanian Embassy and said to handle it any way I wanted. I called the embassy and got the person who was offended on the phone, and he told me that I'd insulted all of Romania. When I questioned how they were able to get the entire population of Romania huddled around the one TV set they had there, he said, "I'll have you know that I've been married to a Romanian gal for fifteen years, and she doesn't have a moustache." To which I answered, "Wait."

Gilda as Emily Litella. As an older Lucille Ball with a deep, raspy voice. As a fireman. As a five-year-old girl doing a soup commercial. Gilda and Chevy in bed after having sex on a one-night stand and her asking, "Who's Terry? In the middle of everything you shouted, 'Oh, Terry! Oh, Terry!' Who's Terry?" And Chevy answering, "I'm Terry."

The closest I came to making out with Gilda.

Literally dozens of characters and sketches over the course of so many dinners. But probably the most successful character that came about from our collaboration was named Roseanne Roseannadanna.

It began with Rosie Shuster, who was one of the funniest writers on *SNL* when I was there. The daughter of Frank Shuster of the Canadian comedy team of Wayne and Shuster, Rosie wrote a lot of very funny sketches with Anne Beatts—like "The Nerds" series with Bill Murray playing Todd and Gilda playing Lisa Loopner. But it was Rosie alone who wrote what I thought to be one of the funniest ideas that never made it on the air, when she pitched a premise about the worst Hanukkah gifts ever—and number one on her list was the Hanukkah that Anne Frank was given a set of drums.

One week, Rosie wrote a public service announcement titled "Hire the Incompetent." In it were three vignettes in which characters who were basically unqualified to do anything told their stories. For hers, Gilda put on a wild wig and a gray suit and while occasionally scratching her armpit lamented being fired from a fast-food restaurant because a customer found a hair in their burger. And then she said, as she wiped her nose, that she didn't think that was so bad, because there were a lot worse things you could find in your food. The sketch played well, and we all went on with our lives, until a few weeks later when I was out to dinner with Gilda and suggested that we take that character, move her into "Weekend Update," and let her do consumer reports, not unlike the local WABC-TV anchorwoman Rose Ann Scamardella did. Without taking a breath, Gilda then asked if we could name the character Roseanne Roseannadanna. I said, "Fine, but where in God's name did you come up with that?"

In the 1960s there was a popular song called "The Name Game" in which the singer, Shirley Ellis, sang a name and made it rhyme. "Shirley, Shirley Bo-ber-ley, Bo-na-na-fanna, Fo-fer-ley . . ." So right there at the restaurant Gilda started singing that song with the name Roseanne, and somewhere in there she insisted was the name Roseanne Roseannadanna. Figuring that life was short, I took her word for it. So that became her name, and, for the record, the character was not a parody of Rose Ann Scamardella. Even though if you google her, it says it was. Trust me. The inspiration began and ended with her name.

So we moved her into "Update," where she was an immediate hit. But, like anything else, it took a few appearances for the writing to find itself. We decided that there would be a viewer letter addressed to Roseanne every week that she would read and then answer into the camera.

For the first few letters writers we used names of people who worked on the show. Doris Powell, who had been the show's secretary when we first started in 1975. And then Bob Van Ry, who was one of the stage managers. By the third time we did it, Gilda suggested we name the letter writer Richard Feder, who was married to my sister Franny and lived in Fort Lee, New Jersey. Gilda liked my brother-in-law a lot but, even more so, liked the sound of his name. So, from there on out, Gilda would begin the segment by saying, "A Mr. Richard Feder from Fort Lee, New Jersey, writes in and says." For me, writing those letters became more fun as we gave Feder a personality by making him, well, an idiot. The stupider his questions, the more it gave Gilda something to play off.

So with legal pad and pen in hand, I'd sit across the table from Gilda and break down the formula that had quickly evolved to be successful. In order for the rant to work, we knew that we had to start with a legitimate news story—usually something topical that Roseanne could use as a jumping-off point before going off on one of her tangents. For example, one week we took on the annual Great American Smokeout event, where everyone was urged to stop smoking because it was so hazardous to your health. The straight line about it would be given to Jane Curtin, then a "Weekend Update" anchor, who would mention it in her introduction.

JANE
This week was the Great American Smokeout. Here to talk about it is correspondent Roseanne Roseannadanna.

The next part of the formula was the letter from Feder that would tell how he related to the story, ending with him asking for Roseanne's advice.

GILDA
A Mr. Richard Feder from Fort Lee, New Jersey, writes in and says,
[reading the letter]
Dear Roseanne Roseannadanna,
Last Thursday I quit smoking. Now I'm depressed, I gained weight, my face broke out, I'm nauseous, I'm

constipated, my feet swelled, my gums are bleeding, my sinuses are clogged, I've got heartburn, I'm cranky, and I have gas. What should I do?

[*to camera*]

Mr. Feder, you sound like a real attractive guy. You belong in New Jersey.

Then the third part of the formula would kick in, with Roseanne saying that when she stopped smoking, she also gained weight and joined a gym, where she ended up seeing a celebrity, in this case Dr. Joyce Brothers, naked in the sauna with a ball of sweat hanging from the tip her nose. I would then navigate Gilda, who, as Roseanne, would start to rant, and I would write down as much as I could for the next half hour.

And then, when dinner was over, the process became dangerous to our personal relationship. Because I would take the nine or so handwritten legal pages back to the office, while Gilda (this was a Friday night, remember) would leave for God knows where, promising that she would call to check in later. Back at my desk, I would embark on sifting through the notes, giving the piece shape, expanding on what was only touched upon at dinner, and crafting it into a coherent draft for the following night's live show. And then, true to Gilda's word, the phone in my office would ring at about 2:00 in the morning.

"How's it going, Zweibel?"

"Fine. Where are you, by the way?"

"What do you mean?"

"I mean, I can hardly hear you because there's loud music wherever it is you are. You at Studio 54? Who are you with? Please don't tell me it's a guy. And that he's touching you in places you always keep covered when you're with me."

"That part doesn't matter. How's Roseanne coming along?"

And then I'd tell her what I was thinking, and she would encourage me to keep going forward and then hang up. I was pissed. I was working, and she was partying. I'd stay at the office for another hour or so and finally go back to my apartment.

The next morning I'd return to 30 Rock and put what I thought were the finishing touches on the piece over breakfast in a restaurant in the lobby called Pastrami 'n' Things. I remember sitting there looking at the tourists who'd come to Rockefeller Center and thinking that they had no idea that we had no material for "Weekend Update" that night. Today, *SNL* has a special staff of writers dedicated to writing jokes for "Weekend Update." Back when I did the show, everyone contributed to that segment, but it was usually the last thing we turned our attention to after our sketches were written, rehearsed, and deemed ready for Saturday's run-through.

⚡⚡⚡

THESE DAYS, WHEN WRITING BOOKS, movies, and stage plays, I'm lucky if they first see the light of day two years later. But a live television show is a high-wire act where you have what's tantamount to instant gratification (or, if what you've written doesn't work, instant humiliation). I would write something on Tuesday and see it play in front of an audience on Saturday. Or even write something on Saturday and see it on television that night.

While I was at *Saturday Night Live*, after the dress-rehearsal audience left the studio, there was a meeting in Lorne's office to determine which sketches would actually be in the live show. The writers would then tweak them and bring the changes to cue cards. Then, if time allowed, I would take an elevator up to my office on the seventeenth floor, watch the eleven o'clock news (there were no twenty-four-hour news networks back then) and check any new AP or UPI wire photos that came in (there was no Internet back then), and if something struck me as funny, I would write a joke, and it would be on "Weekend Update" a half hour later. In fact, there was actually one occasion while we were on the air, that I was crouched under the "Weekend Update" desk scribbling lines and handing them up to Jane Curtin and Buck Henry, who were anchoring during a live show we were doing from the Mardi Gras in New Orleans. Herb and I had written Buck and Jane a number of jokes describing the floats and marching bands in the Bacchus parade that was scheduled to pass in front of their reviewing stand. Unbeknownst to us at the time, something had occurred that necessitated the parade's being rerouted, so every time the lights came on Buck and Jane, hundreds of partying, vomiting college kids started yelling and pelting them with commemorative doubloons while Herb and I handed them jokes about what they should've been seeing. The final line I gave them being that the phrase "Mardi Gras" was French for "no parade."

⚡⚡⚡

OKAY, NOW BACK TO A typical Saturday morning at the show. After my delicious breakfast at Pastrami 'n' Things, I'd go upstairs, find "Weekend Update" jokes that the other writers had slid under my door, and, with Herb Sargent, start to place them in order after I'd given the handwritten draft of Roseanne Roseannadanna to one of the production assistants to type up. A steady stream of jokes would be placed on my desk throughout the morning, and at noon I'd go down to Gilda's dressing room to show her the pages, thinking she'd better like them because I'd stayed up half the night writing while she was dancing with someone I was positive could drink more in one night than I did in my entire life.

"Hi, Zweibel," she'd say, smiling. I would grunt something incredibly unfriendly while placing the pages on the makeup table in front of her and then start to seethe when she'd take out a red pencil and, like a fucking schoolmarm, begin to mark up what I'd written. Checks here, cross-outs there, word changes in the margins, "X"s through entire paragraphs, an occasional "good" scribbled next to a joke followed by "but could be stronger" after it. Then she'd hand me back the pages and run down to the studio to rehearse a scene.

On the way through the halls from her dressing room to the elevator that would take me back to the seventeenth floor, then in the elevator on the way up, and then through the halls that took me to my office I built up a hatred for her usually reserved for an officer of the Third Reich. Wishing her only the worst, I'd sit down, check out her notes, and then curse her wildly upon realizing that she was right, that every suggestion she'd made was better than what I'd written. Oh, yeah? I thought. Well, I'll show her. And then I'd proceed to improve on her suggestions. Make them even better than what she wrote.

I'd do it and then head back to Gilda's ninth-floor dressing room gloating that I had one-upped her. This mood and accompanying shit-eating grin lasted until the exact moment that she took out that godforsaken red pencil again and started to rewrite that which I had rewritten. This routine lasted the entire afternoon, with me going up and down that damn elevator about a half dozen times until she performed the piece during the run-through, then during dress rehearsal, and then tweaked it again in time for the show, where I'd be standing next to the camera she was playing to, my head bobbing like it wasn't correctly attached to my neck, in sync with Roseanne's rhythms and with the mounting laughs and the explosive eruption of applause at the end, in this particular case after she sang a song to the tune of "We Gather Together" in honor of Thanksgiving.

We gather together to ask the Lord's blessing
Please look down upon the Roseannadanna household,
Bring peace to our fathers, good will to our mothers,
And please don't make me sweat like Dr. Joyce Brothers.

And by the time we saw each other at the after-party, Gilda and I wouldn't be talking to each other. The process had been debilitating and demeaning, and we hated what we'd put each other through.

This happened every week. The result of the passion we brought to our work. And had for each other. I once psychoanalyzed the phenomenon as an obvious sublimation of the sexual tension that we still hadn't acted upon. Gilda saw it differently—diagnosing it as being due to the fact that I was an immature asshole in desperate need of an actual girlfriend.

The day after one of these episodes, Gilda and I still weren't speaking to each other when we went to a Sunday brunch hosted by a woman named Boaty Boatwright. At the time, Boaty was a movie executive whose parties were renowned for having the most eclectic guest lists. We *SNL* people would find ourselves in Boaty's apartment with Al Pacino, Diane Keaton, Lauren Bacall, Polly Bergen, Martin Scorsese, Mike Nichols, and Michael Caine—grown-ups, if you will.

By the time we got to Boaty's, Gilda was ready to make up, but I wanted to continue being angry. Beyond the buffet of food was a step down into a living room, where I chose to roam. Gilda remained next to the buffet, making faces and doing little dances every time I looked in her direction—knowing that if she made me laugh, our fight would be over. But I kept averting my eyes in my pathetic need to stay mad. Finally, Gilda couldn't take it anymore and approached Woody Allen, who was loaded down with a plate of food in each hand and a cup of orange juice under his chin. Woody didn't know either of us, but that didn't bother Gilda, who, when she saw I was looking, grabbed him by both shoulders, said, "I'm sorry, Woody, but Zweibel's acting like an asshole, and I have to make him laugh," and shoved him down the step into the living room, which sent bagels, lox, tomato slices, and orange juice flying in all directions. Of course I laughed. The fight was over. And for months afterward, every time Woody Allen saw us walking into a restaurant he was in, he ducked.

ƒƒƒ

SUCCESS SNUCK UP ON US. The great *SNL* writer Marilyn Suzanne Miller used to say, "Hey, kids, let's put on a show," and that's exactly what we did. And we had a lot of fun making one another laugh and finding out that others liked what we were doing. Subways became cabs. Sublets gave way to rental leases. "I'm Chevy Chase—and you're not" became a recognizable catchphrase. I remember Gilda getting a stack of eight-by-ten glossy photos so she no longer needed to lay her head down on a Xerox machine and send the photocopy to fans requesting an autographed picture. In general, doors we never imagined walking through—or even knew existed, for that matter—were now open to us. Studio 54. Opening night after-parties at Tavern on the Green. And Elaine's, that legendary East Side haunt that belonged to the somewhat hefty Elaine Kaufman; there was a famous picture of her heaving a garbage can trying to prevent someone she didn't know from entering her restaurant. She loved writers and had known Herb Sargent for years. And now she knew us, and going there was sign of having arrived that we loved despite the questionable taste of the food. It was there that Gilda and I introduced ourselves to Nora Ephron and Carl Bernstein by sending two glasses of water to their table. And where I saw Chevy do one of the funniest things I'd ever seen anyone do—when a few of us walked in one night and at a front table was director Robert Altman, who was receiving all kinds

With Garrett Morris, Chevy Chase, and Desi Arnaz
during the first season of *SNL*.

of accolades for his just-released movie, *Nashville*. Chevy didn't know Altman, and the show was not yet popular enough for Altman to know who Chevy was. But upon seeing him, Chevy approached the director, excused himself for interrupting his conversation with Gore Vidal and Norman Mailer, and said, "Mr. Altman, I've seen a lot of movies in my life, but I just have to tell you that by far, by far, the greatest film I've ever seen was *To Sir, with Love*." Altman, whose smile had been growing and whose head had been nodding in acknowledgment until Chevy got to the end of that sentence, glared at him with a face that now boasted a rather unhealthy-looking hue of crimson, then turned away and resumed his conversation with the men of letters at his table.

And it was at the Russian Tea Room, shortly into the show's run, that Gilda and I found ourselves out to dinner with Lorne, Chevy, Candice Bergen, Herb Sargent, Paul Simon, and Art Garfunkel. Paul was on one side of me, Gilda on the other. Noticing that I said next to nothing during the course of the evening, as I was in such awe of whom we were with, toward the end of the meal Gilda leaned over and whispered, "Zweibel, pay for the meal." After looking at her in utter astonishment, I whispered back, "Are you insane? This dinner costs more than the house I grew up in." And while the others continued with their own conversations, she then hit me in the leg with her fist, inside of which was her brother, Michael's, credit card. "If you're going to sit at the grown-ups' table, I want you start acting like you belong here."

I understood. I excused myself from the table, gave the waiter the credit card, signed the check with a generous tip, lest they think Gilda's brother was a skinflint, and accepted their thanks with an "Aw shucks" attitude when everyone at the table found out that I'd paid for dinner. Gilda's suggestion worked. It was a step toward being an equal. And it loosened me up. To the point that, when we stepped out onto the sidewalk afterward, I mustered the gumption to say to the vertically challenged Paul Simon, "You don't know it yet, but it's raining." And thank God he laughed.

555

AS LORNE HAD PREDICTED, the show started to find itself. There was less reliance on the hosts as the cast gained confidence and carried more and more of the load. Chevy emerged as our first star thanks to "Weekend Update," on which he was anchor of his own segment, using his real name. Anne Beatts feels that as early as the fourth show, hosted by Candice Bergen, "the show took a turn, as the pretaped short films by Gary Weis and Albert Brooks, and even the commercial parodies became features as the live aspect of the show became more prominent." The very existence of the Muppets sketches came into question. Despite Jim Henson creating characters specifically for *SNL*, the show's edgier tone was incompatible with the Muppets' brand of humor. Explains Frank Oz (who performed Miss Piggy and Fozzie and was the director of such terrific movies as *Little Shop of Horrors, What About Bob?*, and *Death at a Funeral* [2007]): "We had a great first year with Lorne and everyone at *SNL*. It's just that the Muppets had their own rhythms and sensibility that the *SNL* writers were unable to connect with. It was those writers' sensibility that the viewers wanted, anyway. So we went on to do *The Muppet Show*, and *Saturday Night Live* became a huge hit."

As for the writing, Rosie Shuster feels that our sixth show, hosted by Lily Tomlin, was noteworthy, as it marked the emergence of strong female voices, which had been relatively stifled in the previous shows. "My sense is that the show coalesced with the 'Hard Hats' sketch on Lily Tomlin's show. In that sketch, Belushi flat-out refused to walk past a construction site in a tank top and shorts, the target of whistles and catcalls from jeering female hard hats. He felt exposed and vulnerable (much like any female person does in that situation). Danny reluctantly agreed to play the ogled sex object, and the hard hats taunted him, slapping a beam hard: 'Hey, angel buns, come do some squat jumps on this girder.' I felt a distinct female camaraderie emerge that week."

Others felt that the following week's show, hosted by Richard Pryor, was the defining one. Or the tenth and eleventh shows, hosted by Elliott Gould and Buck Henry, for which we eventually won a bevy of awards—and those claims are all valid.

ϟϟϟ

THE SHOW WAS LORNE'S CREATION, as it was he who established a palette where Chevy's falling down and impersonations of a dim-witted President Ford and Michael O'Donoghue's stylized homage to *Citizen Kane* and Samurai Delicatessen could coexist during the same ninety minutes.

For me, however, despite the accolades that were being heaped upon us and the show's growing popularity, I personally feel that *SNL* really defined itself in terms of attitude the week of our eighteenth episode of that first year. A tongue-in-cheek subtlety that was so wonderfully impactful in its understatement. Raquel Welch was hosting, and John Sebastian and Phoebe Snow were the musical guests. For the most part, it was a rather lackluster show, as they sometimes were when there was a host God had not blessed with anything that even resembled a sense of humor. Lorne called me into his office. Again, because jokes were my forte, it was not unusual for him to ask me to write, in addition to my sketches and contributions to Chevy for "Weekend Update," the host's monologue, promos, and the "in-one" pieces that were to be delivered by a person straight to camera. A day earlier, promoter Sid Bernstein, who had first brought the Beatles to America in 1964, had offered them a highly publicized $230 million to reunite. Lorne looked at me and said that he wanted to go on camera and offer them $3,000 to appear on our show. I laughed. A lot. And I still marvel at the thought of him sitting behind a desk holding a certified NBC check to be paid to the order of the Beatles. An understated, straight-faced appeal to the group our generation loved and whose music we'd grown up with. I wrote it up, but the brilliant concept, including the math that it came to $750 apiece, was entirely Lorne. I merely connected the dots he was laying down. I remember asking, "What about Ringo?" and Lorne, without missing a beat, saying, "If you want to pay Ringo less, that's your business."

The joke was continued the following season when George Harrison made an appearance on the show, "expecting" to receive the full amount and Lorne explained to him that that figure was for the entire group and that his share would be one quarter of that.

♭♭

MAY 17, 1976, I went to Los Angeles for the first time in my life. For the Emmy Awards. NBC flew us out first class, the first time I'd ever sat in the front of any plane, and put us up at the Beverly Hills Hotel—the first time I'd ever slept in a hotel room that was bigger than my first car. I remember calling my sister Franny back in Fort Lee, New Jersey, and saying, "Can you believe that right now I'm getting dressed for the Emmy Awards!" while putting on a rented tuxedo whose cummerbund, I found out the next time I wore a rented tuxedo, was upside down.

A limo took us to the ceremonies at the Shubert Theatre in Century City, and I remember the feeling I had as I sat there looking around at the grown-ups who were on prime-time television. Mary Tyler Moore. Peter Falk. Harvey Korman. Bea Arthur. James L. Brooks. We of *SNL*

With fellow *SNL* writers. Bottom row: Marilyn Suzanne Miller, Michael O'Donoghue, Tom Schiller, Rosie Shuster, me, and Bill Murray.
Top row: Anne Beatts, Al Franken, Tom Davis, and Jim Downey.

were in the same room and no longer at the kids' table. I wasn't nervous while checking the program and seeing that they were getting closer to announcing the winners in the Outstanding Writing for a Comedy-Variety or Music Series category. I felt that I hadn't earned the right to be nervous. But by the time presenter Alan King strode onto the stage holding an envelope, I suddenly earned the right to be nervous when he said to writers in general, "As someone who has spoken the written word for thirty-five years, without you we are nothing." And when he opened the envelope and smiled when he said, "From New York!" I leapt to my feet, flew down the aisle with my fellow writers, stopped to hug someone I didn't know, and took the stage.

Altogether that night we won four Emmys, with the other ones for Dave Wilson (director), Chevy (best supporting actor), and best show. And it was all accomplished by simply heeding Lorne's advice to make each other laugh.

For the writers' acceptance speeches, Lorne had us tell Buck Henry, who was watching at home, not to worry that there wouldn't be any material for the show he would be hosting that Saturday, because we were writing even while we were onstage, and then each of us took turns describing the sketches we were working on. I went last and said that the other writers took my ideas, so I had nothing to offer, and it got a laugh.

Afterward, I went to a pay phone and called my parents, but my mother wasn't laughing. She chided me for not saying that I was writing a sketch about how it was she who got me started and that I owed it all to her. At the phone next to me was a man I didn't know who picked up the receiver and asked to speak to Morty Gunty. That's how I met Arnie Kogen, who had been nominated that night as writer for *The Carol Burnett Show*, and who turned my head by saying the name of the first Catskills comic we had both written for. It had all come full circle during this incredible ride, where I went from slicing nova in a delicatessen to getting an Emmy Award in less than a year.

As soon as the show was over, we all celebrated in the private dining room in Mr Chow in Beverly Hills, where we were joined by a young comic I'd never heard of who made me roar with laughter: His name was Robin Williams. When I got back to the hotel, I found a message from Gilda that said, "I got so excited that I threw up."

And when I returned to my apartment in New York, there was a letter from Sid Leinwand, my old boss, that actually had the sentence, "Congratulations, Alan. Looks like you'll never have to slice meat again!"

CHAPTER **4**

SATURDAY NIGHT LIVE

(The Later Part of the Early Years)

MORE SUCCESS CAME with more trappings. Cabs became Town Cars. Rentals became co-ops. Cast members got their own assistants. I remember standing in a Long Island supermarket where the manager was on the PA telling customers about an item that was on sale, realizing she had given the wrong number of the aisle it was in, then saying, "Never mind," à la Emily Litella and getting laughs from suburban shoppers. As fellow *SNL* writer Anne Beatts later said, "You can only be avant-garde for so long before you become garde."

Even I, a staff writer on a late-night variety show, experienced a rather bizarre occurrence attributable to the show's success: I discovered that there were two other Alan Zweibels. One was a very nice comparatively religious guy who worked for the advertising company Young & Rubicam whose relatives would call me from Isreal in the middle of the night to congratulate him upon seeing my name in the closing credits of *SNL*. The other was a pain-in-the-ass lawyer who, to this day, still boasts that he used to get laid by telling women he was me—which I always found ironic, when you consider the difficulty I had getting laid telling women I was me.

During the next couple of seasons, the show grew even more popular. Political satire was now aimed at President Jimmy Carter, the void created by Chevy's premature departure was more than aptly filled by Bill Murray, and new characters like the Nerds, the Coneheads, and Roseanne Roseannadanna were developed. Thanks to Al Franken, who wrote the "Point-Counterpoint" feature for "Weekend Update," the catch-phrase "Jane, you ignorant slut!" worked its way into the culture, while audiences looked forward to Marilyn Suzanne Miller's sketches like "The Judy Miller Show" (in which Gilda was a young girl in a Brownie uniform playacting in her bedroom) that were funny enough to play early in the show, while some of her pieces that had a softer tone played best at ten minutes to one. And though Michael O'Donoghue was now gone, the writing staff added a strong original voice with *Harvard Lampoon* writer Jim Downey—and later Don Novello (who played Father Guido Sarducci), Brian Doyle-Murray, Neil Levy, Peter Aykroyd, Sarah Paley, and Harry Shearer. A few seasons later, it was Jim Downey who recommended the wonderful writing team of Tom Gammill and Max Pross, who were also Harvard alums, after reading some of their sample pages. Says Max about his and Tom's interview with Lorne, "I remember leaving the meeting and seeing Jim and Franken and Davis playing pool. They asked how it went, and we said we weren't sure, Lorne didn't actually tell us if we had the job or not." Tom Davis said, "Then just keep coming in until somebody tells you not to."

At the same time, hosts like Buck Henry, Eric Idle, Steve Martin, and Candice Bergen blended in perfectly with the show's sensibilities

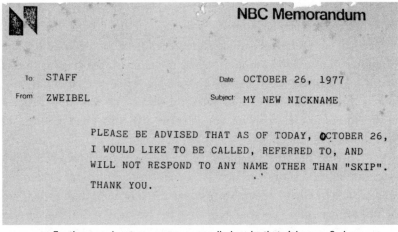

NBC Memorandum

To STAFF Date OCTOBER 26, 1977

From ZWEIBEL Subject MY NEW NICKNAME

PLEASE BE ADVISED THAT AS OF TODAY, OCTOBER 26, I WOULD LIKE TO BE CALLED, REFERRED TO, AND WILL NOT RESPOND TO ANY NAME OTHER THAN "SKIP". THANK YOU.

For the record, not one person ever called me by that nickname. Sad.

to become members of our extended family. The non–show business hosts forced us to flex different muscles, thinking of situations to put them in. Ex-jock that I am, I found athletes like Boston Celtics legend Bill Russell and football great O. J. Simpson (yeah, yeah, the same O. J. Simpson) of particular interest. During the week I would urge them to regale me with details of their heroics as I sat there silently cursing my own limbs for their inability to do what theirs did. So enamored was I of these sports stars that I brought a football to the office the week Hall of Fame quarterback Fran Tarkenton hosted and asked him to throw it to me in a hallway on the seventeenth floor so I could someday tell my grandchildren that I caught a pass from Fran Tarkenton. For the record, I am now the grandfather of five young children who would be more impressed if I told them I'd caught a pass from Ariana Grande.

My personal favorite host was Buck Henry. In college, I used to watch *The Tonight Show* and laugh my ass off when Buck came on as a guest and spoke utter nonsense to Johnny Carson for eight minutes. Smart, discursive, understated non sequiturs that I got to experience firsthand when Buck, who wrote the screenplay for *The Graduate* and co-created *Get Smart* with Mel Brooks, frequently hosted the show, played the perfect stooge to Belushi's samurai, and became a close friend. We had a lot of meals together whenever he came to New York, and he took me to parties at the Playboy Mansion when I went to Los Angeles.

Buck's insights into show business were invaluable. It seemed that he knew and worked with every great writer, actor, and director who ever lived. Mike Nichols. Joseph Heller. Dustin Hoffman. Philip Roth. Anne Bancroft. Paddy Chayefsky. Buck told me that Paul Simon's song "Mrs. Robinson" was originally about Mrs. (Eleanor) Roosevelt but was changed for inclusion in *The Graduate*, told me who was sleeping with whom on the sets of movies he wrote, and also told me how his good friend, the legendary *Tonight Show* writer Pat McCormick, was known to point to what he was purchasing at a supermarket and ask the cashier, "Do you think this is enough toilet paper to handle this amount of food?" I always loved those stories about the generation that came before me and found a certain romance in the lengths they went to to make each other laugh. Bill Persky, who, along with his partner, Sam Denoff, wrote so many of the classic *Dick Van Dyke Show* episodes and created *That Girl*, told me a story about another writer named Bob Ellison, whom others have referred to as the fastest joke mind they've ever known. The best example is when his good friend, Random House publisher Bennett Cerf, died, Bob took Frank Sinatra crony and reputed hitman Jilly Rizzo to the funeral. When someone asked why he would take Jilly to Bennett Cerf's funeral, Ellison, without missing a beat, said, "I wanted Jilly to see what someone looked like when they died of natural causes."

The worst host ever? During the five years I was there? Well, let's just say that on paper I imagine it seemed that there was a degree of poetic symmetry to having Milton Berle host our show. At the infancy of the medium, millions of people stopped what they were doing on Tuesday nights to watch *Texaco Star Theatre* (televised from 1948 to 1956), which gave "Uncle Miltie" the nickname Mr. Television. And now, a full generation later on the same network, legions of *SNL* fans made sure they were in front of a TV at 11:30 on Saturday nights to see our show. So the network suggested it, Lorne resisted it, and it ended up being one of the longest weeks of all of our lives.

Milton was a nightmare. To say he was old-school would be an understatement, unless that old school happened to be one that Neanderthals attended. He was rude to the crew, to whom he barked instructions, claiming he knew more than they did because he had been working in television before they were born. And though that may very well have been true, it was no excuse for his walking around in his boxer shorts, leering at the women on the staff, and calling them names like "Toots" and "Sweet Cheeks." Onstage he was impossible as he broke character in sketches and cracked unwritten jokes that interrupted the flow of dialogue and ruined whatever reality we were trying to create.

"Gilda, Jane, and I were posing for a picture with him," says Laraine Newman, "and he said, 'Why don't you girls do a little soft-shoe?' We said we didn't know how, and he was indignant. I know he came from an era where you had to be able to do it all, and I respected that, but when we said we couldn't tap dance, he said to us, 'Where is your talent?' Oy . . ."

That our approaches to comedy could not possibly be more polar opposite, however, was exemplified when Milton was rehearsing his opening monologue. When he stood on the stage, stopped what he was saying, and said to our director, "Now, when I get to this part, Dave, I'd like there to be a sound effect of a crowbar falling from above, landing on the studio floor, and reverberating until it comes to stop." I remember Dave Wilson's disembodied voice coming from the control room, asking, "Why?" over the PA, and Milton responding, "Because when that happens, I am going to ad-lib, 'Looks like NBC dropped another one.'" In a show that was built around the improvisational gifts of cast members who were geniuses when it came to playing the moment, Milton was *planning* an *ad-lib*! Milton then doubled down on his audacity by requesting that Dave shoot him from the waist up when he was about to mention that he'd recently turned seventy years old, because he was going to make a gesture with his hands below the TV frame so the viewer at home wouldn't see that he was inducing the audience to give him a "spontaneous" standing ovation.

On a more personal level, it was horrifying, because that week Milton actually showed me his seventy-year-old penis. Allow me to explain.

Though Milton and I had never met, I had seen him a number of times at the Friars Club and had written jokes about him for their roasts, a fact that I mentioned to him in his dressing room the week he hosted our show—the same dressing room that Gilda was supposed to meet me at, because we had a sketch we wanted to pitch to him. I got there first and encountered Milton, who was wearing one of those bathrobes that only went down to mid-thigh.

As it is today, comics who perform at roasts do material about one another's stereotypes and what they are known for. With Milton it was two things—his reputation as a joke thief and the size of his dick, a penis with such legendary girth that it once prompted comedian Dick Shawn to say after he walked in on a naked Milton in the Friars Club steam room that he thought he was there with his son.

"It's sort of surreal," I told Milton. "For years I wrote jokes about you and your dick ("After Milton's circumcision they used the foreskin to cover the infield at Yankee Stadium"), and now I'm finally meeting you." It was meant as a passing remark. A mild irony. At most, an ice-breaker in a conversation between a twenty-nine-year-old writer who had little else to say to a seventy-year-old comic. Unfortunately, Milton took it as a request.

"You mean you've never seen it?" he asked, as if his penis was a national monument that parents took their kids to visit on family vacations. "Would you *like* to see it?"

I remember being somewhere between the "N" and the "O" in the word "NO" when Milton, standing on the other side of the coffee table from where I was sitting on his dressing-room couch, parted his robe, took out an anaconda that had somehow traversed the coffee table and was now staring me down, and said, "Pretty amazing, huh?" just as Gilda opened the dressing-room door in time to hear me say, "Yes, it really *is* amazing," before turning on her heels as she said, "See you later, Zweibel."

SNL writer Rosie Shuster had her own run-in with our old-school host. "After dress-rehearsal notes, I was sent to Uncle Miltie's dressing room on a solemn mission to impress upon him that his shtick-laden performance was *way* over the top—and that his (cringe-worthy) broad spit takes were *not* 'our brand of humor.' (Anne Beatts and I had been going for a touching father-daughter scene with Gilda and Uncle Miltie set in an old folks' home.)

"I entered Berle's dressing room," Rosie says, "and he pounced on me, instantly a captive audience. Pacing in his boxers, Berle tried out an endless barrage of jokes on me, testing which ones got a laugh for his opening monologue. The boxers were disconcerting not only because they were TMI, but also because I'd heard that Uncle Miltie had 'the biggest dick in show biz.' Every time I tried to get a word in edgewise, Berle's delivery got more aggressive, and he would poke the air with his index finger. (I felt like George Burns in *The Sunshine Boys*.) Finally, Wardrobe appeared and helped him into pants and suit jacket and led him to home base. I trailed after him, pleading: 'No spit takes in the sketch.' Uncle Miltie went even broader on air. It hurt to watch. I swear

I saw a stagehand cringe. Lorne wisely put the Milton Berle show in the trunk."

That is, that episode has never been repeated.

⚡⚡⚡

THE *SNL* OFFICES THE THIRD year continued to be a fun place to work. The show's mounting popularity fueled our desire to not only do great work but personally changed my world, because *SNL* was where I met my future wife.

Her name was Robin Blankman. She was a production assistant who was beautiful and made me laugh.

Before joining *SNL*, Robin had gotten her master's degree in audiology but decided to take a year off before embarking on her new career. First, she gave guided tours around 30 Rock as an NBC page and was eventually hired to be the *SNL* show secretary by virtue of grossly

Her name was Robin Blankman when I met her.
© Edie Baskin

exaggerating her typing skills—and would often stay late to finish what she wasn't able to get to during the day. One night at about 6:00, while we were still in pre-production before the start of our third season (so we were still keeping civil hours), I was getting ready to leave, when, from the reception area that was adjacent to my office, I heard the click of a typewriter key. And then, a few seconds later, another click. A few more seconds, still another.

I entered the reception area outside of Lorne's office and saw Robin perusing the IBM Selectric keyboard for a letter, finding it, and hitting it before embarking on her search for the next one. Intrigued, I took a seat behind the desk that was facing hers and cleared my throat in an attempt to get her attention. It didn't happen. She kept her head down in pursuit of more keys. I then opened the middle drawer of whoever's desk I was sitting at, found a box of paper clips, took one, threw it at her, and saw it skip away after hitting the typewriter that she remained focused on. She didn't say a thing or even lift her head after I threw another paper clip, this time hitting her in the shoulder.

Frustrated by the non-reaction I was still getting, I then took the entire box, threw it in her direction, and watched as about one hundred clips came raining down on her head. At which point Robin stopped typing, stood up and, still not looking at me, walked around the front of her desk, disappeared into Lorne's office, emerged a few seconds later wearing a pith helmet that had been hanging on a coatrack, retook her seat, flipped a switch on the helmet that made a red light start to flash with a *bee-boo, bee-boo* sound, and, without ever looking up, resumed her typing. I was smitten.

Because we didn't want our relationship to become grist for the rumor mill, we dated secretly. Took different cabs to the same after-party. Different cabs back to one of our apartments after the after-party. We agreed to tell one person, Gilda, who totally endorsed the relationship, because she felt Robin was good for me and that as long as Robin was in the picture, I would stop hitting on her.

The covert nature of our relationship came to a crashing halt, however, the week that Kirk Douglas hosted the show. It was on a Friday when a Bar Mitzvah sketch was being rehearsed in front of cameras. There was a dais that included Kirk as the Bar Mitzvah boy's grandfather and the rest of the cast playing the boy's various family members. As part of Robin's new job as a production assistant, she had to cast a number of extras to sit at tables at the reception and fill out the room. At this point, we had been going out for a while, but our mothers had not yet met. Robin meant well when she cast both of our mothers to play guests at the Bar Mitzvah but had no idea (my God, how could anyone *possibly* know?) that once on the set my mother would flip out, because she thought Robin's mother had a better table. Given that we were rehearsing on camera, the ensuing catfight could be seen by anyone near a television monitor. And since a television network tends to have, perhaps, hundreds of television monitors, upon which we could be seen attempting to pull these two bouffant-hairdo-sporting warriors apart while shouting, "Mom, stop!" and "Mom, you're embarrassing me!" more than one person got an inkling that Robin and I had more than just a professional relationship.

ϟϟϟ

TOWARD THE END OF THAT season I also came to the realization that it was necessary for me to get better representation. But I knew that this was going to be hard. Dave Jonas had been really good to me. And I remembered how I'd felt that Freddie Prinze was an incredible ingrate when he left Dave for a more powerful manager once his career progressed. But I also knew that I was writing for a very hot show that was attracting and featuring the greatest comedy minds on the planet. And that the outside world was taking notice of who we were and what we were doing. So, after some rigorous soul-searching, I came to the sad conclusion that I could no longer be represented by a man who referred to the British comedy troupe as *Marty* Python. And after delaying any action because I secretly hoped he would die peacefully in his sleep so I could avoid an unpleasant confrontation, I realized that I would have to have that talk with Dave Jonas.

My contract with Dave stated that at its expiration it could only be renewed by mutual consent. About a week before that date, Gilda, who knew how guilty and nervous I felt, took me to lunch, made sure that I had a few more white wines than I'd ever had before sundown, and waited in Dave's lobby while I went upstairs and fired him before throwing up in his bathroom.

After some thought, my managerial decision came down to a choice between Jack Rollins and Bernie Brillstein. Jack was a legendary manager whose offices were in New York and whose clients during the course of his career included Mike Nichols, Elaine May, Robert Klein, Billy Crystal, Dick Cavett, Robin Williams, David Letterman, and, probably most notably at that time, Woody Allen, whose movies he produced with his partner, Charlie Joffe. Everyone in New York wanted to be represented by Jack—not only because of the power he wielded with agents, producers, networks, and studios, but because his clients all had original, left-of-center voices, and I knew that if I chose him, I would benefit from being a part of that illustrious group.

On the other hand, there was Bernie Brillstein, who was Lorne's manager. Bernie was a large, jolly man with a white beard—if Kenny Rogers and Santa Claus had a child, it would be Bernie. He played with the big boys yet assumed a gritty style of his own. Bernie called network bosses and studio heads at home, made deals at their kids' Little League games, wore sweat suits to their offices, and loved to laugh. He was one of the last of the breed of show business power brokers who actually loved show business and truly respected talent as opposed to regarding them as commodities.

Bernie was a native New Yorker who now lived in Los Angeles, which meant that if I were to go with him, he would be looking out for me on the West Coast. Aside from Lorne, Bernie also represented Jim Henson and had since the days when no one else was interested in those folded felt puppets he was carrying around in a suitcase. The comedian Norm Crosby, whom Bernie had long ago outgrown, was still a client for old times' sake. I was drawn to that kind of loyalty. Belushi and Aykroyd had recently signed with Bernie. And when Gilda did the same, I got to spend a lot of time with him and immediately liked him a lot. Above all, he had a huge heart to go along with his personality and belly. I felt that he would protect me. In the end, it was these two factors that tipped the scales in Bernie's direction. That, plus the fact that if he ever neglected me, Gilda would yell at him. Okay, so now that I'd decided that I wanted Bernie to represent me, all that was left was for me to see if *Bernie* wanted to represent *me*.

About a month later, in July 1978, Bernie came east for the New York premiere of *Animal House*. The film was hilarious, and Bernie was in an elated mood when, at the after-party, I approached him and asked if I could buy him breakfast the next morning.

"Go fuck yourself," he answered.

"Oh . . ."

Maybe I *will* ask Jack Rollins to manage me, I thought.

But as I began to slink away, he said, "I'll buy *you* breakfast, Shithead!"

The next morning, we met at Pastrami 'n' Things. I ordered scrambled eggs. Bernie ordered pastrami and, well, things.

"Will you be my manager?" I asked.

"Okay, kid."

"Really?"

"Here are the rules. Ten percent commission, I get to be executive producer of anything you create, and if you ever complain to anyone about me without talking to me first, it's over."

"I'm good with that," I responded. "So now what happens? Do we sign a contract? Do I get a lawyer?"

"Shove your lawyer up your ass." He then extended his meaty hand across the table and said, "Here's your contract."

A handshake. That was our bond until he passed away thirty years later. At which time, by the way, when I eulogized him at a memorial before a crowd of 1,400 people at Royce Hall on the UCLA campus, I mentioned that a lawyer was just the first thing that Bernie told me to shove up my ass over the course of the following three decades. I reached into my breast pocket, took out a sheet of paper, and read a partial list

Bernie Brillstein surrounded by friends, clients, and colleagues.
Bottom row: Brad Grey, Richard Dreyfuss, Bernie, Dabney Coleman, Brandon Tartikoff, me.
Second row: Jay Tarses, Garry Shandling, Jim Henson, Norm Crosby, Don Novello.
Top row: Sandy Wernick, Carl Reiner, Jackie Gayle.

of other things Bernie ordered me to shove up my ass, which included
Mike Ovitz, clients who had left him, the first draft of a play I had writ-
ten, the final draft of that same play I had written, a few of my haircuts,
Sepulveda Boulevard, and the internet.

⚡⚡⚡

IN RETROSPECT, signing with Bernie when I did may have also been
me acting on a hunch I had, that a lot of us had, about the world that
existed outside of the walls on the seventeenth floor of 30 Rock. Because
while this claim is purely subjective, I would argue that things changed
at the show at the beginning of that fourth season. After everyone
returned from the summer hiatus during which—on July 28, 1978, to
be exact—*Animal House* had opened. And then, two months later, as

if to drive the point home, Belushi appeared on the cover of *Newsweek*. Alone. No Gilda or Danny or Laraine or any of the other cast members on either side of him. By himself. Wearing a toga and a laurel wreath, Belushi was in a totally different context.

And though not verbalized at the time, there was a subtle shift in the culture at *SNL*. There was a sense that the show could now be a means to an end, a showcase where the actors could create a following and get a film deal. Or maybe their own television series.

The same thing happened to the writers, because movie-studio executives came to rehearsal and inquired who wrote certain sketches. "The nice thing about *Animal House*," Eric Idle says, "is that in the wake of its enormous box office success, Belushi became nicer, and kinder. He had achieved the kind of movie fame he really wanted, and he had envied Chevy going off to Hollywood. This instant fame was something we Pythons never had to tackle. In fact we were over before it achieved its totally unexpected success in America. So we didn't have to go back to a show thinking, I need more for me."

A new era was upon us. *Animal House* had happened. So had *Meatballs*. *The Blues Brothers* was going to happen. So was *Stripes*. And *Caddyshack*. Yes, there was a world outside the confines of the seventeenth floor, and it looked like a lot of fun. And Lorne himself was negotiating a multi-picture studio deal that the writers were not only aware of but wondered if they would be asked to write one of the scripts. Buck Henry recently told me he felt that "if everyone stayed with the show, sooner or later all of us would be movie stars."

As a result, things became a bit more intense. Writers stayed up all night Tuesday to get their initials on top of as many sketches as possible so they would have a piece in that week's show. And some of the actors would also hang around till all hours for fear that a role they might have gotten would be given to someone else who had stayed late and made their presence known. All of a sudden there were stakes that, while pushing the show to grow to greater creative heights with more adventurous sketches and new characters, came with a price. Getting to the office on Tuesdays with the knowledge that we would more than likely not get to sleep until Wednesday night became physically debilitating. Emotionally there were also frustrations, as the writers were prone to casting the actors who were more popular with audiences, since that gave them a better chance of getting their sketches on the air. Personally speaking, I had a tough time, as I hit a dry patch, started pushing, and suddenly felt that I was competing with my colleagues instead of working alongside them as I had in previous seasons. "Weekend Update" was still a place I made my weekly contributions, but, in general, I lost my confidence and withdrew. I had no good ideas of my own, and I became that guy who sucks the air out of the writers' room whenever I'd pitch a joke to insinuate myself into the flow of things.

"When Chevy left, it just seemed like a sui generis event," Al Franken recently told me. "He had been *the* star the first season. *Foul Play* was just an okay romantic comedy as I remember. But *Animal House* was a huge phenomenon, and also it was after the third season. So, that kind of thing was probably inevitable anyway, considering what a big hit the show was by then. I remember that Tom and I were pretty happy doing the show until the fifth season, when we no longer had Danny and John. That was a tough season as you'll remember. And that burnt us out."

My own frustrations mounted. Herb Sargent suggested I get out of the office and go for a walk. Or to a movie. Or across the street to Saks Fifth Avenue to buy something. Anything. He reminded me that sitting alone at a desk for hours waiting for inspiration to strike is a fool's errand—which was in direct contrast to the great director Billy Wilder (*Some Like It Hot, Sunset Boulevard, The Apartment*) who advocated staying put, because "the Muse has to know where to find you."

I chose to heed Herb's advice over Billy Wilder's and went for dozens of walks, saw about twenty movies, and, just to shake things up a little, bought a snakeskin belt from Saks that Gilda insisted looked like it came out of the ass of the bigger snake that had swallowed it.

I looked for diversions wherever I could comfortably find them. When my old friend Freddie Roman called and said that his son, a high school junior, was in a comedy sketch group run by older kids and wanted to know if I could sit in and offer notes, the Muse was going to have to find me up in Rockland County. I rented a car, made the drive up to New City, watched their show, and offered my two cents. And while the kids were appreciative, I can honestly say that no advice I gave Freddie's son Alan, who went on to create the sitcom *Yes, Dear*, or his classmate Phil Rosenthal, who created *Everybody Loves Raymond* and now stars in his Netflix series *Somebody Feed Phil*, had any effect on their ultimate successes.

Thankfully, things got jump-started again a number of shows later, when fellow writer Brian Doyle-Murray wrote a sketch about a local civic organization having their annual awards dinner and booking a fictitious former New York Mets baseball player from the Dominican Republic named Chico Escuela to be their keynote speaker. When called to the podium, Chico, played beautifully by Garrett Morris, looked out at the audience said, "Baseball been berry, berry good to me," and then sat down. Dumbfounded by the rather short speech, the emcee of this event asked Chico if he had anything more to say. At which point, Garret got up from his seat at the dais, retook the podium, said, "Keep you eye on de ball," and sat down again.

I approached Brian the following week and suggested that we make Chico a sports correspondent on "Weekend Update." Not only did that extend the life span of the character, but our collaboration also gave rise to a three-part series that we filmed at the Mets spring training camp in St. Petersburg, Florida, to cover Chico's attempt at a comeback with his former team. This was a parody of the comeback attempted by a former Yankees pitcher named Jim Bouton, who wrote a memoir titled *Ball Four* in which he made many enemies by revealing secrets about his teammates' extramarital affairs, drug use, etc. Brian and I said that Chico did the same in his book *Bad Stuff 'Bout the Mets*, and we wrote a script where the ballplayers snubbed him for it. Like Mets first baseman Ed Kranepool.

BILL MURRAY
[*reading from Chico's book*]

"Ed Kranepool berry, berry bad. He park his car in two spots."
[*to Kranepool*]

Pretty rough stuff.

ED KRANEPOOL
Chico shouldn't have done that. He hurt a lot of people.

⚡⚡⚡

THAT SAME YEAR, 1979, Neil Simon wrote a piece for the Arts and Leisure section of the Sunday *New York Times* that later became the preface of one of his anthologies. It was titled "Portrait of the Writer as a Schizophrenic," and in it, Neil, arguably America's twentieth-century answer to William Shakespeare, given the sheer volume of his work, described the comedy writer as a two-headed monster. The first head is the one that's attached to our shoulders. It's the one that visits the dentist, gets stuck in traffic, squabbles with mothers-in-laws, etc. That head simply goes about its business, when suddenly, without announcement or provocation, a second head emerges and, while hovering slightly above, makes fun of the life the first head is leading and writes about it.

A few weeks before we became engaged on August 2, 1979 (the opening night of Gilda's one-woman show on Broadway, which was also the same day that Yankees great Thurman Munson died in a plane crash), I asked Robin to read that article so she'd know what she was getting herself into—living with a person whose body might be in the same room as hers but whose other head was so often elsewhere.

"That notion is highly unattractive," she said at the time. "Especially to our future children, who would love to have a father with at least one head out of his ass."

Still, I thought it was important for her to know what the future with her life partner would be, despite the fact that she'd witnessed and experienced it at the show. Where the faraway looks took me. The reaching for a napkin to scribble something down in the middle of a serious conversation. Me saying while driving a car, "Can you remember to tell me 'Hitler's tonsils' when we get home? I'll know what it means."

Robin and I got married during the fifth season of *SNL*. The weekend before the wedding, we had a big party for everyone on the show at Sammy's Roumanian Steakhouse, one step down from the sidewalk on Christie Street in Lower Manhattan, which was famous for its singing waiters and the fact that virtually no body part of the chicken, cow, lamb, or turkey was spared from human consumption, and that the resultant gas was enough to make one's boxer shorts billow for about a week afterward.

November 24, 1979. I've tried desperately to keep that smile on Robin's face.

It was a great night. Paul Shaffer acted as master of ceremonies; Tom Schiller recited a benediction in about five different languages; Gilda sang, and so did Simon and Garfunkel. The following Saturday was our wedding in a temple in New Jersey, and then an abbreviated honeymoon, because we had a show the week after. We went to Puerto Rico and returned as husband and wife to our new apartment at about 2:00 A.M. Dead to the world, we had just plopped into bed, not even bothering to unpack, when the phone rang. It was my old pal Rodney Dangerfield.

"Hello?"

"Alan, it's Rodney."

"Hey, Rodney, what's doing?"

"You know, when I was growing up, we were really poor."

"How poor were you, Rodney?"

"We were so poor that on Christmas we couldn't afford tinsel for the tree. We used to wait for my grandfather to sneeze."

I started laughing. At the joke and the absurdity of what poor Robin's life was going to be like. After I stopped laughing, Rodney continued.

"Funny?"

"Yeah, it's really funny."

"That's what I thought."

Rodney then hung up, and I didn't hear from him for about a year.

♯♯♯

DUE TO THE SHOW'S POPULARITY, the NBC censors tended to be a little more lenient with what we did and said. The parameters had expanded, and we were able to do more on the tenth show that we could on the first, and more on the fiftieth than we did on the tenth. Still—and once again it seems absurd in retrospect—there were squabbles, including a classic one that occurred over a Nativity scene.

"Because I liked to flirt with taboos, I was often dancing with censors," says Rosie Shuster. "There was this by-now-famous showdown over the Nerds Nativity play that took place in Lorne's ninth-floor office over the phone while the 1979 Christmas show was on the air. We all tried to hammer home to Ralph Daniels, now the head of Standards and Practices, that this was not the Virgin Mary—this was Gilda playing Lisa Loopner with a red stuffed nose and a paper-plate halo who was playing the Virgin Mary. It did not matter. Over the phone an apoplectic Ralph Daniels really did shout: 'You can't give the Virgin Mary noogies!'"

As she had done that first season with the "Hard Hats" sketch, Rosie continued to write sketches that challenged the male actors to do things that they would rather not do. "A commercial parody I did in year five for 'Mommy Beer' reminded me of the male queasiness that can arise around certain female-centric material. In it, a rowdy bunch of manly men are returning from a hunting trip. They put away their rifles and break out the Mommy Beer. It has a rubber nipple on the top. You could feel the male cast squirm and their knees buckle as they took a long tug from the Mommy Beer rubber nipple to the lyric 'I love my Mommy. She's the queen of all beers.'"

555

PERSONALLY, ALTHOUGH I eventually rebounded from my slump, regained my footing, and, once again, got more than my share of sketches on the show, I became antsy. I started wondering how much longer I could go at this pace. What else was out there? Was it time to move on? For the first time I started writing magazine pieces and thinking of television pilot ideas instead of new *SNL* sketches during hiatus weeks. It was Buck Henry who insisted that I keep my perspective by reminding me how *SNL* was a haven for a writer, because it was a place where the writer got to produce what he or she wrote, having a say in the casting, wardrobe, set design, music, etc. Of course, Lorne made the ultimate decisions, as he had to consider what was best for the balance of the entire show. But the freedom we were given to realize our visions, Buck kept insisting, was rare, if not unprecedented.

"Once you leave this place, it will make you crazy, the control that people who are virtual idiots will have over things you've written," Buck would tell me. "Think about that piece you wrote for last week's show. Where else would you be able to do that?"

Buck was referring to a short film I'd written called "The Walker Brigade," which was one of those defining moments when a writer puts something down on paper and is stunned that people actually take him seriously. I'd pitched an idea for a "documentary" about a little-known group of heroes in World War II called the Walker Brigade who took advantage of a clause in the Geneva Convention (that I made up) that says that you are not allowed to shoot at any members of the military who are using an ambulatory device. Lorne okayed it, *SNL* filmmaker Jim Signorelli assembled his team, and a few days later I found myself at Fort Dix watching dozens of actual soldiers marching in columns with walkers, jumping from a plane with walkers, and, after a huge transport's door opened, sloshing through shallow water as they came ashore using walkers.

So, upon reflection, perhaps there was a certain amount of irony that it was Buck who hosted the last *Saturday Night Live* of the show's fifth year, which ended up being the final year I worked for the show. We had heard rumors, toward the end of the past couple of seasons, that Lorne might not return to the show the following year. Theories among the staff ranged from it was merely a negotiating ploy with NBC to he was signing a big studio deal. But as this fifth season wound down, the mood became even more somber as the rumors grew more intense. The last show of that season took on a surreal tone as we prepared to do a sketch based on an idea that was hatched four years earlier.

I had spent the bicentennial summer of 1976 in Los Angeles co-writing a Beach Boys special that Lorne was producing for NBC that also starred John Belushi and Dan Aykroyd. It was great fun meeting and working with this notoriously dysfunctional musical family, including drummer Dennis Wilson, who had seen fit to allow Charles Manson and his followers to live in his Sunset Boulevard home, and his brother Brian Wilson, who had purportedly written all those great surfing songs while sitting at a piano that was in a sandbox. That's right, he had never actually gone surfing—until we wrote a sketch where John and Danny played California Highway Patrolmen from the "surf squad" who went to Brian's house, read him the charges, then drove him, still in his bathrobe, in their squad car and forced him into the Pacific Ocean.

One night after we wrapped, I took a ride to a house that Al Franken and Tom Davis were renting in Laurel Canyon, and we started thinking of pieces for two *SNL* shows that were going to be done later that summer. I said something about wanting to do a sketch about a party that was attended by historical inventors who had something named after them—like the Earl of Sandwich, Duke of Wellington, the Earl of Chesterfield, Ferdinand von Zeppelin, et al. The three of us then started thinking of who the guests of honor would be and, I think it was Tom who came up with Lord and Lady Douchebag.

NBC was less than thrilled about our idea and wouldn't allow it. Every so often, during the course of the next few seasons, one of us would try to resurrect the sketch but to no avail. But for this show, the last of the fifth season, the censors relented and allowed the Lord and Lady Douchebag sketch, written by a gang of us, to be done. Dressed in historically appropriate garb in an elaborate chamber of "Salisbury Manor, 1730," Buck and Gilda played the lead roles. Bill Murray, Laraine, Jane, and Garrett were also in it. So were Jim Downey, Franken, Brian Doyle-Murray, Davis, Peter Aykroyd, and Harry Shearer. Even me, Robin, and about a dozen other writers and members of the production staff. A grand party. It was the hit of the show, which ended on a final image tight shot of the On Air sign outside of Studio 8H turning off.

The symbolism to a group of people who had never worked elsewhere was the subject of internal debate over the next couple of days until Bernie called and told me that Lorne would not be coming back the next year. The party was over. A few minutes later Gilda, who'd already gotten the same news from Bernie, called and asked, "Now what do we do?"

CHAPTER 5

FORMER SNL WRITER

(Looking for New Voices)

A freelance writer is a man who is paid per piece or per word or perhaps.

—Robert Benchley

NOW A MARRIED COUPLE, Robin and I moved into an apartment on Manhattan's Upper West Side that had sliding doors leading out to a small patio where we had many dinners that were made especially romantic because the back of our brownstone faced the back of the Beresford—a stately pre-war building where the great violinist Isaac Stern, who lived on an upper floor, was known to practice at night with his window open.

And while not too many couples could say they had Isaac Stern serenade them while they were dining, I'd bet a lot of money that the same could be said about Robin's parents' first encounter, in 1980, with our new answering machine, a newfangled contraption they were still unfamiliar with at this point in time. Sure, maybe it wasn't that funny to record an outgoing message that said, "Hey, Alan and Robin aren't home right now and hopefully won't be home for a while, because I just broke into their apartment and am stealing all of their stuff." Still, one Sunday when we came home after visiting friends, when we played back the messages, we heard Robin's mom's voice saying, "Oh, my God!" As if there was an actual intruder who had answered our phone and announced his evil intentions. And then, the next message on the machine was

Robin's mom, once again, this time saying to Robin's dad, "See what I mean, Sam?" As if the same intruder answered the phone a second time and saw fit to make the same announcement verbatim, which was followed by the sound of Robin's father's voice in the background saying, "I'll take care of this, Pearl." And no sooner than I looked at Robin and asked, "What do you think your father meant by that?" when, as if on cue, there was a loud banging at our front door, which I opened to find two New York City cops, who started laughing their NYPD Blue asses off when I told them why they were there.

This was my new life, and I loved it, except for the fact that it didn't have the structure that I'd become used to. The need to be in certain places at certain times. The Monday-night meeting in Lorne's office to try to comfort the host by pitching funny-sounding ideas that we had little intention of writing. Staying up all night Tuesday writing the sketches we actually wanted to write. Read-thru in the conference room on Wednesday. Thursday camera blocking the more easily produced sketches that made the cut. Friday camera blocking the more elaborate sketches that may have needed an extra day for the set to be built. Saturday morning, start putting together "Weekend Update" with Herb, noon, run-thru followed by the dress rehearsal, live show at 11:30, and then the after-party. Sunday we slept until 6:00 P.M., recovering from the week. Followed by breakfast, lunch, and dinner all in one meal. Then back to bed. And the next day we started again. As grueling as it had become, there was comfort in its predictability.

"So now what are we going to do?"

Gilda's words resonated.

And now, well, the absence of structure was daunting. Not so much that summer, because we always had summers off anyway. A few speaking engagements and a week's vacation in Cape Cod gave the illusion that life was normal. But when late August came around and we had no place to go because strangers now occupied our offices on the seventeenth floor, we were thrust into a real world that was suddenly different. Ronald Reagan was the Republican candidate for president, there was a new disease called AIDS, and the decade-long party that had raged during the 1970s came to a screeching halt. The adulthood that I had delayed for so long was here.

♪♪♪

DESPITE ATTRACTIVE OFFERS from Los Angeles–based television shows, I made the decision to stay in New York—much to the horror of Bernie, who yelled at me almost hourly that I should plunk my "fat Jewish ass on a plane" and move to Los Angeles, where show business was located. And to drive his point home he'd allude to fellow *SNL* writer Anne Beatts, who had just created a television series called *Square Pegs* starring a young actress named Sarah Jessica Parker that was going to be shot on the West Coast.

But I dug in. I figured that I could write in New York, fly to LA for meetings, and, if I ever did sell something that went into production, make the move to Los Angeles at that time. To me, there was always something distinctive about being a New York writer. My heroes were members of the New York literati. Woody Allen. Herb Gardner. Nora Ephron. William Goldman. Bruce J. Friedman. Paddy Chayevsky. They spent their days writing or in rehearsal or on a set, their evenings at restaurants like Elaine's or the Russian Tea Room. And that's what I wanted to do. The problem was that after I left *SNL*, I wasn't making enough money during the day to frequent those restaurants at night.

There were no more regular paychecks, a Writers Guild strike was looming, my lecture bureau dropped me because I was no longer an *SNL* writer, and when Robin kept falling asleep at her desk at an ABC show she worked at called *Kids Are People, Too*, we found out it was because she was pregnant with our son, Adam. Suddenly, I was scared.

This was my first real taste of what it was like to be a freelance writer who was no longer on deadline or surrounded by a swarm of other writers and benefiting from the windfall of the energy that comes from collaboration. Therefore, the discipline that had been dictated by the schedule of a TV series now had to be self-imposed.

So I'd wake up every morning, shower, dress, and then commute exactly four steps from our bedroom to the study Robin had set up for me in our apartment. There I wrote various TV pilot scripts and screenplays that didn't get produced and started getting published by writing satirical pieces for magazines like *The Atlantic Monthly*, *MAD*, and eventually *The New Yorker*.

During this time, Gilda was still very much in my life. And though the only thing we actually collaborated on was a book we "ghostwrote" for Roseanne Roseannadanna, she assumed the role of my editor, as I gave her every first draft of everything I was writing. She gave me notes like she did on *SNL*—either by crossing out dialogue and putting her suggestions in the margins, on long phone calls, or by actually coming over our apartment, sitting in a chair across from me, and playing the role of "the girl" with hopes that the dialogue would be funnier and more authentic.

I was working hard. And while I was happy for my former colleagues as the *Saturday Night Live* people were starting to make their marks away from the show, Gilda, who was also fielding movie offers, did all she could to help me make mine.

At this point in her life Gilda also tried her best to establish structure with a secure home life of her own. She married a great guy named G. E. Smith, who, at the time, was the lead guitarist for Hall & Oates (and a few years later would become the musical director at *SNL*). They lived in the apartment Gilda had bought in the Dakota, and we saw them often. One day in particular, December 8, 1980—it was a Monday morning—Gilda called to say her mom was in town and invited us over for brunch. We walked the thirteen blocks from our apartment to the Dakota and, before being admitted through the front gate, saw a handful of fans waiting outside on Seventy-Second Street with hopes of spotting any one of the celebrities who lived there.

"Can you imagine living here with all of these people always hanging out bothering you for autographs or pictures?" Robin mentioned as we crossed the inner courtyard to Gilda and G.E.'s apartment.

Gilda didn't get along that well with her mother, so Robin and I were, in fact, acting as buffers. We discussed Gilda's soon-to-be-released feature film, called *First Family*, written and directed by our pal Buck Henry, in which Gilda played the adult daughter of the president, played by Bob Newhart, as well as the Jean Kerr play *Lunch Hour*, which Mike Nichols had sent her and that she would eventually star in with Sam Waterston on Broadway.

We stayed a couple of hours before this otherwise forgettable brunch came to an end. We said goodbye and left, and when we stepped back out onto Seventy-Second Street, Robin indicated a heavyset man wearing a hat with earmuffs and holding a camera.

"Something wrong?" I asked.

"That guy was standing here when we arrived."

"He's been standing out here for two hours? He must have a lot of spare time on his hands," I said before we started walking home.

The next time we saw that same guy was on the news, when the police released the photo of Mark David Chapman—the psychopath who assassinated John Lennon when he and Yoko returned from a recording session to their home in the Dakota that night. Like everyone else who was stunned by the unexplainable that night, Robin and I sat speechless while watching television, wondering how such a thing could happen.

Around midnight, the phone rang. It was Gilda, weeping as she described how scared she was being alone in her apartment while hundreds of people were gathering outside of the Dakota holding candles and singing "Give Peace a Chance."

"You want us to come there?" I asked her.

"Yes . . ."

"We'll be right over."

"But you can't. The cops aren't letting anyone into this place."

"Okay, but . . ."

"Zweibel . . . ?"

"Yeah?"

". . . Can I come over there?"

So Gilda came over, and the three of us watched TV until Robin said good night and headed for bed. Gilda and I talked until about 3:00 in the morning. About the Beatles. About how John and Paul supposedly saw Lorne make that $3,000 Beatles offer while in John's Dakota apartment and considered coming to the studio before realizing they'd never get there in time. We talked about God. About what happens after you die. About how in six weeks an actor who had starred in a movie called *Bedtime for Bonzo* was going to be sworn in as the leader of the free world. About everything except the state of her marriage, which she avoided every time the conversation even came near it.

"I'm having a good time being married," she finally told me before changing the subject again.

I then made a bed for her on our couch, and we spoke a little more until she fell asleep.

ƒƒƒ

WHEN I DID WORK, I didn't stray too far and was grateful that Lorne had given me jobs as a staff writer for a live NBC special called *Steve Martin's Best Show Ever* and later on a short-lived series called *The New Show*—both of which reunited many members of the old *SNL* cast and writing staff. We had our production offices in the legendary Brill Building, where so many of rock 'n' roll's earliest hits were written by the likes of Carole King, Barry Mann and Cynthia Weil, Jerry Leiber and Mike Stoller, Neil Diamond, and scores of others. I loved being in the same space where such classic songs as "You've Lost That Lovin' Feelin'," "Stand by Me," and "Will You Love Me Tomorrow" were written two decades earlier. Its intriguing history was later described in Ken Emerson's book *Always Magic in the Air* and in the Tony and Grammy Award–winning *Beautiful: The Carole King Musical*, whose book was written by Douglas McGrath.

Steve's special was a lot of fun. We were doing live television again. In Studio 8H. And since it was produced only a little over a year since we'd left *SNL*, so many of us felt like we were picking up where we'd left off and were excited to be writing together again. Since *The Elephant Man* was a huge Broadway hit, Steve had an idea about playing the elephant guy—a sketch I wrote with Franken and Davis. And I

STEVE MARTIN

November, 1981

Dear Alan,

This letter is to express my deepest appreciation for your contribution to <u>Steve Martin's Best Show Ever</u>. I felt during the show that people were giving a greater effort because they loved the show, and your gift of time and talent was wonderful. Usually, I give lavish gifts at the end of an experience like this (on my last show, everyone received large screen TVs and video-disc players), but I'm between jobs right now and being so close to Christmas there's extra strain on the pocket-book. I'm sure on my next show people will be receiving lavish gifts because I'm expecting a big check in a matter of weeks. It's unfortunate that you had to devote all your great energies at a time when I'm caught a little short, but I heard you love perma-plaque, so I hope this will do.

Your friend,

Steve

A laminated and mounted letter from one of the funniest people on this or any planet.

met a really funny writer named Jack Handey, who had written a lot for Steve and later created a hilarious inspirational segment for *SNL* called "Deep Thoughts" that appeared between sketches. (*"It takes a big man to cry, but it takes a bigger man to laugh at that man."*) Since the special aired the night before Thanksgiving, Steve wanted to do a monologue listing the things that he was thankful for. And though I had his voice in my head from all the times he'd appeared on *SNL* and from being a huge fan of his, I actually found myself imitating Jack's style when I had Steve say, "I am thankful that small children don't burst into flames when they say the number four," and, "I am thankful for the Atlantic Ocean, because without it a lot of people from Portugal would just come strolling into our country."

The New Show was another story. When I'd heard that Lorne was assembling the gang again to do a weekly taped variety show in prime time, I let it be known that I wanted to be a part of it. Lorne was kind enough to hire me, and I was grateful to be in the company of others again. So many of the writers that I'd worked with before: Franken and Davis, Jim Downey, Tom Gammill and Max Pross, Jack Handey, Sarah Paley, and Buck Henry. Writers I hadn't worked with before, like George Meyer and Dave Thomas. And a few exciting actors like Kevin Kline and John Candy. But the show didn't work. For the creative team, it lacked the frantic energy of what had excited us about live television. Where the show is over and done with at 1:00 A.M. As writer Max Pross puts it, "When Tom and I heard Lorne was doing a new show, we felt loyalty to the man who'd given us our first job in television. So we, along with Jim Downey and George Meyer, left the Letterman show for a series that only lasted a few months. I never kept track of Letterman; I assume he was canceled and never heard from again."

Aunt Gilda and Gene visiting Lindsay hours after she was born.

Shortly after *The New Show* was canceled, Robin gave birth to Lindsay. We now had two children and were really happy, in what had suddenly become an apartment that was a little small for a family of four. Writing-wise, I kept at it and started expanding my circle by working with new people. I wrote an off-off-off-off-Broadway play called *Between Cars* that was produced at the Ensemble Studio Theatre and starred a twenty-two-year-old then-unknown actress named Elizabeth Perkins. Followed by another play called *Comic Dialogue*, which was included in the theater's Marathon of One-Act Plays—an event that included other playwrights like David Mamet, Richard Greenberg, and Shel Silverstein. At this point the theater started to really intrigue me, as it was the closest I could come to live television—there was immediate feedback from an audience, with the luxury of do-overs, as material could be tweaked or even totally rewritten if it wasn't received with the unbridled pandemonium I'd envisioned when writing it.

There was also a brief stint with a giant in the musical theater when my old friend, the great Broadway choreographer Pat Birch, who'd staged so many of the classic *Saturday Night Live* pieces (such as the one in which Gilda and Steve Martin danced across the entire studio floor), asked if I wanted to write a short movie for the twenty-fifth anniversary of PBS's *Great Performances*. It was to be a seven-minute musical starring Matthew Broderick called "A Simple Melody" that I collaborated on with Cy Coleman, the legendary Broadway composer whose contributions to the culture included the music for *Little Me, Sweet Charity, On the Twentieth Century,* and *Barnum*. I worked with him in the office he kept around the corner from Carnegie Hall, where the walls boasted posters of his shows and the original Hirschfeld pen-and-ink drawings that he was featured in alongside caricatures of other Broadway luminaries like Hal Prince, Neil Simon, and Mike Nichols. I watched as Coleman sat at his piano, banging out one melody after another, trying to figure out which would be best for our purposes. I sat in awe while studying someone using a vocabulary that differed from mine. And when I asked him how it worked for him, if he heard notes in his mind, he told me about his then six-year-old niece who had asked him essentially the same question a different way.

WKWZ 88.5 FM

COMMUNITY RADIO

Southwoods Road
Syosset, New York 11791
(516) 921-8850

Walter M. Yannett, Ph.D.
Principal

Jack De Masi
Faculty Advisor

Agnes Hennessy
Station Supervisor

Ann Merz
Station Manager

October 3, 1983

Dear Mr. Zweibel,

I would like to thank you for doing an interview with me last Saturday. When it is all edited and made into a show, I will send you a copy of the final product. I hate to even edit into one half hour program because the interview went so well, so what I will probably do is make three shows out of it with none of the interview edited. Part of the interview will be used in a special, consisting of interviews with you, Jim Downey, Al Franken, Tom Davis, Michael O'Donoghue, Anne Beatts and Don Novello. So I'll send you a copy of it in whateve form it finally takes

I would also like to thank you for helping me set up other interviews, I don't think you realize what a great help it will be. I will call you on the thirteenth about Bill Murray, Dan Akroyd, Buck Henry(Who I'm watching now in Heavan Can Wait.),Brian Doyle Murray and Rodney Dangerfield.

I would just like to say that I don't understand why you said you only performed in skits like Spud. I saw you in a skit the other day about a conducters club and I think it showed the kind of energy and enthusiasm you can put into a part.

Well thank you again for everything, I really appreciate it.

Yours truly,

Judd Apatow

— Member of Associated Press News Wire Serv.ce

— Member of Intercollegiate Broadcast System

— Longhorn Radio Network

I wonder whatever became of this kid.

"Uncle Cy, do you always have a song in your head?" she'd asked.
"I guess I do, angel."
"Wow, that means you'll never be lonely."
From the mouths of babes.

I got a similar response years later when Eric Clapton scored a movie I wrote with Jessie Nelson called *The Story of Us*. I was in the recording studio with my eyes glued to Clapton, who sat on a stool look-ing up at a TV monitor with a guitar lying across his lap. "Okay, run the scene," said Eric.

While they ran a scene from the movie, Eric Clapton sat there and plucked a few notes.

"Please run it again."

They did, and he watched the scene again, playing a few more notes.

He asked a third time. And then a fourth. And a fifth. Each one building on what he had previously discovered. He did this a few more times, and then, maybe ten minutes after this process began, the world had a new song.

"What the fuck was that?" I asked Eric Clapton.

"What the fuck was what?" he said, laughing.

"You just wrote a song right in front of me."

"No, I didn't . . ."

"But I saw you . . ."

"Those songs are out there," he said, gesturing skyward. "The tunes, the melodies. All I do is channel them."

"You channeled 'Layla'?" I asked a little too loudly.

He smiled.

"Jesus, Eric!" I remember yelling as I shook my oversize head in amazement.

⚡⚡⚡

AND, NOT TO BE DENIED, on the flip side of this genius, there lay the abject cretinism I encountered during that post-*SNL* period that renders me stunned to this very day.

I had written my first book. A novella called *North* that was about a nine-year-old boy who didn't feel appreciated by his parents, so he declared himself a free agent and wandered the world, offering his services as a devoted son to the highest-bidding set of moms and dads. It was now time to promote it, and I worked hard at overcoming my fears about being on live television. My fear of fainting. Of excessive sweating. Of losing control of my verbal filter and blurting a stream of dirty words that would forever shame me and my progeny. To help prevent such occurrences, beta blockers were called upon, and I eventually felt comfortable being in front of the camera. So the publisher's publicity department started booking me on a number of television talk shows, including a local New York midday one where the host's first guest this particular day was civil rights activist Rosa Parks. I sat in the greenroom, watching her on the TV monitor, fully expecting that when her interview was over, she would leave the set during the commercial and then I'd replace her. Nope. During the commercial a production person came into the greenroom and led me to a backstage area from which I would enter and take a seat next to Ms. Parks, who moved maybe a foot to her right on the same couch that I would be sitting on.

After the commercial, I heard the host introduce me as the writer of a new book called *North*, which was my cue to enter. I came through the curtain, acknowledged the thunderous applause from all thirty-five people in the studio audience, and took a seat that I nearly fell off of when the host, who wore an ascot and had a suntan that looked like it had been sprayed on through a fire hose, started the interview by saying, "Well, Alan, I guess it's safe to say that you owe Rosa Parks a huge debt of thanks, because if she had given up her seat on that bus, you couldn't have written your book, because there wouldn't have been a civil rights movement and no liberties like childhood free agency."

I sat there, stunned. Not from nerves but from almost throwing my back out trying to follow the logic of this host, who was trying to show his audience of thirty-five that there was actually a connection between a large Long Island Jewish jokester who used to write for a children's comedian named Roger Riddle and this most venerable woman of color who had public schools named after her. *I* had written a dirty joke about licking a stamp, while this courageous woman, on what would have been her hundredth birthday, was actually put *on* one.

The silence in the studio was thunderous as all eyes were upon me.

"Alan . . . ?" urged the spray-tanned host.

I took a deep breath, turned to my right, and somehow mustered the energy to form words.

". . . Thank you, Ms. Parks," I said, not knowing why.

". . . You're welcome, Alan," Rosa Parks answered, equally clueless.

And then the host, whose widened smile revealed about, say, 267 capped teeth, started nodding, and then his audience started clapping.

As shocking as this may sound, given the crowd-pleasing connection we made on that couch, Ms. Parks and I did not forge a friendship after this appearance.

"You mean you didn't get her number?" Robin joked when I arrived home. She knew that I was getting nervous again. Adam was four years old; our second child, Lindsay, was almost one; and the phone wasn't ringing. But, as usual, my wife did all she could to pull my head out of my ass.

"No, and I had such high hopes about writing for Rosa," I said, playing along.

"You mean like a Las Vegas act?"

"I'm sure she can sing and dance. Or maybe even star in her own sitcom. *Oh, That Rosa!*"

It was 1986. Popular sitcoms had names like *Mama's Family*, *Who's the Boss?*, *Gimme a Break!*, and *Charles in Charge*, so a series whose theme song was "Ring Around the Rosa" was within the spirit of what was being offered on the networks.

After the Rosa Parks jokes were mercifully over, Robin looked at me, read my silence, and said not to worry. That something would come along. That sooner or later I would find an exciting new voice to write for.

CHAPTER **6**

LIGHTNING STRIKES AGAIN

(It's Garry Shandling's Show)

IT STARTED WITH a call from Bernie.

I was sitting in the dining room at the Friars Club, when I heard my name being paged. A waiter then approached with a phone and plugged it into a socket under a portrait of Alan King on the wall behind me.

"Hello?"

"Hey, kid."

"Hi, Bernie. What's doing?"

"Do you know who Garry Shandling is?"

"Yeah. I've seen him on Carson and Letterman. He's really funny."

"Well, he's doing a special for Showtime that's heading straight for the shithouse unless they get some help."

This happens all the time. A script is written and then given to another writer, who looks at it with fresh eyes to offer suggestions for rewrites, new scenes, jokes, etc. I've personally been invited to sit at many roundtables where a television or movie producer invites a group of writers to go page by page through a script suggesting changes. There have always been writers like Aaron Sorkin, Nora Ephron, William Goldman, Babaloo Mandel, and Lowell Ganz who have been paid to doctor feature-length scripts. And though often not credited, their contributions are impactful enough to attract better casts and tip the scales that the movie would even be made in the first place.

This is true in the theater as well, where other writers, especially if a play is already on its feet but floundering, are called in to help. My favorite story about script doctoring involves the legendary wit George S. Kaufman, who, with Moss Hart, wrote a number of the Marx Brothers movies and classic Broadway plays like *You Can't Take It with You* and *The Man Who Came to Dinner*. Kaufman was asked to come to Pittsburgh to watch, in an effort to help it, a struggling play being produced by the Bloomingdale family that they hoped to bring to Broadway. After watching it, an underwhelmed Kaufman met with the Bloomingdales and made only one suggestion: "Close the show, and keep the store open late on Thursdays."

So Bernie sent me the script for *The Garry Shandling Show: 25th Anniversary Special*, which was a "retrospective" of a fictitious talk show Garry had hosted, a parody of the kind of anniversary specials that Johnny Carson's *Tonight Show* did. I liked the script (written by Shandling and Marc Sotkin) a lot and thought I could help; I liked the idea of adding some fake "vintage" film clips that could be produced as if they were highlights of past shows through the years as well as a handful of jokes I thought could be incorporated into already existing dialogue.

A few days later I flew to Los Angeles, drove to a restaurant in Westwood, and met Garry, who seemed like a nice enough guy. We discussed the script, and I told him my ideas, but I really couldn't get a sense of whether he liked them (or me, for that matter). All of my suggestions were received with slight nods that I was unable to interpret.

After we left each other, I checked into a hotel and immediately fell asleep. At 1:00 A.M., which was actually 4:00 A.M. for my huge East Coast body, the phone in my room rang.

"Hello?"

"Alan, it's Garry."

"Hey, man . . ."

"Alan, my dog's penis tastes bitter. You think it's his diet or what?"

That morning I called Robin and said, "I think I found a writing partner."

✱✱✱

THE CHEMISTRY WAS PALPABLE. I liked Garry. A lot. A Jew from Tucson, Arizona, he was of a species I had never encountered before. A kind, self-deprecating, tortured soul who would get overly animated while discussing southwestern furniture but approached my young children as if they were filled with plutonium.

And he was funny. Very funny. In his own way, as funny as anyone I'd ever met, as the writer in him spoke through the character I was getting to know.

"I always shave one of my legs," he'd say, "so when I'm lying in bed it feels like there's someone else in there with me."

ϟϟϟ

WHILE HE WAS AN ELECTRICAL engineering student at the University of Arizona, Garry started writing comedy in his spare time. Kelly Carlin, the daughter of George Carlin and writer/performer of the solo show *A Carlin Home Companion: Growing Up with George*, told me, "One day Garry read that my father was appearing at a club in Phoenix. Garry wrote a few pages of material for George and made the two-hour drive to try to show it to him. When George was pointed out sitting in the bar, Garry introduced himself and said he wanted to share the material with him. My dad thanked Garry but said that he wrote his own material. However, he also added that he'd be willing to look at the pages and give him notes if he came back the next night. So Garry drove the two hours back to Tucson and two hours back to Phoenix the next night. True to his word, Dad sat down with Garry and told him there was a lot of great stuff on each page—that he should keep writing because he definitely had a gift for comedy. Years later, while introducing George Carlin when he received the American Comedy Awards Lifetime Achievement Award, Garry told this story. And when my father took the stage, the first thing he said to the audience was, 'I apologize for Garry Shandling.'"

ϟϟϟ

ALMOST BY DEFINITION, writing teams are eccentric couplings. Two people who view the world similarly, yet with an appreciation for the differences that give their product an alchemy that neither could achieve individually. From the outset, Garry and I built on what each other said and recognized our potential.

Garry asked a lot of questions about my time at *Saturday Night Live* and its process. I told him about my partnership with Gilda—that our sensibilities matched, and we always felt that I brought out the guy part of her and that she appealed to the feminine part of me. Not only did Garry understand, but, after a lengthy discussion, we decided that he and I would take turns being the woman.

That contrast is important for writing partners. Bill Persky, who with his partner, Sam Denoff, wrote for *The Steve Allen Show* and *The Dick Van Dyke Show*, says, "Sam was acerbic, and I was adorable. He'd throw a hand grenade into the room, and I'd go in and ask if anyone needed help."

"Another nice thing about writing as a team is that if I'm not with Tom, I'm off duty," says Max Pross of the writing team Gammill and Pross. "I never lie awake at night trying to figure out an ending or act break. I just figure Tom will think of something the next time I see him. In fact, I probably won't even finish this quote."

ʄʄʄ

IT WAS DURING THIS TIME that I met Brad Grey, who was Garry's manager and Bernie's partner. Only twenty-nine years old, Brad was very funny and as smart as they come. "How did you and Bernie get together?" I asked him during a meal break. As he told me, he laughed about his moxie. Brad said he was in a weekly doubles tennis game with Bernie, Mike Ovitz, and William Morris agent Jeff Witjes. After one game he told Bernie that he'd like to have breakfast with him the next morning.

"I told Debbie," Bernie told me he said to his third wife, "I wonder how much this is going to cost me," thinking that Brad was going to ask him for a loan. But when they met, Brad pointed out that Bernie represented an older guard that included Jim Henson, Lorne, Dan Aykroyd, Gilda, Norm Crosby, et al., while Brad had a roster of young, unknown clients like Garry Shandling, Dennis Miller, Bob Saget, Bill Maher, Jon Lovitz, Kevin Nealon, and Dana Carvey whom he felt were the next wave. When he suggested that they join forces, Bernie asked for the weekend to think about it and on Monday morning called Brad in agreement.

Brad told me how excited Garry was about the prospect of working with me. It was a partnership that Brad encouraged. I told him how I, too, wanted to explore it. So after I helped out on his Showtime special, Garry and I decided to figure out what we wanted to do next. We started hanging out. Dinners. Lakers games. I became more familiar with him and how his mind worked when I drove with him down to the Comedy & Magic Club in Hermosa Beach and watched him make audiences roar with laughter while intermittently referring to the yellow legal pages of handwritten new material he'd brought with him onstage: "I don't want to say I have a big penis; I want you to say it."

I was intrigued by his persona. Sure, it had been done before. The flawed, hapless character who was constantly striking out—especially when it came to affairs of the heart. But his was somehow different. It was better. More intelligent in its construction and insight. Personality that got laughs by virtue of attitude and nuance. The writing was honest, with slowly evolving stories with embedded jokes, as opposed to so many other comedians who tried to portray similar inadequacies by merely sprinting from one punch line to the next. There was an innate awareness of human feelings and relationships that Garry acknowledged and then personalized with a unique spin of hardship. Like saying that he and his girlfriend broke up after having big fights about who was more disappointed. Or taking things a step further with patented tongue-in-cheek sarcasm when he said, "I broke up with my girlfriend right after she moved in with some other guy. I said, 'That's where I draw the line.'"

"One of the things I found the funniest and admired most about Garry, which is true about most great comedians," says Bob Saget, "is that no matter how you wanted to figure it out, the source of that joke or premise, it came from truth."

And those times that he did venture into fantasy, the audience went along for the ride, because it was still within character, albeit an exaggeration. For example, one night at the Comedy & Magic Club Garry did something that, to this day, I had never seen anyone do before. In his car on the drive to the club down in Hermosa Beach he offhandedly said, "Look, when I'm onstage, about three quarters of the way through my set, I'm going to scratch my ear. That's going to be your signal to shout out, 'Tell us about your chimp.'"

"Tell us about your chimp?"

"Yes, and no matter how much I dismiss you and try to change the subject, you keep insisting that I tell the story about my chimp."

". . . Sure."

So when Garry took the stage, he immediately had the audience laughing at routines about his mom, his hair, and his sexual inadequacies, and about thirty minutes into his set, after he got to the part where he lamented his inability to sustain relationships, he subtly tugged his ear.

"Tell us about your chimp!" I shouted from my seat at a back table.

Garry paid no attention to me and started talking about his shrink.

"Tell us about your chimp!" I shouted again.

"No!" he shouted back and tried to resume.

"Come on, we want to hear about your chimp!"

"Please, sir. It's embarrassing," Garry pleaded.

But by now the audience was intrigued and started yelling, "Tell us about your chimp!" and, "Hey, we want to hear about your chimp!" segueing to a chorus of "Chimp! Chimp! Chimp! Chimp!" and would not allow Garry to go further with his act until he told them about his chimp.

"Okay," he said with feigned reluctance. "I have a pet chimpanzee that imitates everything I do," he told the audience. "The other night, when I brought this girl home for the first time, the chimp took one look at me, hopped up onto my dresser, dipped his fingers into a jar of

Vaseline, smeared it on his butt, bent over, and started pointing to his ass. And then I yelled, 'Bad chimp! Naughty, naughty chimp!' And I said to my date, 'I don't know what's gotten into him. He's never done this before. I swear.'"

I was shocked at the audience's reaction. The great majority of them howled, a bunch shook their heads with incredulity that he'd actually said what he did, and a few others just sat there, stunned but smiling. They all enjoyed it. Out of context or delivered by another person, such urgings allegedly made by a pet chimpanzee might have produced different results. But since Garry had just spent the preceding half hour speaking as someone who often finds himself in peculiar situations, the audience was more than willing to go along with whatever he had to tell them

$$\mathcal{f}\mathcal{f}\mathcal{f}$$

WE ALSO WENT TO LAS VEGAS. Strangely enough, I'd never been there before. Even when I was writing for those Catskill comics who were opening acts for the headliners in those rooms. Back then, I wrote their jokes, they delivered them onstage, and then they'd call me when they got home to tell me how they fared. This time I went with Garry, who had appeared there many times before, sharing the bill with the likes of Donna Summer, Jim Stafford, and Joan Rivers.

He knew the town well, and everyone there loved him. I'm still not sure of the route I followed him on once we got to the strip, but it was one that took us underground from one hotel to another by way of their kitchens. And not only did security guards greet Garry and allow him entry, but the cooks, dishwashers, et al., all greeted him by name, welcomed him back to Vegas, and offered us food.

This particular night he was at Caesar's Palace performing in front of 1,700 people at a Toyota convention—the most staid, conservative crowd I'd ever seen. But they laughed their asses off when Garry strode to the podium and said, "There's nothing I like doing more right after I masturbate than performing at a Toyota convention."

On the flight back to Los Angeles, he told me he had an idea for a series where he played himself, Garry Shandling the comedian, who talked to the camera and showed the life of a single guy. Coincidentally, I had been developing an autobiographical show about a comedy writer with a family who also broke the fourth wall. We decided to meld the two thoughts and see where it took us. Garry, thanks to the success of specials like *Garry Shandling: Alone in Vegas* and that twenty-fifth-anniversary show, had a six-episode commitment with Showtime, which, in 1986, was regarded as the cable network that was not HBO. But they were in the market for an original comedy series. And we had one.

�§§§

IN THE MID-1980S, cable television was still relatively virgin territory for original comedy programming and a likely home for what we wanted to do. In this case, the word "likely" is a euphemism for "last resort." In 1986 shows like *Cheers, Perfect Strangers, The Cosby Show,* and *Who's The Boss* dominated the networks, but just as late-night was the perfect off-center place for *SNL,* what was then regarded as "experimental" found a welcome home on cable.

In fact, before Garry and I joined forces, he, Brad, and Bernie had pitched this idea to Brandon Tartikoff at NBC. I knew and admired Brandon. He was incredibly smart and funny and was unafraid of expanding what were then the parameters of television comedy. I'd first met Brandon when he was part of Fred Silverman's regime my last year at *SNL* and then again in 1983, when Brandon himself was president of the network and I wrote an ill-fated pilot titled "Big Shots in America," which was produced by Lorne, starred Joe Mantegna and Christine Baranski, and was directed by the great James Burrows. An awful lot of talent. Yet the biggest laugh, as I recall the experience, came at the rather dismal read-through, when, despite my pulling an all-nighter in my Brill Building office, a siren could be heard from outside, and Jim Burrows said, "It's the comedy police," and then Lorne whispered back, "They're coming for the script."

The "Big Shots in America" pilot was shot in front of a live audience and then shown to a test audience, who was less than enthused. And apparently Brandon was as well. Not that low test scores were necessarily the end-all to Brandon. The man was a true visionary who had the temerity to disregard low ratings, go with his gut, and stand behind initially struggling shows like *Cheers* and, later on, *Seinfeld* (which tested horribly) because he believed in them and put his faith in their creative teams. He gave those series the opportunity to grow with hopes that audiences would ultimately find and embrace them, and they did.

That said, his suggestions for what would have to be changed for him to even consider buying Garry's idea are horrifying in retrospect. He didn't want Garry to use his real name. He said Garry should play a character with another name. He didn't think the audience could relate to or care about the life of a comedian and, instead, suggested that Garry's character be a baby photographer. And Brandon further recommended that Garry not talk to the camera but to his dog. For those of you who think you may have misread those sentences, fret not. Brandon wanted Garry to play a baby photographer who confided in and shared his innermost feelings with his dog.

After Michael Fuchs, then the president of HBO, also passed on the show, it found a comfortable and excited home at Showtime, where its president, Peter Chernin, along with Allen Sabinson and Gary Keeper, encouraged us to present them our vision with promises of support. Those promises were kept as they understood what we wanted to do and appreciated the quirky, satirical lens through which we wished to tell our stories.

ƒƒƒ

GARRY AND I WERE WELL aware that a comedian playing himself in a situation comedy and speaking into the camera, despite Brandon's admonitions, was hardly a revolutionary concept. Jack Benny had stood in front of a curtain and addressed his audience at the beginning of every episode of *The Jack Benny Program* (1950–65) before joining the rest of his cast for that night's story. And Garry insisted I read the book *Say Goodnight, Gracie! The Story of Burns & Allen* by Cheryl Blythe and Susan Sackett to learn more than I already knew about George Burns and Gracie Allen—a husband and wife comedy team who not only bookended their show (1950–58) with conversations played outward to the audience but also had George, cigar in hand, eavesdropping on the other cast members on his television set during the episode we at home were watching and then saying something to the camera like, "There's Gracie. This is the first time I've seen her on television. She looks cute. I'm going to watch her every week."

By peering through his "twenty-seven-inch keyhole," George was also able to affect the story depending on his whim—by injecting other characters to complicate the plot or telling one of the actors to make a choice with full knowledge that it would result in comic confusion. And on more than one occasion he admitted that he could easily solve a problem, but he wouldn't do so "because then the show would be fifteen minutes short."

The takeaway from this was that Garry, like George, would have an intimate relationship with the camera as well as the ability to control the world we would create for him.

⚡⚡⚡

OUR PLOT FOR THE PILOT episode was simple. Two days after Garry moves into a new apartment, he comes home to find that all of his furniture was stolen by Vanna White.

We beat out the story and divided up the scenes in Los Angeles. I then returned to Robin and the kids in New Jersey, and we wrote the script three thousand miles apart and then sent our scenes to each other using a new service FedEx offered called Zapmail that guaranteed delivery door to door within three hours. Given that it takes a plane six hours to fly across the country, in those pre-internet days of 1986 we were dumbstruck as to how such a thing was possible. Much later we realized that FedEx had a new contraption called a fax machine, but we remained baffled during the ten days it took for us to write the pilot. That pilot script was the first of seventy-two shows that we would do together.

Both Garry and I were completely anarchistic in our approach to situation comedy. We were the same age, we both had great affection for the classic sitcoms we grew up with, and we venerated their creators, like Carl Reiner (*The Dick Van Dyke Show*), Nat Hiken (*Sgt. Bilko* and *Car 54, Where Are You?*), and my old pal Buck Henry, who, along with Mel Brooks, gave us *Get Smart*. But since it was Garry who actually wrote scripts for situation comedies like *Welcome Back, Kotter* and *Sanford and Son*, it was he (*Big Shots in America* notwithstanding) who was more familiar with what was standard fare. We were by no means passing judgment on the quality of the shows at the time. We were both fans of James L. Brooks–created series, like *The Mary Tyler Moore Show* and *Taxi*, and Susan Harris's series, like *Soap* and *Empty Nest*. It's just that Garry and I had a strong desire to play with the form in which they were presented. So where at *SNL* we used to say, "*The Carol Burnett Show* would do it this way; how should we do it?" it was Garry who was more apt to say, "*Three's Company* would do it this way; how will we do it?"

My response was usually to go theatrical. To make use of Garry's ability to speak to the camera. And, since he controlled the narrative of his life, instead of dissolving to some scene that takes place later, I would suggest that Garry merely tell the audience, "So here's where we are in the story. It's two days later, and now I have to deal with this cop," and then have him turn back into the scene with the cop, who's already standing there.

Again, this was in homage to George Burns, who actually replaced a cast member, Fred Clark, on the air, in the middle of a scene, by stopping the action and saying to the audience:

> Ladies and gentlemen, I have a very important announcement to make. For the past two and a half years, the part of Blanche's husband, Harry Morton, was played by Fred

Clark. But this year Fred went to New York City to appear in a Broadway show, so we had to get a new Harry Morton, and I'd like you to meet him. Ladies and gentlemen, it gives me great pleasure to introduce Larry Keating.

After Larry was greeted with applause, George called the actress playing Harry Morton's wife, Bea Benaderet, over and made the proper introductions, "Larry, this is Mrs. Morton. Bea Benaderet. Bea, this is Larry Keating, your new husband."

ƒƒƒ

JUST AS IT WAS WITH *The George Burns and Gracie Allen Show*, the show we were creating was going to acknowledge the fact that it was on television, and I thought the title should convey that. *The Garry Shandling Show*, which Bernie suggested at a meeting in his office, didn't do it for us.

"Why the fuck not?" Bernie bellowed.

"It's too ordinary," I remember saying.

"Too ordinary, my fat Jewish ass! His name is Garry Shandling, and it's his fucking show!" he bellowed again.

"Do you have any suggestions?" Brad asked me. In contrast to Bernie, Brad was quiet, soft-spoken. He never bellowed.

"What if we called it *Garry Shandling's Show*?" I said. "I mean, you're playing yourself, and this is your show."

"Close," said Garry before retreating to that mysterious place he sometimes went while sitting in front of you. Even this early in our relationship, I already knew that when he returned, he'd have a better suggestion.

It was during this brief interlude, maybe ten seconds altogether, that I heard, coming from where Bernie was sitting, what I was more than certain was a fart. Not a real earth shaker, which I'm sure Bernie had the potential of delivering, given his considerable girth, yet loud enough for me to look over at Brad for confirmation. Brad, who at this point had been in countless meetings with Bernie, offered only a slight shake of his head and then held up his hand as if to convey, "We'll talk about it later." Totally flummoxed, I held my gaze until I heard another fart, this one perhaps a single decibel louder than the previous one. It prompted me to look over, once again, at my esteemed manager, who caught my dumbfounded glance and responded by winking at me. To this day, I can honestly say that I have no idea what that wink meant, whether it was some sort of power display or if it was his reaction to the titles we were suggesting. All I know is that in the middle of all this, Shandling came back from wherever he was.

"How about *It's Garry Shandling's Show?*" he offered.

"*It's Garry Shandling's Show*," I repeated. "Yeah, that's it. *It's Garry Shandling's Show.*"

"Makes sense," said Brad, nodding.

"Who wants lunch?" Bernie bellowed.

⚡⚡⚡

"WE'RE GOING TO NEED A THEME SONG," Garry said. We had just finished lunch in Bernie's office and were going down in the elevator at 9200 Sunset Boulevard at the time.

"Any thoughts?" I asked.

"Since our television show is sort of about television, maybe our theme song should sort of be about our theme song."

"Makes sense . . ."

And that's when Garry started reciting.

GARRY

This is the theme to Garry's show, the theme to Garry's show,

Garry called me up and asked if I would write his theme song . . .

And that's when I started reciting.

ME

I'm almost halfway finished; how do you like it so far?
How do you like the theme to Garry's show?

GARRY

This is the theme to Garry's show, the opening theme
to Garry's show,
This is the music that you hear as you watch the
credits . . .

ME

We're almost to the part, of where I start to whistle,
Then we'll watch It's Garry Shandling's Show
[*five seconds of us whistling*]

BOTH OF US

This was the theme to It's Garry Shandling's Show.

By the time that elevator got to the lobby and the doors opened, the show had a theme song that Joey Carbone eventually put to music. Shandling and I had our Eric Clapton moment. Okay maybe, it wasn't "Layla." It probably wasn't even "These Boots Are Made for Walking" by Nancy Sinatra. Still, we were content with our day's work, which took all of three minutes in an elevator. So we smiled, nodded and went to a Lakers game.

⚡⚡⚡

THIS RELATIONSHIP WAS GROWING and getting more exciting every time we got together to write or simply discuss the new show. There was, however, a defining moment in our new partnership, one that had nothing to do with our work. Garry had been staying at a hotel in New York City when we were working on the pilot story. One afternoon he wanted to check on the flight he was booked to take back to Los Angeles that night.

Not bad for something written in an elevator.

"Here's my travel agent's number," he said to me. "Call her and see if my plane's on time."

"Excuse me?"

"Call my travel agent," he repeated, pointing to the phone.

His tone indicated he wasn't kidding, and I was stunned. I knew that Garry was starting to become a hotter property and that this project had the potential of being a huge break for me and my stalled career. But

I also knew that how I handled this moment would set a precedent for our new relationship going forward. So I took a beat before responding.

"Listen, Garry, I'm going to be your partner on this thing. Creatively. I'll work hard with you and for you to make this the best product possible. And hopefully, we'll also grow to be closer as friends. But please don't confuse that with me being your assistant. Because that's just not going to fucking happen."

Now it was Garry's turn. I remember being a little nervous about what his reaction would be. Even this early in my career, I had seen a number of comedians change as they went from obscurity to feelings of entitlement as their careers and public profiles took off. And I sort of held my breath as I awaited Garry's response, which, when he finally offered it, surprised me completely.

"Good."

"Good?" I asked, almost smiling.

Another silent beat. So I spoke again.

"You mean I got it right?"

Garry nodded.

"This was a test?" I added.

"I need you to be strong," he said.

As bizarre as I thought this was, I let it pass. We had work to do. For the record, this would not be the last time I let something pass because we had work to do.

ϟϟϟ

CASTING FOR *IT'S GARRY SHANDLING'S SHOW* was fun, as even the actors auditioning sensed that this was going to be something different. Our instincts were to lean toward actors with an improvisational background. Taking that page from Lorne's playbook when he created *SNL*, Garry and I both felt that this would enhance the script—by creating an atmosphere where the cast felt comfortable ad-libbing during rehearsals with hopes that they will provide better dialogue and jokes while they were in the moment than the writers were able to imagine from the desks in their offices. Ultimately, improv players Bernadette Birkett and Paul Willson (who portrayed Garry's sidekick in the *25th Anniversary Special*) were chosen to round out the cast with actors Michael Tucci and Molly Cheek.

In our quest to cast actors who looked like ordinary, relatable people, an interesting situation ensued when it came time to decide between two eleven-year-old boys for the role of Grant, Michael and Bernadette's son. One boy was Scott Nemes, an awkward-looking, heavyset kid with glasses and curly hair. The other boy's name was Fred Savage (yes, *that* Fred Savage), who was thin, dark-haired, and adorable. After some discussion, we decided that while Fred looked like a typical sitcom child who could go on to be a teen heartthrob in a series like, oh, *The Wonder Years*, we would go with Scott, as we figured that more kids looked like him and might have the relatable insecurities that we planned on giving him.

But the most bizarre moments came when we auditioned older actresses to play Garry's mom, who would have a heart attack upon entering her surprise birthday party in the third episode. Each woman came in and read the sides with Garry to see if there was chemistry. Callbacks were more interesting, however, as six elderly actresses returned to merely clutch their chests and fall to the floor for us to determine whether their myocardial infarctions looked credible. No dialogue, just waiting for one of us to say, "Now!" and then dropping onto the mat we'd put on the floor. Barbara Cason, the wonderful actress who got the part, told us later on that she had spent the night before the callbacks purposely collapsing in front of her husband, the actor Dennis Patrick, who kept asking, "What the hell kind of show is this, anyway?"

ƒƒƒ

USING *THE BURNS AND ALLEN SHOW* as a jumping-off point, we ended up with a series in which Garry played himself, broke the fourth wall, drove a golf cart from set to set, recalled memories by jumping into a flashback booth, and lived in a condo complex where neighbors like Tom Petty or Rob Reiner would pop in to return a hedge clipper or do their laundry.

The critics gave it rave reviews and dubbed it "the anti-sitcom."

The New York Times, Los Angeles Times, and Tom Shales (arguably the most respected television critic in the country from the *Washington Post*) were all enthusiastic about our little show. In addition to People Magazine grading it an A+, possibly the most rewarding reaction was expressed by one of our comedy heroes, Larry Gelbart, who said in *TV Guide* that *It's Garry Shandling's Show* "defies comparison with any other program on the air today . . . it is audacious, satirical, hip, sophisticated, and wonderfully silly, and, often miraculously, all of the above at the same time."

And because of these creative liberties we were permitted to take, so many writers who had felt frustrated by network limitations now wanted to write for cable. As a result, Garry and I were able to assemble a terrific team who, following *It's Garry Shandling's Show,* went on to write *Bill and Ted's Excellent Adventure* and *Men in Black* (Ed Solomon, *Mosaic*); produce *The Simpsons* (Sam Simon, Al Jean, Mike Reiss, and Jay Kogen, who was only a production assistant, worked for our show before he went on to write and eventually become co-executive producer of *The Simpsons*); write for *Seinfeld* (Tom Gammill and Max Pross—who've also written for *The Simpsons* for more than twenty years), as well as direct *Curb Your Enthusiasm* (David Steinberg) and *The West Wing* (Tommy Schlamme). Thanks to all of their inspired efforts, *It's Garry Shandling's Show* won dozens of awards. In those early days, cable shows were not eligible for Emmy Awards, so we won a bevy of what were then called ACE Awards—chrome statuettes shaped like the icon in the upper corner of the ace of spades that looked like the hood ornament on a 1955 Buick mounted on a thick block of wood that weighed more than I did when I was born. There were also Television Critics Association (TCA) Awards. And in the final season of the series, *It's Garry Shandling's Show* was the first cable comedy show to ever be nominated for an Emmy.

Equally rewarding was how people such as Edie Adams—whose husband, the late, great Ernie Kovacs, was television's first great innovator when it came to playing tricks with the medium itself—would hang out in our studio claiming that our show was something that Ernie would have gotten a kick out of. Says Edie's son Josh Mills, "When my mom was asked to appear on *It's Garry Shandling's Show*, she jumped at the chance, because it challenged the viewers' expectations by turning the camera upside down; or when it was tilted, Garry would almost fall off the set. That's pure Kovacs."

And how, as Terri Miller, who was a production supervisor on the show, recalls, a twenty-year-old kid named Quentin Tarantino worked at the best video store down in Manhattan Beach, "so Peter Barth (the show's stage manager) and I would put Quentin on the guest list in exchange for free video rentals. He came to our show quite a bit."

And how—and this is my personal favorite—Buck Henry (who wrote the screenplay for *The Graduate*) told me that he showed our parody of that movie to Mike Nichols (who had won an Oscar for directing it), and Mike became an instant fan of what Garry and I were doing.

"It was so much fun writing a fourth-grade play every week," says Ed Solomon. "But what I learned was that if a story has an emotional truth, then you can use all of the video tricks and gimmicks you want, because they come out of character and aid in the resolution of that story. To this day, that's a lesson that I repeat to myself when I'm writing."

⚡⚡⚡

AS EXCITING AS THAT FIRST year of the Shandling show was, it was tough on me and Robin and our two young children, who were back in New Jersey. On any series you are generally working on three shows at the same time. That is, while you're producing this week's show, you're editing last week's and preparing the script for next week's. So what had begun as cross-country flights every weekend during pre-production became once a month for a few days during our hiatus weeks. That, coupled with the fact that this was pre-Skype and FaceTime, meant I missed chunks of their young lives that letters and phone calls couldn't replace. Because the initial order for the show was only six episodes, our reasoning had been, why uproot the family if we weren't picked up and I was back home in two months? And by the time the show was picked up for twelve more episodes to complete an entire season, we didn't want to uproot the kids in the middle of the school year.

So the weekends were particularly lonely. I lived by myself in a home on Doheny Drive above Sunset Boulevard that I rented from the singer Freda Payne, who had a big hit in the 1970s called "Band of Gold." And though I am loath to make any assumptions, on occasion my loneliness was interrupted by late-night knocks on the front door by an assortment of singers like Tom Jones and Luther Vandross who looked incredibly disappointed when I told them that Freda wasn't home.

Hiatus weeks were a little easier, because I still went to the office most days to edit the previous week's show or meet with the staff to try to get a leg up on the next few scripts we'd be producing. I'd also accompany Garry to *The Tonight Show* when he'd be the guest host for a vacationing Johnny Carson. It was during one of these weeks that I was introduced to the *Tonight Show* writing team of Al Jean and Mike Reiss, both Harvard alums, who came to work for us on our show.

But no matter how I filled my days, I still went home to Freda Payne's empty house at night. So when Showtime gave us an order for fifty-four more episodes of *It's Garry Shandling's Show*, which was essentially three more seasons, we closed up the home we had just built in North Caldwell, New Jersey, and moved the family to Los Angeles.

We chose to live in Brentwood, enrolled the kids in schools, and tried our best to adjust to West Coast life. Los Angeles is a company town that the greater majority of my friends had already made the move to, because, as Mel Brooks told me, "If you're a coal miner, maybe you should live in West Virginia."

It took a while to adjust, although the family got its Los Angeles indoctrination the very first night we were there. Robin and I took the kids to dinner at an Italian restaurant in Westwood called Matteo's that was often frequented by the likes of Dean Martin, Sammy Davis Jr., and other members of the famed Rat Pack. We found a booth not too far from the bar and ordered, and while waiting for the food to come, Lindsay, who was three years old, started misbehaving. Kicking Adam. Not sitting still. Throwing bread. And despite repeated admonitions, she persisted until I issued a final warning that if she didn't calm down, she would be sent away from the table. She acted out again, and I told her, "I've had it! You are to stand in that corner and not come back until you can sit here like a big girl." Lindsay left the table just as the waiter came with our first course. I put my head down for a second to taste the soup when I heard the voice of an older man saying, "This young lady says you're giving her a hard time." I looked up and saw Frank Sinatra holding Lindsay's hand. Although I'd never met him, I said, "Mr. Sinatra, please listen to my side of the story," and I proceeded to inform him of Lindsay's behavior. Sinatra then asked, "Is that true, Lindsay?" and when she sheepishly nodded, Sinatra asked her to apologize, hug her dad and retake her seat, and told us to enjoy our meal before he headed back to the bar.

As much as I appreciated Ol' Blue Eyes' parental assistance, suffice it to say that I didn't see the need to tell him any of the jokes I'd written years before for a comic named Pat Henry for a Friars roast about the shady characters Sinatra was said to have associated with.

I really like telling jokes about Frank Sinatra—it gives me the occasion to wear cement shoes with my tuxedo.

ϟϟϟ

NOW THAT THE FAMILY was in Los Angeles, I segued into expanding my hyphenate to "writer-producer-husband-father," as I had been forced to fulfill the last two titles long-distance the year before. It still wasn't easy, given the unorthodox demands of the Shandling show that so often kept us at the office until 2:00 A.M. a couple of nights a week. Frustration came from the fact that when a script was sent to the studio floor for rehearsal (when so many writing staffs are tweaking the script for the following week's show), I would often have to come upstairs to tell the writers lines that Garry, ever the writer, had ad-libbed and wanted incorporated into this week's script. And while a joke here and there is easy enough to accommodate, lines that affect the plot and, consequently, the scenes that follow it are a different story. Literally. So then the question became whether to change the following scenes at that time or wait until after we all went down to see the late-afternoon run-thru, hear more lines that none of us had ever heard before, and then go upstairs and wait for Garry to finish his phone calls before telling us more changes that he'd like. Often Garry would then stay at the writers' table just to hang out, and after we finally coaxed him into getting the hell out of there, our rewrite session would start at 9:00 P.M.

Quite different than so many other shows. For example, Phil Rosenthal, who co-created *Everybody Loves Raymond*, says, "I sent everyone home at six every night. Sometimes we left earlier. The whole point was that if you were going to write about real life, you should have one. And everything that you saw on the show happened to me, or Ray, or one of the other writers. Took this idea from Carl Reiner—it's how he ran *The Dick Van Dyke Show*."

I didn't have that luxury. As the show runner, I was in a bind, as the buck didn't always stop with me. I spoke to Garry more than once—in fact, dozens of times—about how demoralizing these last-minute changes were to the staff, especially when the changes appeared to be lateral, even arbitrary. With no marked improvement of the same script that had been such a hit only a few hours before when he and the rest of the cast sat around the table reading it. However—and here was the greater frustration—Garry's requested changes, many times, made the show better. And funnier. Even the drafts that he and I wrote together. While closer to the mark because of his initial input, they, too, were subjected to the same onstage editorial process. Again, if it was a matter of coming up with new jokes, we had fun. Going around the table with each writer pitching jokes over pizza and, as was a staple around virtually all writers' tables in those days, telling tales about Danny Thomas and his renowned scatological affection. But when the script needed an overhaul, I often had to assign scenes—have Tom Gammill and Max Pross go into their office, Al Jean and Mike Reiss go into theirs, Janis Hirsch

Yes, at one point, Garry and I were so close that we
walked around this way.

go into hers, etc., to do rewrites. And when they finally emerged, we sat
with the scenes, formed them into a coherent story, and then started the
joke writing. Hence, the early-morning returns to our respective abodes.
Once again, I cite Marshall Brickman, who says, "I've come to believe
that there's no such thing as a totally equal collaboration. There has to
be a dominant party, so that the result has a consistent tone and voice."
Therefore, it's safe to say that no matter how much I prided myself in
how close I came to capturing Garry's voice, I was still, at best, the vice
president of the show I'd cocreated.

Says Paul Feig (creator of the TV series *Freaks and Geeks* and the
director of movies such as *Bridesmaids, Spy,* and *A Simple Favor*), who
got his first job in show business as an actor on *It's Garry Shandling's
Show,* "When I sold *Freaks and Geeks* to NBC, they said they loved the
script and not to change a thing." Those are the words that every writer

dreams of hearing from the people in charge. So when we went into our first day of prep, Judd said, "All right, let's tear the script apart." I was floored and thrown. I argued against it, but Judd told me Garry's philosophy, which was, basically, be as hard on the script as possible and try everything you can and if you mess it up, you still have the original script to go back to. Tearing it apart doesn't make it disappear . . . I've never forgotten that and always tried to work that way on any other projects I'm doing."

⚡⚡

DESPITE THE UNGODLY HOURS, since Adam and Lindsay had school, I made sure I was awake to see them at breakfast, because it was a pretty sure bet that I wouldn't see them that night.

I remember one particular morning, after their carpools filled with the children of movie stars and other show runners picked up the kids and before I headed to the studio, I stopped into the nearby Brentwood Country Mart, a quaint place with a handful of stores and restaurants where you can eat outside at one of the wooden tables they have in the common area. In a corner of that quad was a small luncheonette, where I took a seat in a back booth and had coffee while reading the sports section of the *Los Angeles Times*. In the booth across from me was a group of older men who, I ascertained from their conversation, were once comedy writers for such classic shows as *The Jack Benny Program* and *Burns and Allen*. I was fascinated, and my instinct was to introduce myself and ask a million questions about their wonderful careers and their collective contributions to the culture. But then I listened closely and detected the bitterness in their tones. Their resentment about no longer being able to get work. Them bitterly putting down everything that was currently on television, saying, "This generation has no idea what's funny!" A haunting omen? The comedy writer's version of those older comics I used to see playing cards at the Friars Club while bitterly cursing the younger audiences who no longer found them funny. Was this going to be me one day? I decided not to introduce myself. And I started going elsewhere for coffee and the paper.

ϟϟϟ

IN ADDITION TO ALL OF the plaudits and excitement surrounding our series, it was also the last television appearance by my old pal Gilda.

I was angry at her. I'd been in Los Angeles shooting the pilot for *It's Garry Shandling's Show* and was excited by the prospect of reuniting. Gilda had moved to Los Angeles a few years earlier, married Gene Wilder, and established a brand-new life for herself on the West Coast. Our communication had dwindled in those pre-internet days when different time zones and work schedules reduced our communication to occasional phone calls and visits whenever one of us was on the other's coast. And now that I'd be in LA for an extended period of time, I figured that we could make up for lost time.

But after accepting every dinner invitation I extended, she would ultimately cancel. When this happened three or four times, I remember telling Robin that I thought Gilda didn't want to be my platonic friend anymore. Robin spoke to Gilda on the phone, then insisted that I call her. It was then that Gilda told me she hadn't been feeling well. That she had Epstein-Barr virus. She apologized for breaking all of our dates. I told her I understood, and she made me promise to call her the next time I came to Los Angeles.

Six weeks later I was back in LA to start work on *It's Garry Shandling's Show*. The day I was moving into Freda Payne's house, Gilda showed up at my door holding a housewarming gift. A big potted plant reminiscent of the one we had met behind in Lorne's office that first day of *SNL*. We both laughed, put it in a corner of the living room, and sat on my newly rented couch to have one of our talks. I was excited to be with her. She then told me that she didn't have Epstein-Barr virus. I was thrilled to hear that—with Robin and the children three thousand miles away in a new house we'd just moved into in New Jersey, I started to list all the fun things Gilda and I could do together. Dinners. Movies. Lakers games. It was then that she politely smiled and told me she had been diagnosed with ovarian cancer and said she'd like me to help her with this part of her life. Stunned, scared, and doing all I could not to cry, I asked her, "What should I do?" and she said, "Make me laugh."

And this was my role in my platonic friend's life while she was sick. Garry and I produced a show every week and sent her the VHS cassette as if it were a Hallmark card. I told her jokes on the phone, trying to get her mind off of, if only for a few minutes, whatever horrors she returned to after we hung up. And then, in our second season, we asked her to appear in an episode. She loved the show and thought Garry was hilarious but was nervous that, since she hadn't been seen on television in some seven years, people would not remember her. And just as I was beginning to say, "Don't be ridiculous . . . ," she answered her own question by saying, "But I have to do your show, Zweibel. My comedy is the only weapon I have against that fucker." That's what Gilda did: She personalized her battle with disease by calling it "that fucker." And then she made a request.

"Zweibel, could you help me make cancer funny?"

♪♪♪

ROBIN DID ALL SHE COULD to help Gilda when she moved out with the kids. Lunches. Trick-or-treating with Lindsay. Shopping trips in Beverly Hills when Gilda felt strong enough between her treatments.

Plus, as an unexpected highlight one night when I was in the editing room, Robin went over to Gilda and Gene Wilder's house and urged her to accompany her to a party Laraine Newman was having where there would be some of the old *SNL* people. Since Gilda had moved to Los Angeles, it had been years since she had seen the *SNL* people, and she was nervous.

In effect, she had forsaken them for her new life, where she dedicated herself to auditioning for the role of Mrs. Gene Wilder. And

Gene felt that Gilda's old friends represented the unhealthy life she led before he met her. So she turned her back on her past as Gene sent her to a battery of doctors. Counselors to help cure the bulimia. Dental surgeons who gave her new teeth to replace the ones destroyed by the bulimia. She stopped drinking. Started playing tennis. She swam every day. She wanted to get healthy.

So much so that she got angry at Belushi when he died. She had loved John. No one ever made her laugh more than he did. And she was pissed that he'd destroyed himself. She wanted to live. Now more than ever.

"I think you'll enjoy seeing everyone again," Robin told Gilda, who remained silent during the entire ride. And when they arrived, Gilda just sat there in the passenger seat. Until Robin came around to her side of the car, opened the door, and said, "We don't have to stay long."

And when Gilda entered Laraine's house, she was greeted with hugs, kisses, cheers, and tears. A parade, led by Bill Murray, ensued, with everyone holding Gilda aloft as they chanted, "You're not going to die! You're not going to die!" Gilda ended up staying a lot longer than she thought she would.

Back in the car, Robin reminded a gleeful Gilda that the old gang still loved her. "You may be in a different chapter of your life," she told her, "but these people love you and you love them and they miss you."

When they returned to Gilda's house, Robin and Gilda tiptoed in so as not to wake up Gene, who they thought might be asleep. But when they entered the master bedroom and discovered him sitting up in bed next to their dog, Sparkle, Gene looked up and asked, "Did you guys have a good time?"

"We said we had a blast," recalls Robin. "And then, like two excited kids coming home from a middle-school dance, we got onto the bed and started jumping up and down while saying, "It was so much fu-un! It was so much fu-un." Not long afterward came a similar scenario, this time with a group of people Gilda had no history with.

The week that Gilda came to appear on *It's Garry Shandling's Show* was arguably the most anticipated one in the four-year history of the series. Garry told me more than once that he was nervous and wanted to make sure that we didn't disappoint her. Our director, Alan Rafkin, who was usually unflappable, admitted that he was having trouble sleeping. And the cast was in awe—collectively relishing the chance to be on the same stage with a hero. "It was no surprise to find Gilda adorable and twinkly and sweet," says actress Molly Cheek. "And it shouldn't have surprised me to see her fragility, but I don't think I understood how sick she really was."

As for me, well, where I had assumed the part of the younger brother on *SNL*, now, some thirteen years later, our roles were reversed as she looked to me for the strength she no longer had. The writers' room also showed deference to my relationship with Gilda, and I had to remind them that the script was still the most important thing and that they should try to approach this as they would any other episode.

But it was hard to. Onstage, during rehearsals, she was the old Gilda. Ad-libbing with Garry lines that found their way into the script.

GARRY

I haven't seen you in a while. Where have you been?

GILDA

Oh, I've had cancer. What's your excuse?

GARRY

Just a series of bad career moves—for which there is no cure, by the way.

And as she became more comfortable and regained her confidence onstage, Gilda reached back to her roots and started improvising scenes, which elevated the comedy to a higher level. Just like the old days. For example, when a flashback from the Vietnam War took place in her living room, the script had Gilda motioning for the palm trees that were lowered with accompanying jungle sounds to be lifted, because she was sick and considered it an intrusion. But it was her suggestion that while the trees were being raised, a coconut fall on her head, at which point she segued into a character that on *SNL* she called Colleen—a stunned woman with crossed eyes who exists in a dazed world of her own and whose index finger incessantly taps on her thigh.

But offstage it was a different story. My visits to Gilda's dressing room found her lying on her couch, holding her belly. I remember one Monday in particular, she was in pain because the night before she and Gene had gone to a restaurant, and she ate some lettuce that she was now having the hardest time digesting. Her attempts to downplay the pain were unconvincing. Yet she wouldn't go home early when I suggested it, and the next night, when we taped the show, I stood with her behind the door to Garry's living-room set before she was to make her entrance in front of an unsuspecting audience. "You okay, honey?" I asked. "Yes," she replied. "Now get your fat ass out of here, because I have a show to do."

⚡⚡⚡

THOUGH I WATCHED THE TAPING with my back to the stage, my eyes trained on the four monitors showing the different angles that the cameras were shooting, I could feel my tension mount as Garry's monologue about sea monkeys was about to be interrupted by Gilda's knock on the other side of the door to Garry's apartment. And then, as Garry approached the door, I abandoned my duties as producer and turned to see my old buddy appear in front of a live audience for the first time in many years.

[*Garry opens the door and sees Gilda*]

GILDA
Hi, Garry.

GARRY
Oh, hi, Gilda.
[*to audience*]
Hey, everybody, it's Gilda Radner!

The studio audience, three hundred strangers she'd feared wouldn't remember who she was, erupted with the loudest, most sustained applause we'd ever gotten. When the cheering subsided and Gilda told that first cancer joke, the audience, for the briefest of moments, hesitated at the sound of a word that was hardly the subject of humor. And then, as if they all processed it exactly the same way, thinking, "Oh, she has cancer, so it's okay for her to joke about it," they laughed, started applauding again, and got emotional about what she was publicly going through. Her heroism. Appearing on the cover of *LIFE* magazine smiling with short hair. Sitting courtside at a Lakers game with a bandana on her head, kidding around with Kareem Abdul-Jabbar, who'd told her not to be embarrassed—that he's also bald but led the league in scoring the year before. Doing everything she possibly could to get the word out that you can live a substantial, productive life even though you had this "fucker." A few days later, while editing the episode, I noticed that the picture from the angle I wanted to use showing Gilda's entrance was jumping ever so slightly, and I couldn't figure out why— until I remembered the mood in the studio on show night and that the big burly man operating that camera had been crying, and his hands were shaking.

ϟϟϟ

GILDA LOVED DOING THE SHOW and was nominated for an Emmy Award for best guest appearance. She felt revived and ready to pursue her career again. After Bernie and Brad spoke with Michael Fuchs at HBO, Gilda, Garry, and I started meeting about creating a series for her. She wanted to play the star of a variety show, and we'd depict her life at the office as well as at home. I still have those notes.

She also continued to thumb her nose at cancer. One night, Bernie was being honored by the Big Brothers, a Los Angeles charity, and Gilda was asked to speak at the event. I wrote this poem for her to recite.

The Big "C"

I was going through life,
As free as a lark,
In the world of acting
I was making my mark.

In Second City,
And then on TV,
Not thinking once,
About the big "C."

I saved up my money,
An apartment I bought,
My wealth was my own,
Or so I thought.

I can't even tell you
How often you cry,
When the dreaded "C"
Starts draining you dry.

Friends try to console,
And tell you they care,
But deep down you feel
That this is unfair.

Now before I upset you,
And lead you astray.
I just want to tell you,
I'm feeling okay.

Cancer's no problem,
'Cause I'm in remission,
The "C" I refer to,
Is Bernie's commission.

She never got to deliver it.

✦✦✦

DURING THE LAST MONTHS of Gilda's life, we were not as close as we had been. We'd speak on the phone a lot, but since my role was to make her laugh, she would let my questions about her well-being go only so far, as there were things happening to her body that she felt more comfortable sharing with Robin.

In our last talk, one night walking along a Santa Monica beach, she allowed herself to be reflective. About her life, which she knew would soon be ending. She said that if she came back, she would like to be a ballerina. Said that comedy was about what's wrong with the world. Things that are too big, too small, too stupid, too clumsy. But a ballerina has total control of her body. That moved to music. In complete concert with her surroundings.

She had sent me the manuscript of her memoir, *It's Always Something*, and I'd finished reading it that morning. She seemed pleased that I thought it was so wonderful. Her voice somehow resonated with every sentence. So candid. So emotional. So Gilda.

I apologized to her. Saying that I didn't know all the details of what she'd been going through. All of the procedures. All of the pain. And that I wish I had.

"And you would've done what about it?" she asked.

"I don't know, but . . ."

"Oh, you just wanted to see me naked, and you know it."

"Yeah, you're probably right."

She then asked if I could do her a favor. To put my arm around her. I asked if she was cold. She said, "A little."

✦✦✦

THE CALL THAT CAME to our house at 6:00 A.M. Saturday was not from Garry Shandling. It was from Gene Wilder. Gilda had died. It was my birthday. She'd hung on until shortly after midnight and then passed away. Just like her. As if to make sure I would not forget the day she left this world. After the morphine could no longer do its job. When my buddy's pleas of "Get me out of this body" were mercifully granted.

It seemed as if the world mourned. People who had never met Gilda felt sad. *Saturday Night Live* that evening was hosted by Steve Martin, who paid tribute to Gilda in his opening monologue by showing the famous dance across the studio floor he'd done with her.

Robin and I flew back east for the funeral in Connecticut. So strange to be in someone's home when they are no longer there. Even stranger was the absence of emotions I felt as a pallbearer for my old pal. Who as a little girl would say the words "Bunny Bunny" on the first day of every month to bring her good luck, to stave off any bad thing that could happen. It was a childhood superstition that she still practiced as an adult. I remember trying my best to conjure up what I thought would be the appropriate sentiments for someone I loved so dearly. I came closer when speaking at her memorial in Los Angeles. A eulogy I concluded, because it took place on June 1, by saying "Bunny Bunny" for her.

It was, however, the first time I ever saw Garry cry. Openly. So unashamedly overcome by grief that he couldn't finish his prepared remarks. In that moment, I loved him. No jokes. No spin. Just raw Garry.

As I write this, I now understand that that feeling harkened back to when Shandling and I first met. The ingredients of initial attraction in a relationship. Best feet forward. The desire for acceptance. The excitement in realizing that we were both on to something special. The affirmation from others encouraging us to keep going.

But then the stuff of life crept in, and, well, by the end of the show's four-year run, Garry and I were barely speaking to each other. I'll assume more than my share of the blame for that situation. Almost by definition, when a writer writes with a comedian *for* that comedian, the dynamic of the relationship is that the writer has to fully immerse himself in the comedian's psyche to know how he feels and how he thinks, so when the comedian speaks, it sounds as if *the comedian* wrote it. It requires the writer to compromise his own ego, recede to the shadows, and yet remain on call. It sometimes reminded me of the stories I'd heard about Bob Hope, how, well into his nineties, he made his writers wear beepers so he could call them in the middle of the night to say he was doing a fund-raiser in Akron and he needed forty jokes about the mayor and his wife by morning. When I asked Bill Persky about this, he cited how it was not unusual for a couple of Hope's "regulars to show up at his house in their pajamas at three in the morning."

When a writer is producing a television show for a star, he also has to step back and objectively look at the material and make sure that it doesn't betray the comedian's character. One particular joke, albeit funny in the moment, may be inappropriate for the comedian overall.

Years later I was collaborating with Billy Crystal on his one-man Broadway play *700 Sundays*—a poignant tribute to his parents and extended family—and we were debating whether or not to use certain jokes that Billy's uncle, who was known for his wildly inappropriate humor, told him when he was five years old. And while certain jokes got big laughs, we were careful to make sure that it was not the wrong kind of laugh that would undermine the audience's ability to sympathize with the uncle later in the play.

To his credit, Shandling the writer was also smart enough to have a good degree of detachment, as he referred to his character as "Garry" as opposed to "I." Yet Garry, the actor playing himself in scenes with other actors, not only tended to stay in the moment by personally getting as many laughs as possible but also wanted to remain faithful to his real-life character, who was in his forties, single, and lived alone.

But at this point I had other muscles I wanted to flex. Robin and I now had three children, I was the beleaguered commissioner of our son Adam's Little League, I had "secret lunches" with our five-year-old daughter, Lindsay, every Saturday afternoon because I wanted to let her know she was still special after the birth of her younger sister, Sari, and stories that grew out of those experiences did not fit into the Shandling show's format. I was frustrated. So I really couldn't blame Garry for his growing resentment about my divided focus, given the other projects I was keeping in the bottom drawer of my desk or the precious hours I carved out on a Sunday afternoon to be with my family, only to come home to a ringing phone.

"Hello?"

"Where were you today?" asked Garry. "I called three times."

"We took the kids to Disneyland. What's up?"

"Nothing's up. I just wanted to get together and start breaking some stories for the next cycle of shows."

"We can start tomorrow, Garry. We have a two-week hiatus until we go back into production. There's plenty of time."

". . . Fine."

ϟϟϟ

WE WERE DRIFTING APART. For me, this was probably best exemplified late one night in an editing room. Garry and I had both grown frustrated that no one was seeing our series. Sure, the reviews were terrific, as was the word of mouth. So much so that Showtime's subscriptions went up markedly, which was their truest indicator that a show was successful. But many places across the country were not even getting Showtime, and that included a lot of cities that people we knew lived in. Like Manhattan. That's right, huge chunks of the Upper East Side of New York City did not get Showtime. Neither did where we lived in New Jersey. Or where my sister Franny lived in Rockland County, New York. And I was personally going broke FedEx-ing cassettes to Herb Sargent and a handful of others to prove that I indeed had a job.

So when the FOX network came into existence, a deal was struck where Showtime would have exclusive rights to air our show for thirty days, and then FOX would televise it on Sunday nights at 10:00 as part of a one-hour package coupled with *The Tracey Ullman*

Show. So, in effect, *It's Garry Shandling's Show* made the gigantic leap from no one watching it on Showtime to no one watching it on FOX.

Still, to accommodate its next incarnation on commercial television, the episodes had to be edited for time. On Showtime, our half hours sometimes ran as long as twenty-eight minutes, as opposed to the network length of twenty-two. Cable provided the luxury of playing out our stories to their conclusions as long as they ended in time for the show that followed at its scheduled time. But now they had to be shortened to allow for commercials and, on a few occasions, to remove any jokes that might be deemed objectionable on a broadcast network.

So now it was 2:00 A.M. in a dark, windowless editing room. We were into the fourth season of a series that was all about Garry. I had devoted myself to writing for him, learning every aspect of his being, and trying my best to serve his every whim. Sure, that's the nature of the job. But at that late hour, when Garry was vacillating between two close-ups of himself that looked exactly the same, I just couldn't resist asking him a question.

"What college did I go to?"

"Huh?"

"I'm serious. I know you went to Arizona. Where did I go?"

Garry kept his sunglasses on when he turned to me and said with no uncertainty, "Dartmouth."

It was delivered as a declarative statement. Not a guess. Not even the hint of a question mark. Just a direct answer that, if anything, had the slight intonation of annoyance that I would even dare to ask such an insulting question that of course he knew the answer to. Garry then turned his attention back to the monitors.

"What if we make that a two-shot?" he asked the editor.

"No," I said.

"What do you mean, no? Why shouldn't that be a two-shot?"

"I mean, no, I didn't go to Dartmouth."

A beat. He knew that I knew that he didn't know. (Is that a sentence?) As usual, we were on the same plane.

". . . Sorry. I meant Florida State."

We continued editing, but he knew I was upset. Like Gilda, Garry also knew that if he made me laugh, things would be better between us. So that Sunday, our phone rang at 6:00 in the morning. These were the days before caller ID, so when anyone phoned our home at that hour, it meant one of two things: either someone was dead, or Shandling was calling. Robin and I had more than one debate as to which of those options was more disturbing. Since the phone was on the night table on Robin's side of the bed, she robotically lifted the phone and passed it over her body to me.

"Hello?"

"Alan, it's Garry."

"Hey, man, what's—"

"Alan, I had a date last night."

"God, help me . . ."

"We were in bed, and she says to me, 'No fingers in the ass.' And I said, 'Look, it's my finger and my ass, and if that's where I want to keep it, you don't have a vote in the matter.'"

Of course I laughed. I was a sucker for Garry and was easily seduced by the tormented mind that could write a joke like that. But the reality was that we'd both had enough. Garry felt betrayed, I felt unappreciated, and after our final show of the fourth season we angrily went our separate ways.

Garry's history was that relationships ended by crashing and burning; whether with girlfriends or business associates, drama came along with the termination. Things rarely glided to a halt with both parties shaking hands, hugging to commemorate a job well done, and then seguing to an enduring friendship. The venerable writer Peter Tolan (*Rescue Me, Outsiders, Analyze This*), who worked closely with Garry as director and executive producer on *The Larry Sanders Show* for six seasons, told me that he was one of the few whom Garry didn't turn on. "I remained in Garry's trusted circle from the start, until he passed. And I never really knew why until I saw the HBO documentary about him. I certainly knew about the brother, Barry, who died when he was young, but I never pieced together the idea that we (male writers, actors, comedians—anyone) were all his replacement brothers, and he was sitting there counting the hours waiting for us to disappoint him—or betray him or leave him the way Barry did. I honestly think that's what that issue was all about." And now it was our turn to be embattled.

Until Robin couldn't stand it anymore.

In those days, we would spend our summers at our home in New Jersey (that's right, we left Los Angeles to summer in suburban New Jersey) so we could be near our families and our kids, whom we sent to sleepaway camps in Maine. One day Robin saw in the newspaper that Garry was going to appear at a hotel in Atlantic City and called him.

"Listen, I'm bringing the big lummox down, putting the two of you in a room, and neither of you is coming out until you're friends again. You've been through too much together to be acting like such idiots."

Robin and I drove to Atlantic City. And while she stayed downstairs depositing an untold number of coins into a rigged slot machine, I went up to Garry's suite. Where we sat silently, like two petulant children, not looking at each other for several long minutes. And then I heard him mutter under his breath, "Notre Dame."

Once again, for those of you who may not remember what I said on page 2 of this book, I had gone to the University of Buffalo.

And then, after a few seconds, I uttered, "Close enough," under *my* breath.

We both stayed stoically silent before, as if on cue, we turned in each other's direction, held our stern expressions for a few beats, and then started laughing.

"You're such an asshole," he said, still laughing.

"As are you."

"I know."

And that was it. Our rapprochement. No discussion or analysis or even any apologies. We both just knew, and any more words would've been redundant.

CHAPTER 7

GOOD SPORTS

(Writing for the Wrong People . . . Again)

THIS IS NOT GOING to be an easy chapter for me to write. Kind of like hearing a song that was popular when an old lover broke up with you. But in this particular case, if that lover also murdered your pets.

First, a little context. The success of *It's Garry Shandling's Show* made me attractive to the studios that, in those years, were signing creative producers to long-term overall deals. I had gotten a few offers, most notably from Castle Rock. Rob Reiner, one of the company's partners, had hosted the third *Saturday Night Live* ever. We had met that week, liked each other a lot, and had stayed friends since.

So during a rehearsal break from an episode of *It's Garry Shandling's Show* that Rob was guest appearing on, he told me that Castle Rock (named after the town in so many of Stephen King's books) wanted to sign me, and I was more than interested. In the early nineties his company was a virtual haven for people to do their best work. Long gone were the days when Rob was called "Meathead" by Archie Bunker in *All in the Family*; he had gained enormous success and respect as a director with such hits as *This Is Spinal Tap*, *Stand by Me*, and *The Princess Bride* and was now in pre-production for *A Few Good Men*.

Billy Crystal wrote and starred in movies like *When Harry Met Sally* and *City Slickers* at Castle Rock; Larry David had just co-created *Seinfeld*, which was also a Castle Rock production; and Christopher Guest would soon be making brilliant movies like *Waiting for Guffman* and *A Mighty Wind* for Castle Rock—so it seemed like the perfect place for me to end up. I had just come off of writing and producing seventy-two episodes of a highly acclaimed weekly television series and was really excited to start developing some new ideas of my own with good friends whose work I greatly respected.

So now comes the part where I totally screwed up. It was in April of 1991 and, once again, it started with a call from Bernie Brillstein.

Hi, kid.

Hey, Bernie. What's doing?

I have two words for you.

"Castle" and "Rock"?

Better. "Farrah" and "Ryan."

"Farrah" and "Ryan"?

That's right, kid.

As in "Fawcett" and "O'Neal"?

You got it! CBS wants a series for them, and they want you to create it!

Bernie, are Farrah Fawcett and Ryan O'Neal funny?

Ryan can be.

But what about her? I've only seen Farrah in *Charlie's Angels* and in TV movies where her husband beats the shit out of her and then she sets his bed on fire.

I think they can be great in a romantic comedy.

I don't know about this.

Hey, Tracy and Hepburn made some pretty great romantic comedies . . .

That was different.

Why?

Because Tracy and Hepburn were in those romantic comedies.

Stop being a wise guy . . .

Bernie, Tracy and Hepburn were great actors, they were funny, and they were in love. Farrah and Ryan are in the tabloids all the time. They're always fighting.

I'm sure Tracy and Hepburn had their moments, too.

Bernie, to the best of my knowledge, Katharine Hepburn never pulled a gun on Spencer Tracy and emptied the clip into the side of his car!

CBS loves Farrah and Ryan . . .

That's why CBS is in third place!

Farrah and Ryan are Hollywood royalty.

They're Hollywood hooligans!

This is a great opportunity, kid.

To what? Create a romantic comedy for a couple who are neither romantic nor comedic?

You're not looking at this the right way.

There's a right way to look at this?

Yes, because if this show is a prime-time network hit, you can form your own production company and become an entity like your friends Rob Reiner and Jim Brooks.

Yeah, but . . .

And that's what you want, right?

Yeah, but . . .

Well, this would put you in a great position to do that. Look, right now your hits have been in late night and on cable. But if you can show that you can reach a mass audience, Jesus, you can write your own ticket.

So, what you're saying is that I should do a show I don't want to do so I can start doing shows I really want to do?

Something like that.

Come on, Bernie . . .

I can't believe I have to talk you into this when there are writers who would give their left nut to create a series that has a twelve-show order.

Twelve episodes . . .?

That's right. This can change your whole career, kid.

CBS ordered twelve episodes of a show that doesn't exist?

It's done all the time, Alan.

Jesus . . .

So should I tell CBS that you'll do it?

Yeah, I guess so . . .

Attaboy!!

But on one condition . . .

What's that?

That Farrah and Ryan die and come back as Tracy and Hepburn.

Alan!

Okay, okay, let me think about it.

f f f

IT WAS THE ONLY TIME in my career that I ever went against my instincts and didn't listen to every fiber of my being when they were screaming, *Have you lost your fucking mind?*

Let's be honest, once something is written and produced, it's in the hands of a different god as to whether it will succeed or not. But I'd always prided myself that the intent going in was a noble one: to believe in the concept and be excited about every phase of the writing and production process to see it to fruition. This time, however, every shred of pride I had was nowhere to be found.

Bernie and Jeff Sagansky (the president of CBS) arranged a few meetings for me with Farrah and Ryan. While I found them likable enough, in my heart I knew that they were, in fact, two people who represented a clichéd Hollywood couple I would usually parody. Perpetually tan, great hair, about 267 very white teeth between them. Yet, in deference to Bernie and this opportunity he was offering me, I nearly threw my back out trying to look at this from an angle that made sense. Was it possible that I could figure out a way to present these two mannequins in a way that would hit a nerve and surprise everyone with their *unique* chemistry?

Or did I do it for purely commercial reasons? In 1991 a network success could conceivably launch me into a stratosphere where I could create my own company, I could start my own Castle Rock. I thought about it. It was tempting. Years earlier, after I'd left *Saturday Night Live*, I was asked by the Carsey-Werner Company to run *The Cosby Show*. I turned it down. While I was doing the Shandling show, I was offered the opportunity, also by Carsey-Werner, to create a show for Roseanne Barr. I turned it down. Now, there's no saying that either of those shows would've been the huge successes they were with me at the helm. But I ultimately agreed to do *this* show because I didn't want to feel stupid a third time while everyone on the continent stopped what they were doing on Tuesday nights at 9:30 to watch Ryan and Farrah.

Still, no matter what spin I put on it, I knew in my heart this was wrong. I'd wake up in the middle of the night, and Robin would say, "You don't really want to do this. So don't." When I'd call Herb Sargent, he told me the same. When I'd call anyone else I had ever met in my entire existence, they told me the same. Still, I said yes and tried every way imaginable to make it work.

Ryan *can* be funny, I thought to myself. I liked him in light comedies like *So Fine* and *What's Up, Doc?* forgave him for *Love Story*, and thought he was great when he played a con man with his daughter, Tatum, in *Paper Moon*. Okay, so I'll make his character a charming scoundrel, I figured. A former NFL player named Bobby Tannen who was a reckless party animal who often had run-ins with the police, and, as hard as he tried, everything he touched turned into a spectacular failure.

And Farrah? Was it possible that her disgusted reactions to him would be enough? And that despite her strong attraction to this lovable, well-intentioned bad boy a lot of the comedy would lie in her approach-avoidance? That even though she knew he was wrong for her no matter how seductive his appeal, there was a part of her that gave in to temptation with hopes that she could ultimately tame him? I could write that, I thought. It could even be cute in an old-fashioned romantic-comedy way. So I decided to adjust my approach to this whole thing. Write a script that I loved and then "cast" Ryan and Farrah for the parts. Let the script show them how I wanted the characters to behave. Was it possible that it could work that way? I wrote the script and was thrilled with it. So were Farrah and Ryan and CBS and Bernie. As was the creative community.

The series was called *Good Sports*, and it was set in a fictitious ESPN-like cable sports network. For Farrah and Ryan's characters, I drew from their real lives. Two combative ex-lovers whose love and hate spilled over into their roles on the *SportsCenter*-type show they were co-anchoring. This was 1991, and though an ex-jock had worked incredibly well in a sitcom when Ted Danson played Sam Malone in *Cheers*, at this point in time a sitcom about a sports workplace had not really been done on television (this was years before Aaron Sorkin created

Sports Night), and it was theoretically exciting. We had the cooperation from CBS Sports for footage and access to games, and they helped us book top-flight athletes like Kareem-Abdul Jabbar, football great Jim Brown, and Yankees owner George Steinbrenner to appear on the show to lampoon themselves.

The supporting cast was comprised of great character actors like Lane Smith, my old *SNL* colleague Brian Doyle-Murray, and Tony winners Lois Smith and Cleavant Derricks; the writing staff was comprised of top-flight scribes who had earned their street cred on highly successful television shows and features, including Monica Johnson, who co-wrote a lot of the Albert Brooks films.

Expectations ran high. Or, probably more accurately, guardedly high. There was a press buzz anticipating this show. Dear Lord, was it possible that Bernie was right? We found out the answer to that once production began, when *Good Sports* became a classic example of a show that existed because it had "stars" and, conversely, failed because of those very "stars."

Simply put, they were not funny. At least not funny in the way I wanted them to be funny. That's not to say that was their fault. Maybe I was just unable to make them funny in the way they could be funny. Or in the way that any living organism with the correct number of chromosomes might think was funny.

The saddest part was that I'd had a strong hunch about this even before the first show aired. I remember the exact moment that I knew we were doomed.

It was when they appeared on Arsenio Hall's talk show to promote the premiere of *Good Sports*. Shortly after they were introduced with a fanfare traditionally afforded couples who live in Buckingham Palace, Ryan saw fit to describe his and Farrah's first make-out session by saying that they had kissed so hard, his gums and lips started bleeding. That's right, he was telling a talk-show anecdote about how there was blood all over his mouth while he was kissing Farrah Fawcett. And as if that attractive image wasn't enough to make the studio recoil in horror, a few minutes later he moved in for the kill by saying that Operation

Desert Storm, which was being televised live by CNN, wouldn't affect the show's reception, because people were so apathetic. "We'll get good ratings, anyway." It was at about that time, when you could cut the audience's non-reaction to America's favorite couple with Ryan's bloody incisors, that I turned to Brad Grey, who was backstage watching this on the monitor next to me, and said, "We're fucked."

"*Good Sports* was by far the worst work experience I ever had," says producer Terri Miller. "It started out as such joy and became pure stress. The work on the page was good. Then to see Ryan butcher it was so frustrating. We would put in sixteen-hour days Monday to Friday, and then Alan and I would come in for eight- to ten-hour days on Saturday and Sunday to edit. I remember that the Gulf War happened during that time; I never knew which was going to be worse, the battle unfolding on CNN or the battle unfolding on the stage."

And while prognostication is not generally one of my strong suits, it pains me to this very day that I was right. Again, as my friend Rob Reiner always says, it's the process that you remember. The day-to-day work experience you had is what stays with you. Obviously, everyone wants the product to be received well. Appreciated. So they can take pride in a job well done.

But what people sometimes don't understand is that professionals work just as hard on a television show that's unsuccessful as they do on one that's a hit. Writers write and endlessly rewrite scripts. Directors break down those scripts to determine the camera angles to effectively bring that vision to life. Actors make choices for the same reasons. The crew, casting, wardrobe, production staff; maybe a hundred people who take pride in their talents work very late hours making their contributions. And producers spend Sundays away from their families sitting in an editing room staring at two actors on a monitor who, under the best of circumstances, they enjoy looking at.

But what I remember is Farrah taking over an hour to have her hair redone between scenes, making the studio audience antsy and hostile, which aren't exactly attitudes conducive to laughter. Ryan referring to the writers as "career killers" and hearing that he punched a member of the crew. Each day presented us with an adventure that no one wanted to be on.

One incident that I really didn't mind, however, happened on a morning that I was talking to Farrah in the studio. Apparently she and Ryan were fighting again, and, when she saw him approaching from behind me, obviously to make him crazy, she picked up her shirt and flashed me. That happened twice. Milton Berle's penis, Farrah Fawcett's chest. Yes, it's been an interesting ride.

But you also know that a show was a total nightmare when one of its highlights was casting an actor on someone else's show. Jeffrey Tambor came in and read for the role that ultimately went to Lane Smith. While he was just not right for that particular role, I asked if he could stay for a few minutes. Terri Miller and I went into another office, where I picked up a phone, called Garry Shandling, and asked if he was still looking for someone to play his sidekick, Hank, in the upcoming The Larry Sanders Show. Garry said yes, and I told him that we had someone we thought he should see. So we sent Jeffrey to Garry, and, well, we all know that he ended up becoming the huge star that he is from that role. Another nice part of this story? Every year Robin and I knew when the first day of shooting was for a new season of Larry Sanders, because a gift basket filled with wine and cheese and a thank-you card from Jeffrey would come to the house.

Okay, now back to some bad stuff.

"She stole an ankle bracelet," I told Robin.

"What are you saying?"

"I'm saying that Vic Kaplan (the show's line producer) told me that Farrah went to Tiffany, bought an ankle bracelet, and charged it to the production. When I asked Farrah about it, she said she planned on wearing it on camera, so according to her way of thinking, it was technically a prop."

"Does that mean you have to cut to a close-up of her ankle to justify the write-off?"

"Either that or just hand out magnifying glasses to everyone watching at home."

Then again, there were not that many people watching at home. After a respectable rating when we premiered, probably due to a spate of promos, some very favorable reviews, and a general curiosity about this couple doing a television series together, our audience began to slowly dwindle. No, that's being too kind. The audience left in droves. It seems they didn't much care for Farrah and Ryan as a couple, which was a bit of a problem, since the show was about them as a couple.

The writing staff, despite the high salaries they were making, told their agents to start looking for jobs on other shows. In fact, I can still remember the sound of desk drawers slamming in writers' attempts to hide the other projects they were working on when I entered their offices. I felt bad. Responsible for the miserable time they were all having. I am sorry that, to this day, it is the one credit that virtually everyone who worked on that show leaves off of his or her resume. As Russ Woody, an incredibly highly regarded writer-producer for such shows as *Murphy Brown* and *Becker* and the author of a very funny/poignant memoir about his father called *Tuesdays with Ted*, says about his stint on this show, "*Good Sports* was a near impossible situation that turned into a lousy experience for all. The main problem was the stars. The stars always have undue powers. If they're unpredictable or moody or angry, they can say, 'No, no homeless characters. Make him an out-of-work mime.' Then they go home to Malibu, and the writers are stuck there unraveling an entire script and putting it back together before the next morning's run-through."

"What would Gilda say about this?" Robin used to ask in an attempt to help me find humor in this god-awful situation.

"My guess is that Gilda, Tracy, and Hepburn are up there laughing their heavenly asses off at this mess I've gotten myself into."

♪♪♪

MY RELATIONSHIP WITH BERNIE SUFFERED. Sure, he called every day and came to the filming of every show, but it was awkward. He knew that I was angry for allowing myself to be talked into doing this series. He said he was sorry. And I said thank you. For trusting me with this undertaking. It was a huge monetary loss for his company, as Brillstein-Grey had to assume a lot of the financial responsibility for the wasted time and the extravagance of the show's two stars.

And when he called to say that *Good Sports* had been canceled by CBS, we were both relieved. Everyone was relieved. Which was sad in itself, because usually when a television series is canceled, you're really disappointed.

But this was, in effect, a mercy killing. A series that I knew was in deep trouble when my sister Franny said it didn't make her laugh.

CHAPTER **8**

CRASHING AND BURNING IN ANOTHER GENRE

(North Goes South)

I WRITE. This is what I'm wired to do. To awaken at 5:30 every morning, sit down with my vocabulary, choose words, and arrange them in an order that would not only hold a viewer or reader's interest, but also afford them a laugh or two along the way. And if I succeed, well, mission accomplished. There's no greater feeling. But if I fail, well, I'm sorry, but it's not a war crime. I swear, I tried my best.

In a writer's head, all ideas are praiseworthy. It is during the leap from the cranium to the page where trouble can occur. I learned to handle criticism early on when jokes I'd written, whether for others or myself, didn't get a laugh or when sketches didn't make it past the read-through at *SNL*. Or when entire episodes of sitcoms I was doing had to be rewritten the night before they were to be taped in front of a live audience. Or when scenes of a play had to be rewritten after the first preview because at some point the audience stopped laughing and started looking for the exits. Or when editors of books or various magazines I wrote pieces for reacted as if English was not my first language.

But those moments were nothing compared to the reception I received for a movie I wrote called *North*.

First, a little background. After the demise of *Good Sports*, I was, as Bernie so eloquently put it, "colder than whale shit in television." Although no one really blamed me for that show's failure, no one was exactly planning any ticker-tape parades for me either. The one exception to this was my friend Rob Reiner, who always claimed that, at various times during the course of a career, a good writer may not be a hot writer. That he or she may not be attractive to television networks and movie studios due to a recent flop really had no bearing on whether that writer had talent, as so many other factors come into play when a production doesn't work: casting, timing, miscalculating what audiences will want to see so many months or, in some cases, years down the road. It's not unlike, say, how the great poet Emily Dickinson died penniless, but her poems are so beloved today. Not a great analogy? Well, I pray you get my point.

Thankfully, Rob's faith in me from the year before had not waned, so he and his Castle Rock partners signed me to a television deal and I moved into one of their offices, where I shared a suite with my old pals Larry David and Billy Crystal. The odds of such an occurrence, that three guys who started out together some twenty years earlier should now be in this situation, was not wasted on us. We were giddy and thankful at the same time.

As part of my deal, Castle Rock also bought the rights to *North*, a book I'd written years earlier about a boy who becomes a free agent and

With Robin and the kids in 1991. We're all smiling. Must've been the day *Good Sports* was cancelled.

travels the world looking for new parents. The book was inspired by our son, Adam, who was at that age when he would look at me and Robin while we were all sitting at the dinner table, and, from the expression on his face, it was easy to tell that he was thinking, "I can do better than *these* two."

My literary agent at the time, Esther Newberg, sold the book to a wonderful editor named Peter Gethers at Villard/Random House. Peter has edited a number of my books, and, because he's a writer himself, he's an author's dream.

Writing books is a mostly solitary endeavor. A personal vision that the writer feels is best expressed with words to be read as opposed to dialogue to be spoken. As a result, it requires him to go deeper in his specificity. Digressions into the internal lives of characters give understanding as to motive and behavior. Descriptions of wardrobe and demeanor may take pages versus being conveyed in an instant when seen on the screen or stage. So the process is slow and long with extended periods before I ever feel comfortable showing the pages to another human. But with Peter it was different, as working with him was almost like having a collaborator. Someone who didn't stand in judgment but, rather, gave feedback and suggested what else I could do to accomplish what I wanted to convey. As my friend Tom Hanks, whose bestselling book of short stories, *Uncommon Type*, Peter edited, puts it, "'Is this anything?' I would ask. Because it's not a test and comes from my head and my own typewriter, the question is as legitimate as a motorist asking, 'Is this the way to the Hoover Dam?' We both know the destination but need information. Am I on the right route, not necessarily the shortest way, but, the way? My editor would say, 'Sure, but take the third left, and ignore the signs. You'll see the Hoover Dam in the distance.'"

You hold on to people like Peter. And on the television and movie side, I've found that the same could be said about Andrew Singer, who is the president of television and head of West Coast operations for Lorne Michaels' company, Broadway Video. It was Andrew who championed Fred Armisen's hit show *Portlandia* when few others believed in it. But Andrew, who thinks like a writer though he doesn't write, did.

North was a thin novella I wrote while I was a staff writer on *The New Show*. I kept the manuscript in my bottom desk drawer, worked on it before others got to the office or during hiatus weeks, and when it was time to get a quote for the book jacket, I sent the advance galleys to Rob Reiner for a blurb. Rob really liked the book, gave me a very funny blurb ("If you read only one book this year, I would say that you're not a very avid reader"), and expressed an interest in directing a movie version of it. I was beyond thrilled. I had written the book with a movie version of it in mind, keeping an eye toward the visuals. The book was even illustrated by the cartoonist Alex Tiani. Rob came to New York, we discussed what the movie would look like, and we were both excited about its prospects.

Then eight years passed.

Studios were less than thrilled to finance a movie version of a book whose sales were meager despite the endorsements of my celebrity friends and all of the publicity I was doing. But after Rob and his partners formed Castle Rock, they had the luxury of selecting the movies *they* wanted to make. When we all met to discuss an overall television deal they wanted to offer me, Rob asked if the movie rights to *North* were still available. I told him they were, he said he wanted to develop it into a screenplay, and, after I wrote the first draft with Rob's producing partner Andy Scheinman, Rob attached himself as the movie's director.

A writer's dream! To be hired to adapt your own book into a screenplay. Given Rob's track record, I had every reason to believe that the movie would have a great chance of being a hit. And God knew that after *Good Sports* I was in dire need of redemption.

Rob and I did dozens of rewrites together—going over every beat and every line time and again to make sure the script was as good as it could possibly be to attract the best possible cast.

It worked. Jason Alexander and Julia Louis-Dreyfus, Bruce Willis, my old pal Dan Aykroyd, Jon Lovitz, Alan Arkin, Kathy Bates, Elijah Wood, and John Ritter all signed on, and *North* would also mark the first movie appearance of an eight-year-old actress named Scarlett Johansson.

I had initially envisioned this film, not unlike the book, to be small scaled, a simple tale that took place inside of a young boy's head. I thought it would have the look of a low-budget independent film, something that would be embraced by children but could also be watched by adults who remembered feeling more appreciated by parents other than their own. In my mind, this was a $7 million movie, something that could open small and, by virtue of great reviews and word of mouth, slowly gain traction. These were pretty much the hopes that Peter Gethers had for the book—that it start with a cult following, then grow to be mainstream, and ultimately become a classic.

Rob had a grander vision, a $45 million picture that implied a big advertising and promotional budget to help assure a big opening weekend.

Though it took a little while to adjust to Rob's way of thinking, I understood that it was now Rob's movie. Television writers become producers so they can have the ultimate word on all creative aspects of a show. From casting to wardrobe to music, etc., all departments report to the executive producer who, even after consulting with his trusted creative team, makes the final decisions as to how the series should look. But film is the director's medium. It was now my role to support and do everything I could to be in tandem with Rob. So I shifted gears, came to embrace what he wanted to do, and even became enthusiastic about it. I came to feel like an equal partner, as Rob considered all of my suggestions, and he included me in every part of the process, from casting to location scouting.

And once production began, I got the same feeling I'd had when we first started *Saturday Night Live*. Something I'd written was being taken seriously. People woke up early. Sets were being built. Big burly men were carrying long planks of wood. Other men, not quite as big and burly, were standing atop scissor lifts angling klieg lights. There were catering trucks. Wind machines. Extras wearing makeup to make them look like Eskimos. There were painters. Wardrobe women hurriedly walking, holding three different choices of cowboy hats. People whom I had no idea what their jobs were talking into walkie-talkies. Trailers

With Rob Reiner, who was either pointing at the monitor or the food on the craft services table. I honestly can't remember.

containing eight fetid toilets being used by a crew who curiously referred to them as honey wagons. All because a writer slapped down a bunch of words on paper.

Hopes were lofty. The actors were happy, the rewrites I was doing on the set seemed right, and the enthusiasm among the crew, even the most jaded veterans, was palpable. As we drove to work every morning, Rob and I had visions of classics like *The Wizard of Oz* and his own film *The Princess Bride*. As a result, the buzz about this movie around town was so good that Bernie Brillstein's phone kept ringing with offers for me to write more scripts, and, even better, we were invited to a ton of parties given by people we'd never met.

"But we don't know the Schwarzeneggers," said Robin.

"So what? The Stallones are going to be there."

"We don't know them, either."

"Why are you being so difficult?"

⚡⚡⚡

AFTER SEEING A MOVIE THAT doesn't work, people often ask—and I've done so myself—"Didn't they see that this was going to be horrible?

Shouldn't they have, at some point, realized they had a huge turd on their hands and pulled the plug instead of continuing to throw good money after bad?"

There's an old saying in the movie business that no movie is as good as its dailies or as terrible as its first cut. Well, *North*'s dailies were great. Because the movie tracked North's visits to a series of prospective parents in Alaska, Hawaii, Africa, etc., the episodic nature of the material seemed to work in the viewing room as individual vignettes. And even the first cut played well to an audience comprised of friends, family, and employees of the studio, who were thrilled to be out from behind their desks.

But the moment the final cut was shown to people we weren't related to, it was a different story. Test audiences who came to the screenings excited to see Rob Reiner's new movie exited somewhat stunned—not only giving the film scores that implied that they wouldn't recommend it to friends but also demanding we return the ninety-one minutes of their lives they'd wasted watching it.

Some new scenes were written and then shot. Some existing scenes were rewritten and then reshot. The great composer Marc Shaiman (*Sister Act, A Few Good Men*, and, along with Scott Wittman, *Hairspray*) wrote a beautifully moving musical score. And Rob, his four Castle Rock partners, and I kept our sixty collective fingers crossed with every hope that we'd not only salvaged the movie but that it would actually be embraced by a mass audience.

We held on to that belief straight through to the premiere, which was a screening of the movie followed by a big party. Sorry, I just lied. It was a screening of the movie followed by a wake. By the time the lights came up in the theater, the audience hightailed out of there as if the place was on fire. And those few who felt obligated to look us in the eye afterward were as euphemistic in their praise as one would be after seeing a picture of an extremely disfigured infant. I heard comments like, "Boy, that's what I call a movie!" The fact that very few people stayed for the after-party and that both of my parents—whom I'd flown in from Boca Raton for the big night—were weeping in the limo on the way back to our house gave further indication that *North* was not destined for the classic status that Rob and I had envisioned.

Any shred of hope I had that I might be spared public humiliation was dashed the following morning when the premier film critic in the country, Roger Ebert, was somewhat less than enthusiastic in his assessment of my baby. At the time, Roger's syndicated television show "At the Movies" with fellow film critic Gene Siskel was highly rated, and their "thumbs-up" opinions were sure to be boasted in all print advertisements, while a "thumbs-down" verdict was tantamount to a box office death sentence.

For those of you who don't recall Roger Ebert's published review of *North* or didn't carry an original clipping of it in your wallet until it yellowed and became brittle and disintegrated with age so you replaced it with an internet copy printed on heavier stock as I did, here is an excerpt:

> *I hated this movie. Hated, hated, hated, hated, hated this movie. Hated it. Hated every simpering stupid vacant audience-insulting moment of it. Hated the sensibility that thought anyone would like it. Hated the implied insult to the audience by its belief that anyone would be entertained by it.*

Now, because I have a tendency to be a tad hard on myself, I took the time to reread it. Slower this time. Looking for a hidden adjective. Or perhaps the phrase "I'm just kidding" that I had somehow overlooked the first twenty-five times I read this obituary. But no. There was no getting around it. There was something about *North* that apparently rubbed Roger Ebert the wrong way.

To say the least, Ebert's review was embarrassing and hurtful. And my guess was, there was no way that other Alan Zweibel was even coming close to getting laid by anyone literate enough to have read that review.

Don't get me wrong, Roger had every right to dislike, or even hate, this movie. It was his job to give his opinion, and he was a good writer, so maybe part of the reason it bothered me so much was that a fellow wordsmith had been so personally negative about how I defined myself.

To be fair, this was not the only negative review that the film received. There were a number of them. Okay, I'm lying again. There was a veritable avalanche of them. But because that review was written by Roger Ebert, it was the one that everyone on the planet read.

And quoted.

Quoted to me by friends who called to express their sympathies. ("It's like Ebert stuck two thumbs up your ass and then ran in opposite directions.")

Quoted to Robin; when she returned home from the supermarket we'd been shopping at for years, she said, "I'm wondering if maybe we should order in for a while."

And quoted to our son, Adam, who, when he grew tired of defending his dad to his Los Angeles classmates, asked if I'd be offended if he changed his last name to Sorkin.

It seems that Adam's main nemesis was none other than Mike Ovitz's son, who attended the same school. At that time, Mike was the head of the Creative Arts Agency and arguably the most powerful and feared agent in Hollywood. The taunting that Adam was the target of reached an absurd Hollywood low when the two eleven-year-old boys got into a shouting match.

At dinner at home, it was our nightly practice to go around the table, with each of us telling the others what our high and our low was for the day. Adam recounted the scene from school:

Young Ovitz: You're stupid!
Young Zweibel: You're stupid!
Y.O.: You're ugly!
Y.Z.: You're ugly!
Y.O.: Oh, yeah? Well, your father wrote *North*, which only did $7 million at the box office!

Adam claimed that this was his low. I asked him how he responded to Young Ovitz, and he said, "Well, at least people like my father." To which I nodded and said, "That was definitely your high." And mine, too.

⚡⚡⚡

STILL, THE DELUGE CONTINUED. From all directions.

"Hello?"

"Alan?"

"Hi, Dad . . ."

"Alan, don't read *TIME* magazine. Page sixty-seven. Third column on the right. Right next to the Subaru ad. Boy, that guy really ripped you a new asshole."

This was the first I'd heard about the *TIME* review. After Ebert, I'd vowed not to subject myself to this form of masochism, but it was to no avail, as well-intentioned friends, family members, and every person with the ability to read made a point of conveying their condolences to me in the most random places—like Vicente Foods, the same Brentwood grocery store where Robin had been accosted.

"You okay, Alan?"

"Sure."

"You look terrible. Is anyone sick?"

"No, everyone's fine, Rabbi Freiling."

"I read the reviews of your movie . . ."

"Uh-huh . . ."

"Terrible. Just terrible . . ."

"Well, I tried my best . . ."

"I'm sure you did . . ."

"Well, it was nice seeing you, Rabbi . . ."

"I was talking to a colleague of mine about your reviews . . ."

"You were?"

"Yes, a rabbi from Northridge—a scholar who's an expert on the Holocaust, mind you—who started comparing the reviews you got for *North* with the ones Hitler got for *Mein Kampf.*"

"He what . . . !"

"And apparently Hitler did better."

ℑℑℑ

ROBIN TRIED TO HELP by citing films, now considered classics, that had received negative reviews when they were originally released. For a while she even gave thought to putting together a book titled *Critically Incorrect*, compiling those horrible critiques next to the iconic posters of those films.

"It has dwarfs, music, Technicolor, freak characters, and Judy Garland. It can't be expected to have a sense of humor as well, and as for the light touch of fantasy, it weighs like a pound of fruitcake soaking wet" was what *the New Republic* thought of *The Wizard of Oz*.

"It's a Frankenstein monster stitched together from leftover parts. It talks. It moves in fits and starts but has no mind of its own . . . Looking very expensive but spiritually desperate" is how Vincent Canby of the *New York Times* felt about *The Godfather Part II*.

Was it possible that *North* would also eventually defy its detractors, stand the test of time, and be embraced like those beloved classics? That one day things would be reconsidered? That one day, a critic would write . . .

> *"Savagely maligned when first released a half century ago,* North's *rediscovery as an American treasure is reminiscent of how a lot of people initially hate Swiss cheese but eventually crave it"?*
>
> —*Hubert Ebert*
> (Roger Ebert's great-grandson)

Maybe.

In the meantime, Rob felt bad for me, as I did for him. After a string of heralded hits, he now had to endure his first failure. So we called on our friendship and leaned on each other during the ensuing onslaught.

"Well, even Babe Ruth struck out," I said, trying to console him.

"True," Rob said, "but this wasn't a strikeout. It's more like some-one drilled Babe in the nuts with a fastball."

"Poor guy," I remember saying. "Then again, the Babe may have been so drunk when he got hit in the nuts that he didn't feel it."

⚡⚡⚡

SHOCK GAVE WAY TO PARALYSIS, and I couldn't write. Few noticed. Banks stayed open, children weren't sent home from school, and the flag in front of our post office remained at full mast. But for a person whose earliest filmed speaking role is a home movie of the three-year-old version of himself shouting "Writer" when asked by a grandmother what he wanted to be when he grew up, this was devastating. Or, to be more exact, I allowed this to be devastating.

"Stop being a self-indulgent idiot," said one of my idols, James L. Brooks, who wrote and directed *Terms of Endearment* and *Broadcast News*, when he called to congratulate me about the movie, even though I tried my best to talk him out of it. But he wouldn't listen.

"Listen, there was a void in the universe, and you created some-thing to fill it. Don't give those people the power to affect you like this. Come on, it really doesn't matter what Ebert or *TIME* or that guy on Channel 4 thinks."

"The guy from Channel 4 didn't like it?"

"Oh . . . Hey, that's not the point. Now get back on the horse and do what you were meant to do."

The best advice, however, came from our then ten-year-old daugh-ter, Lindsay. Tired of seeing her father lying on the couch in his study, gaining weight and basically conceding all his power to those who don't create but, rather, criticize those who do, she approached me after arriv-ing home from the fourth grade one afternoon.

"Daddy?"

"Hi, angel."

"Have you moved at all today?

"What do you mean?"

"This is the same position you were in when I left for school this morning."

"Of course . . ."

"Yeah, that's a different flavor of Häagen-Dazs, so you must've moved."

"Well . . ."

"Dad, if I tell you something, do you promise not to punish me?"

"Ah, sure."

"Promise?" "Promise."

"Fuck 'em."

"Lindsay!"

"You promised."

"Okay."

"Dad, didn't you once tell me that Angie Dickinson never sold any of her poems while she was alive but kept on writing them anyway because deep down she knew they were good poems and that she was a good writer?"

"Emily Dickinson."

"Hey, you smiled . . ."

⚡⚡⚡

TIME PASSED. And, like all wounds, Roger's words receded into the past, where they eventually became shielded by scar tissue.

And life went on.

Ebert went on to give other movies both good and bad reviews, and I tried my best to take back the power I had given him by saying on one of my early David Letterman appearances that O. J. Simpson claimed that he went to see *North* the night of the murders but there was no one else in the theater to corroborate his story. I've even read Ebert's review on talk shows and during speaking engagements, not only because it's laughably bad but also to convey that wounds such as these, though painful, are only temporary. It's like the quote by Henry Wadsworth

Longfellow that my old friend Herb Sargent sent me: "The strength of criticism lies in the weakness of the thing criticized."

Or as Hyman Roth told Michael in *Godfather II*, "This is the business we've chosen." Yes, if we are willing to accept the excessive accolades and awards bestowed upon us for work that's lauded, we have to brace ourselves with the expectation that we can be publicly criticized for work that is, well, unappreciated. Or even, well, abhorred.

Still, in the spirit of Hyman Roth, for years I wondered whether there'd be any bloodshed if I ever ran into Roger Ebert.

Eventually I did.

It was March 2006, and I was on a book tour promoting a novel I had written called *The Other Shulman*, when someone I was having lunch with in a Chicago restaurant pointed him out. Yes, there was Roger Ebert, about three tables away from us, wearing an absurd-looking sweater boasting every autumn color imaginable—three different shades of brown, muted gold, burnt orange, baby puke green—a sweater that not only was far too big even for his rather portly body type, but that also made me immediately envious of anyone who was color blind.

I became transfixed. I watched him eat. I watched him laugh. And when he got up, I watched him as he worked his way to the men's room. Within seconds, I excused myself and did the same.

So there we were. Downstairs in the men's room of a restaurant and, as if I was now a spectator to this scene, I was consciously curious as to how I would behave. Completely detached. As if a second head hovering above me was saying, I wonder what Alan is going to do to Roger Ebert?

"Roger?" I heard myself saying as we were both washing our hands afterward.

"Yes," he answered, as he looked up into the mirror on the wall above the sink in front of us.

A beat of silence.

One during which he appeared to be trying to figure out where he may have seen my face before. And one during which I tried to figure out what I was going to say next. It was clearly my turn to talk. Some twelve years after that review.

"Alan Zweibel," I said.

Another beat of silence.

Roger appeared to be using *this* moment to tighten every muscle in his body.

A moment that I broke by saying, "And I just have to tell you, Roger, that I hate, hate, hate, hate, hate, hate, hate, hate, hate that sweater you're wearing."

One last beat of silence.

Then I smiled.

And then he smiled.

Then I started laughing.

And then he started laughing.

And then we shook hands.

That was the last time I saw Roger Ebert, who passed away in 2013. I'm happy he and I met that day.

Rest in peace, Roger.

CHAPTER 9

BUNNY BUNNY

(Even in Death Gilda Saves My Ass)

I BELIEVE IT WAS Prime Minister Winston Churchill who once said, "Success isn't final; failure isn't fatal. The courage to continue is what counts."

Sagacious and inspiring words indeed. It was just unfortunate that Churchill had died some thirty years before *North* was released, or I would have asked him to fly to Los Angeles and keep whispering those words in my ear as I lay vegged out on a couch devouring fistfuls of what we usually handed out to trick-or-treaters.

Instead, my tailspin was mollified by the ever-soothing Bernie, who was quick to inform me that I was now "colder than whale shit in television *and* movies." In a business sense, this was less than great news, given that television and the movies were the main businesses I was in. Then again, that point was somewhat moot, as I was numbed into a state of creative catatonia. In effect, I had no new ideas to write about, so what difference did it make that I had no place to sell them?

Writer's block? Dry as a bone? Shooting blanks? Call it what you wish. It's an occupational hazard that at one time or another visits all who deal in words. How do they work through this temporary condition? "I do the same thing I do to end constipation," Dave Barry tells me. "Just sit there until something comes out."

For the comedy writer? In a time of emotional upheaval? Like after the death of a loved one? Or while going through a wrenching divorce? When the very thought of trying to be funny seems blasphemous?

On a television show, other members of the writing staff can compensate for your lapse. Still another advantage of the group effort. Where the process marches onward while the affected writer can recede and present a softer voice. Even temporarily hide. I did that a number of times when I was on *SNL*. In particular the fourth season, when Robin and I had a big fight and broke up for a while. I was distraught to the point where the softer voice I presented was, at best, spoken in broken English. So I would slip into rooms where sketches were being written by gangs. Occasionally I'd suggest a line of dialogue that effectively brought the momentum of the room to a screeching halt. And I endured the humiliation of repeating jokes that were just pitched and agreed upon as if I could insinuate myself back into the effort by merely speaking.

Eventually, as it often happens, the atmosphere of those writers' rooms coupled with the collective adrenaline rushes of everyone involved as it gets closer to the time the audience will be entering the studio and even the personal embarrassment associated by not contributing can help expedite a writer's reemergence from those depths. In my particular case, my recovery was further expedited by one of my colleagues taking me aside and making me laugh by saying, "Listen, either shut the fuck up or go home—you're killing us."

"Only writers feel they have the right to get their own block," says Mike Reiss. "Dentists don't get dentist's block. Tax attorneys don't get H&R Block. One of the prerequisites of being a television writer is not to get writer's block. TV not only needs material, it chews through about five times as much material as makes it to the air."

But for the writer who works alone? In a home office where he is supposed to be developing scripts but has, in effect, no deadlines? As one of my favorite playwrights, Herb Gardner (*A Thousand Clowns, I'm Not Rappaport*), once said, "Your days are spent making up things that no one ever said to be spoken by people who do not exist for an audience that may not come."

ƒƒƒ

"YOU SHOULD WRITE SOMETHING about your relationship with Gilda."

The speaker was Robin, and she said this one afternoon upon discovering my now thirty-five pounds heavier carcass lying on the couch staring blankly at a television that was not turned on. She was right. It was time to start emerging from the self-pity and go back to doing the only thing I knew how to do. But I had absolutely no desire to heed Robin's suggestion.

"I don't want to capitalize on Gilda."

"Who said anything about money? Your best friend died over three years ago, and you still haven't cried."

Well, that part was true. I had filed Gilda's death in that remote part of the brain where facts are stored without emotional attachments.

"Do it for yourself," she continued in that way she has of continuing without giving me even the slightest opportunity of responding. "I think it's time you took your head out of your ass and dealt with it."

I hated her for being right. We now had three children, the youngest of whom, Sari, was not only Gilda's godchild but was held in her arms in what was to be the last photo taken of Gilda. If I didn't feel up to creating, maybe I'd have better luck remembering.

So I deftly removed my head from my ass and started writing for Gilda again. Not as Emily Litella or Roseanne Roseannadana or any of the other characters that I used to put words into the mouths of. This was for the private Gilda. The one that only I knew. The relationship I wanted to visit just one more time as best I could recall it.

I chose to write in pure dialogue: Gilda talks, I talk, Gilda talks, I talk. I wanted our words to touch each other again without the cold formality of structure, semicolons, or complete sentences. This was just for me, so I felt no need to be anything but casual.

Where did we meet? Oh, that's right, when I was hiding behind that plant in Lorne's office.

"Can you help me be a parakeet?"

"Excuse me?"

*"Yeah, I think it would be really funny if I stood on a
perch and scrunched up my face and talked like a parakeet. But I need someone to help me figure out what the
parakeet should say. Are you a good parakeet writer?"*

I wrote mostly at red lights. I'd pick up the legal pad from the passenger seat and scribble until the driver behind me honked. It was like
a diary that I'd make entries into late at night and even during breaks
from a script I was working on at the time. How accurate was it? Well,
since I can honestly say that I wasn't wearing a wire when I was friends
with Gilda, it's impossible to claim the words are verbatim. So while my
memories of the events were vivid, I could only do my best to recapture
the essence of what was spoken between us.

My friend Mary Karr, the great writer of *The Liars' Club, Lit,* and *The
Art of Memoir,* who is an undisputed master of the form, says, "Memoir
is not an act of history but an act of memory, which is innately corrupt."

I found that to be so true. We write the story we wish to tell, stress
the memories that best serve that story, and deemphasize, even omit,
those that don't. Such is the romance of recollection. We glorify our first
loves, our parents, and our hometowns.

Besides, this was an exercise for me alone. My private therapy.
Because of the intimacy of the writing, I felt it would never be read by anyone else. So I wrote with abandon. Without the need to censor. Or impress.

This is where writers are lucky. Without trying to sound too lofty
or, even worse, like a pompous turd, this is where his or her so-called
gift can be used for personal advantage. Because whatever the mood,
no matter the longing, the writer can use his words to connect himself
to any world he wishes to visit.

I was talking to Gilda again. I wrote slowly, because I didn't want
her voice to end. As long as I was writing, Gilda was alive. I even drew
pictures of us in different settings that I thought would make her laugh.
I can't draw for the life of me, but I felt that my pen-and-ink stick figures
somehow captured the sensibility of, well, us. Of the kids inside of us
that we tried so hard to recapture and hold on to. And how we always

comforted each other when we experienced our lives changing. Like we did at the onset of her fame. In particular the night we went to Carnegie Hall to see Billy Crystal and Melissa Manchester perform, and, upon entering, she was shouted out to by so many audience members who recognized her. How we sat in our seats after the audience left, and she was on the verge of tears.

> I'm scared, Zweibel. It's a weird feeling, having strangers call me by my name and knowing all sorts of things about my life that I never told them. So it would make me feel better if you didn't call me what everyone else did.
>
> Sure. Thanks.
>
> Excuse me . . . miss?
>
> Yeah?
>
> Any thought about what I should call you?
>
> . . . Gilbert.
>
> Gilbert?
>
> Yes, Gilbert.
>
> Makes perfect sense to me.

Or how so many years later, when Gilda was very sick and I went to Cedars-Sinai Medical Center to donate blood, the nurse handed me a pen and paper, telling me that Gilda liked to know whose blood she was receiving and that I should write something nice to my platonic pal, because she was having a tough time.

> Dear Gilbert—
> I knew I'd get some fluid of mine into you one way or another.
>
> Love,
> Zweibel

And then, about six months after I'd begun, the writing was over. I had finished. I had two hundred and twenty handwritten pages that spanned from the moment we met behind that potted plant through fourteen years of eccentric friendship that ended with the eulogy I gave at her memorial. Fourteen years of the words that had passed between us.

As far as I was concerned, I had completed my mission. The catharsis was complete. Closure. It was time to move on.

ƒƒƒ

FOR THE HELL OF IT, I sent the pages to a few friends—those who knew Gilda and who also knew Gilda and me together, because I thought it might elicit a memory or two. I sent the pages to Mel Brooks, Carl Reiner, Rob Reiner, Garry Shandling, and Bernie Brillstein—all of whom had the same reaction: that I should publish what I'd written. "No," I kept repeating. "This is not meant for strangers."

But after everyone, including Robin, insisted that my book was a nice tribute to Gilda, especially after another book by a former acquaintance of hers was published that was highly inaccurate and upset her family a great deal, I began to entertain the idea of actually publishing this book. First I wanted the blessings of a few people.

I sent the pages to Gilda's brother, Michael. He and Gilda's mom read them and, with the exception of one minor tweak (I'd described their dad as a "mountain of a man," when, in fact, he was only 5' 6"), encouraged me to publish the book.

Then I called Gene Wilder, Gilda's husband, and merely told him I was FedEx-ing something that I'd like him to read. Giving no hint as to what it was, I sent it and held my breath. Until he called back the next evening and said, "I hope you plan on publishing this." He also asked what the book's title would be. That's right. Now that it was going to be a book, it was probably a good idea to give it a title.

"Bunny Bunny."

"Perfect," Gene said.

✦✦✦

THE MOMENT I AGREED to publish *Bunny Bunny*, there was a sudden shift. What had been a subjective outpouring, an unbridled voice of recollection, was now going to be a product. Which meant that my most personal piece of writing would have to go through an intrusive process to ready it for reading by strangers. I was now about to embark on the deliberate task of modifying things without changing what was my truth, which was not easy, considering the new cast of characters who were now in my life.

An editor who said, "We can use a better joke here," or a fact checker who wanted to see my driver's license to prove that Gilda did indeed die on my birthday. Not to mention a publisher who asked a question that, to this very day, stuns me with its abject idiocy.

"Does she have to die at the end?"

"What are you suggesting? That she had a bad cold?" I asked.

"No, she could have had cancer. But it would be great if she beats it and then dies in the sequel." To this day I'm still shocked that this executive was actually allowed to vote.

Sure, some changes were easy to make, as they were innocuous. Freda Payne's house became the home of Larry Fine from the Three Stooges, because I thought he was a funnier landlord to have. *("See that dent in the wall? Moe did that.")* I also figured I wouldn't get a lot of hate mail for changing the Carnegie Hall scene to take place in an empty Madison Square Garden, because I thought that Gilda's "Call me Gilbert" speech would resonate better after enduring the louder shouts from more raucous fans during the course of a Knicks game. Plus, it would be easier for me to draw basketball players in shorts vying for a jump ball than a fully clothed Melissa Manchester and Billy Crystal.

But the inclusion of certain personal things had to be handled deftly. This was my life we were talking about. The names of my wife and children were going to be in this book, and I had to be careful about the context they were in. As parents, Robin and I warned our children about the dangers of drug use. So as a memoirist, how do I convey that my use of cocaine had been only a temporary, regrettable phase I had gone through?

More important, I had to be protective of Gilda. This was a story about shared experiences, secrets, and feelings. How do I reveal her vices and demons without betraying her? Her family trusted me with her memory. I was more than aware of my responsibilities.

Still, since this was going to be a book read and judged by others, I had to slightly lower the bar in regard to its literal accuracy; so I allowed for tweaks and edits that would still maintain the integrity of the relationship.

That said, I lost a lot of sleep over this. Despite the encouragement of Gilda's mother and brother and Gene Wilder, I wrestled with the prospect of this kind of exposure and second-guessed the moral compass that was guiding me. For reassurance, I reached out to the members of our *SNL* family for both the support and good will of all who knew and loved her. I knew that they would be direct and let me know whether they deemed this book exploitative.

I sent the manuscript to Lorne and requested a blurb. And to Laraine Newman. And Jane Curtin. Paul Shaffer. Franken. Chevy. As well as members of the extended family like Candice Bergen. Carl Reiner. Rob Reiner. Billy Crystal. Whoopi Goldberg. Mel Brooks. And they all obliged. And were wonderfully positive. As Dan Aykroyd said at the time, "Zweibel was really her best friend. I remember. I was there. Herein he succeeds in capturing the warm, humorous, generous essence of the person around whom all the positive elements of *Saturday Night Live* pivoted." So I slept a little better.

***

PETER GETHERS, who was now an editor-at-large for all of Random House, took a personal interest in this book and was curious about the title. "It makes perfect sense once you read the book, but it really doesn't mean anything until then." In effect, he was asking, what would make people buy the book? Say, "By Alan Zweibel, author of *North*"? No, not unless Random House wanted potential book buyers to go running for cover. Peter thought that we should put Gilda's name in the subtitle, so people would have a clue as to what the book was about. He asked me for some suggestions. I was at a loss.

"How would *you* describe this book?" Peter asked me.

"Well, it's sort of a love story."

"Then maybe that's it," Peter said. "*Bunny Bunny—Gilda Radner: A Sort of Love Story.*"

The "sort of" was not only accurate, given the platonic nature of the relationship, but also reflected the sensibility of what Peter referred to as an eccentric memoir. This was further exemplified by those primitive pen-and-ink drawings that ran throughout the book. The ones I drew (scrawled?) because I felt that they would've made Gilda laugh. In effect, they collaborated with the writing and added another dimension to the words spoken between us.

Then the cover became an issue. The publisher wanted a picture of Gilda. That I understood. They showed me an actual photo with her arms outstretched, with a splash of red to make the picture pop. That I hated. And I knew it was something that Gilda would also have hated, because it was a misrepresentation that bore no reflection of her or the book's personality. Gilda was quirky. Whimsical. Francesco Scavullo photographs were not.

So I reached back to our *SNL* days and contacted Edie Baskin, whose hand-painted photos of the cast and hosts were a signature look of the show back in the seventies. She teamed up with my wife, Robin, and created a cover with an ethereal-looking Gilda dressed as she once appeared in a sketch as Dorothy from *The Wizard of Oz* floating above two sets of footprints, mine and Gilda's, in a trail on a beach.

Now the book would be mine. For better or worse, no matter its reception, it was a memoir that I could stand by. The cover, the drawings, and, most important, the dialogues that attracted attention even before the book was in galley form.

Credit: Robin Zweibel and Edie Baskin

⚡⚡⚡

I RAN INTO DIRECTOR James L. Brooks at an Oscar de le Hoya fight
one night in Los Angeles and told him I wanted him to read something.
He did and got excited. Because the book was in pure dialogue, he felt
that it would be effective read aloud, and he directed staged readings as
fund-raisers for the recently founded Gilda's Club—a support community
for cancer patients and their families that was started by Gene Wilder;
the great actor Mandy Patinkin; a woman named Joanna Bull, who had
been Gilda's wellness advisor; and newsman Joel Siegal.

With Julia Louis-Dreyfuss and Jason Alexander
after their staged reading of *Bunny Bunny*.

For the first readings Julia Louis-Dreyfus and Jason Alexander read the parts of Gilda and Alan in front of sold-out audiences at the Geffen Playhouse in Los Angeles and then at the Walter Kerr Theatre on Broadway. Subsequently, Jim staged a reading with Woody Harrelson and Holly Hunter—two actors who couldn't possibly be more dissimilar to Gilda and myself. Yet the fact that the audience was incredibly enthusiastic about what they'd heard served to prove that impersonations were unnecessary. If the spirit of Gilda was captured and the relationship between the actors worked, the piece would work as a play or even a film.

Finally the book was published and was a big seller. People were not only interested in reading about Gilda Radner but also related to having a friendship with someone they continued to love even after they both married other people. And even after one of them passed away.

I started appearing on the late-night talk shows to promote it. The movie rights were purchased, and I eventually opted to adapt it as a play that had a successful off-Broadway run. The stage adaptation compromised the book's literal accuracy even more, as the dialogues, which played so effectively when left to the reader's imagination, now had to be visually compelling. Late-night phone calls that were intriguing when simply read aloud by Jason and Julia sitting in chairs on a bare stage now had to be rethought as scenes, with movement that had never occurred. So now the standard shifted to one of whether any manufactured scene could very well have happened to these two characters. I often envision that when I die, Gilda will be waiting for me in heaven with copies of the book and the published play and indicating various places, saying, "What the hell is this? I never said that. Zweibel, this never happened!" Then, if I had to guess, she would take out a red pencil and start to rewrite the new material, making it funnier than I ever could have without her.

Forgive me for bragging but I drew that illustration.

CHAPTER **10**

700 SUNDAYS

(Billy Crystal and the Rise of the One-Man Show)

THE FIRST ONE-MAN PLAY I ever saw was *Clarence Darrow* by David Rintels. It was 1974, and Henry Fonda portrayed the famed attorney reviewing his life and career, including his roles in the Scopes "Monkey" trial and the Leopold and Loeb murder case. It was the first one-person show of its kind, as the ones that came before it, such as Hal Holbrook's *Mark Twain Tonight!* and James Whitmore's *Will Rogers' USA*, weren't plays but readings of their subjects' material.

In that pre-*SNL* year, I saved my deli earnings to buy a ticket and sat there mesmerized while Fonda, under the direction of John Houseman, created Darrow's entire biography by first establishing eye contact with the audience and then alternately receding into his 1890s apartment and a 1920s courtroom, where he addressed an unseen judge, pleaded his case to an empty jury box, and referred to invisible defendants.

It was magical. The drama of a man's life brought to a stage via the marriage of words and effective lighting. The play was surprisingly funny with a touch of pathos, too, as Fonda's warmth exposed the heart within Darrow's bold exterior.

> Darrow: I've never hoped to see any man meet his Maker before the appointed day, but there may have been one or two obituary notices I've read with approval.

Afterward, I remember wondering, should I ever consider writing a one-person show, whose singular voice would I want to capture? Hal Holbrook as Thomas Edison? Alan Arkin as John Wilkes Booth? Lily Tomlin as Amelia Earhart? Richard Pryor as Moses? James Earl Jones as Gilbert Gottfried? Okay, maybe not the most inspired (or funny) ideas in the world, but I was intrigued nonetheless.

It seemed like a natural form for me. Storytelling. Dialogues with other characters embedded within a long-sustained monologue. Jokes, but not stand-up, as there's a narrative to service. With an emotional ending, of any kind, that has to be earned.

But I didn't do anything with that idea until decades later.

In 1998, Billy Crystal, Larry David, and I were still sharing that suite at Castle Rock. At the time, I was working on a script with Jessie Nelson that would become a Rob Reiner–directed movie starring Bruce Willis and Michelle Pfeiffer called *The Story of Us*. It was a script I had started writing alone—about a couple with two children whose marriage was slowly eroding as the stuff of life chipped away at what was once a loving relationship. It would be evenhanded. There would not be a good guy or a bad guy. "Can a Marriage Survive Fifteen Years of Marriage?" would be its thematic subtitle.

I am happy to inject at this point that *North* did nothing to affect my friendship with Rob. We had a great time: Robin and Rob's wife, Michele, became good friends; we shared a house in Hawaii; and Rob and I did a few more projects together. An ill-fated pilot for CBS. As well as one of the great thrills of my existence on this planet when we wrote jokes for Carl Reiner and Mel Brooks's classic "2000 Year Old Man" routine. This came about when Rob and I wrote and produced a one-hour documentary/special for ABC about early childhood development and the importance of nurturing called *I Am Your Child*. To assure a good rating for a rather academic subject for prime-time network television, Tom Hanks hosted, and we loaded up our sketches with roles played by Billy Crystal, Robin Williams, Oprah Winfrey, Michael J. Fox, Rosie O'Donnell, Marty Short, Jon Lovitz, Gen. Colin Powell, who read

Goodnight Moon to his young grandchild, as well as President and Hillary Clinton in the Roosevelt Room in the White House talking about whether they did everything they could as parents to emotionally prepare their daughter Chelsea to go to college in the fall. After Rob asked his dad and Mel to appear, he and I made a list of people in history that Carl would name, and Mel would answer whether or not that person had been hugged as a child.

CARL

Shakespeare?

MEL

Hugged.

CARL

He got a lot of physical attention?

MEL

You don't write sonnets like that without an occasional squeeze and, "Way to go, Will."

CARL

Attila the Hun?

MEL

Not hugged. His mother didn't even talk to him.

CARL

Gandhi?

MEL

Hugged. Thrown up in the air and kissed all over.

CARL

Jesus?

MEL

Hugged.

CARL

Moses?

MEL

Hugged.

CARL

Buddha?

MEL

Hugged.

CARL

Hitler?

MEL

Kicked.

CARL

Not hugged?

MEL

Not hugged, not read to, no one bought him an ice cream cone in the summer, no one ever said, "Adolf, would you like your bed turned down?" I've always said that if someone—a mother, a father, a good-looking neighbor, anyone—had tucked him in and said, "Sweet dreams,

little Adolf," maybe he keeps those tanks out of Poland
and takes in a movie.

So one day over lunch when I casually said to Rob that if Robin and I were
ever to get separated, I thought we should do it over a summer, when
the kids were away at camp and wouldn't know about it, he immediately
said, "Let's do that script."

So I went to work. For two years. But the first few drafts I wrote
were incredibly lopsided. The guy was deserving of sainthood. His wife
was a complete bitch. Not exactly what I was trying to do, but I just
couldn't capture the voice and mind-set of the woman. Every word she
said sounded like a man had written it, so the character's credibility
and empathy were totally undermined. To gain the balance I wanted, I
asked Jessie Nelson to co-write future drafts with me. I had long been
an admirer of her work as the writer and director of *Corrina, Corrina*.
(She would subsequently serve in the same roles for *I Am Sam* and was
the book writer for the hit Broadway musical *Waitress*.)

But aside from her obvious talents, what convinced me that Jessie
might be the perfect writing partner for this script was when she and
her husband, the director Bryan Gordon, were seated across from Robin
and me at a dinner party celebrating Larry David's fiftieth birthday. I had
never met them before, but the moment I saw Bryan whisper something
to Jessie, and she rolled her eyes the exact way Robin does when I say
just about anything, I knew. I approached her as we were leaving the
restaurant and said, "Look, we really don't know each other, but how
would you feel about revealing your most personal secrets to millions
of people with me?"

Jessie smiled and was game enough to say yes.

So the collaboration began, with me saying that nothing I had
already written was sacred and should only be preserved if it fit into what
she and I were now doing. The only scene I lobbied for from my original
drafts, and I was thrilled that Jessie liked it, was the one where our lead
characters, Ben and Katie, met each other as Robin and I did—with Ben
throwing paper clips at Katie and her putting a pith helmet on her head.

Jessie was the first woman I'd written with since Gilda, and our approach was different, as she is a disciplined writer. We kept regular hours, and where with Gilda I let her run off at the mouth, navigating her outpourings and then sculpting them into coherence by myself afterward, Jessie was very protective of the characters we were writing for and often kept me in check when I was the one who'd go astray.

During the course of our process, she grew to be a close friend, and she brought her and Bryan's marriage to the script. We would often playact the parts, and our writing became those reactions to each other in the situations we put Ben and Katie in. As we did in a scene where they went to a marriage counselor who had a birthmark that looked strikingly like the state of California.

> Dr. Hopkins
> This cycle of closeness and estrangement you've
> both told me about. What instigates it? Triggers it?
> The first thing that comes to your mind?

> Ben
> (staring at his forehead)
> Sacramento.

> Katie
> Governor Gray Davis.

It was during one of these sessions that Billy stuck his head into my office.

"You got a second?"

I asked Jessie to excuse me, and I went next door.

Mind you, Billy had been my good friend since 1974, but during the ensuing twenty-three years we still hadn't worked on a project together. During that span of time, Billy had become an international superstar who had starred in the 1984–85 season of *Saturday Night Live*, hosted the Oscars a record number of times, and acted in some of the most iconic and largest-grossing films in the history of cinema, such as *City Slickers* and *When Harry Met Sally*. Billy had, to be frank, done quite nicely without my help.

From 1992–98, aside from seeing each other every day in the Castle Rock offices, Billy and I spent a lot of time together the way middle-aged guy friends do (he was "Uncle Billy" to my children), and I still couldn't help but notice that we had absolutely no overlap between our personal and professional lives. Why? Hard to say, except perhaps we both didn't want to jeopardize our friendship by subjecting it to the ill feelings that can arise due to creative differences. Or perhaps it was simply that Billy thought the other writers he was working with, all of them first-rate, were better suited for the projects he did. I accepted that possibility as well. Just so you know, for the purposes of this book I, asked Billy why, in his mind, we hadn't worked together for so long, and he said, "Sexual tension." So, needless to say, I still don't know the real reason why.

So once inside Billy's office, he said, "I'm thinking of doing a one-man show about my father that I'll call *700 Sundays*. Would you like to help me write it?" I was honored, said yes (with the caveat that he give me some notice before we started, so I could clear my schedule), and then happily went back to work with Jessie.

That was the last I heard of the project for four years. And it's not like I didn't drop hints along the way. Every so often I'd see Billy and say, "Hey, I'm ready whenever you are!" And Billy would respond with a noncommittal, "Okay."

So I'd wait a few months. Then I would say, "Hey, I'm ready to dive in!" Again, Billy would respond with the same, nonchalant, "Okay."

After a while I stopped mentioning it. I started to feel like one of those dorky kids in a touch football game who's told to go out for a long pass and, as he runs and waves his hands to indicate he's open, is told to go farther and farther until the other kids decide to scrap the game and go to lunch.

But after his mom passed away in 2001, Billy was finally ready to talk about his family. Perhaps her death completed the story that he was now able to tell. Maybe he now had perspective, a complete overview. And why, after all of those years, did he still turn to me for the role of his collaborator? According to Billy, "When you are close friends, you want a working relationship to be just right. *700 Sundays* was the most personal work of my life, and I knew you were the perfect choice. I trusted you with the joys and sorrows of my life."

More than anything, I was touched that my friend would trust me with his life. I knew what Billy's family meant to him, so the invitation to help him present them was one I took seriously with the utmost respect for its delicacy and for the range of emotions that this memory play was going to evoke. And for the surprise that awaited Billy Crystal fans who'd buy tickets to his Broadway show expecting to laugh their butts off for a couple of hours, as they had while seeing the one-person shows of Whoopi Goldberg, John Leguizamo, Lily Tomlin, and Mario Cantone—without any expectation that they would tearfully call their parents or children afterward to say "I love you."

⚡⚡⚡

THE SHOW'S TITLE SET THE TONE: *700 Sundays*. Because Billy's father worked six days a week, he was only free to spend time with him on that remaining day: Sunday. Going to ball games, the Long Beach boardwalk, the movies—it was their one day to be together. Billy was fifteen years old when his dad died suddenly. So he calculated that he and his father had had roughly seven hundred Sundays together. And once this was explained after a few very funny anecdotes, Billy's story added a new dimension.

Capturing Billy's voice would not be an issue. Decades of friendship certainly gave me enough time to know how Billy spoke and what he would find funny. Putting words into the mouths of his deceased family members whom I'd never met would not be difficult either, as I simply channeled the broken-English voices of my own immigrant relatives. As we deftly observed in *700 Sundays*, all of us have the same families—they just jump from album to album.

The most unusual part of the development process that began in 2003 was the script. That is, there was none. Forgive me: When we began, there were four pages filled with Billy's concepts. Anecdotes. Bits of dialogue. A blueprint for something very powerful, funny, and special.

We met at night. Billy spoke, and I listened. As close as we were, I hadn't known about the jazz musicians who were always at his house when he was growing up. I had heard some of the stories about his relatives but certainly not all of them. I asked a ton of questions. Billy answered them with more stories. I took notes. Wrote a joke here and there. The length of the script swelled to four and a half pages.

Rehearsals soon followed. First in a small black-box theater on the grounds of Pepperdine University. Then in a stark room at the Geffen Playhouse in Los Angeles. Billy, the great director Des McAnuff (*Jersey Boys, Tommy,* and, later, the musical *Ain't Too Proud*), a production assistant (Lurie Horne Pfeffer), and myself. These were tough work sessions. Through the years, I'd seen Billy Crystal onstage in coffeehouses, Las Vegas nightclubs, Carnegie Hall—virtually every venue imaginable with the exception of a stark room in Los Angeles in front of three people sitting behind a table taking notes as he performed. We watched Billy as he created a show in front of our eyes. The stories he'd told me were now growing into scenes, coming to life while Des, Lurie, and I tried our best to pretend that we were a thousand people to provide Billy with laughs to indicate how we thought it was coming along.

At about this time my role began to clarify itself as being twofold. On the one hand, in order for me to write for and about these people, I had to embrace them as much as Billy did. I had to try to capture the essence of what made them unique as individuals. Their voices. Their points of view. Their wonderful ability to find the humor in a world that was not always humorous. I had done that in both the book and stage versions of *Bunny Bunny,* so that part was easy.

Billy's affection for them was infectious, and, since it could be said that we all live slightly different versions of the same lives, I also grew to love them for how they reminded me of some of the phlegmatic immigrants I'd had in my own family. So just as I had done many years

before, writing monologues in the voices of different comedians, now I
was doing the same thing, except the cast was Billy's family.

On the other hand, I had to also view the play in denial of those
feelings. To look at Billy's life as a dramatic piece of writing. With the
unanticipated responsibilities of urging him to dig deeper, to get in touch
with an emotion that the play needed to have expressed at a specific
moment. The one who had to take a step back to the edge of objectivity
and point out that a certain cherished anecdote was redundant or, even
worse, be the one to say, "I think we can use a laugh at your father's
funeral." And I remember being more than nervous the day I felt it
necessary to have this particular discussion.

"Look," I said, "I want to ask you a question. And you don't have
to answer right now, but this is important. When you were fifteen, you
had a fight with your dad, he got upset, left the house, went bowling,
and had a heart attack. In your fifteen-year-old brain, did you think it
was your fault?"

Billy said yes. So it became a very emotionally effective part of
the show when Billy, upon viewing his dad in an open casket, wrote and
said the following:

". . . And he was so still. When just hours before we were fighting
about the girl. And I kept thinking: Is this my fault? Did I make this
happen? Our argument, did I bring this on? Why didn't I get a chance
to say 'I'm sorry'? Why didn't I get a chance to say goodbye?"

I found it exhilarating to plumb the depths of my good friend's
memory and together create a stunning moment of theater.

$$\sharp\sharp\sharp$$

ULTIMATELY, THE PROCESS BECAME a dance. I followed Billy's
lead and serviced the growing script with dialogue and jokes where
needed and then tried to expand the boundaries by exploring the different roads that the new material was now providing.

The time then arrived for the play to be seen by more than three
people. Billy and Des arranged for a fourteen-show performance about

an hour and a half down the road from Los Angeles, at the La Jolla Play-house (where Des was the artistic director) in a program called Page To Stage. It was an exciting time for me. No matter how many years I've been working, to see my words come to life in concert with other elements of a production like music, lighting, and an ingenious set that replicated Billy's childhood house—with photos and home movies displayed in its windows—where the memories were made.

My process settled into its own rhythm. During the performances, I'd sit in the back row of the theater, next to Des, with a pad and a pen that had a little light attached to it, writing jokes. New ideas worthy of exploration. Embellishments on themes that Billy ad-libbed as he made five hundred people laugh and cry while talking about his life and family. I spent intermission eavesdropping. In the lobby. At concession stands. Hanging out in the men's room much longer than a respectable father of three really should, trying to hear what people were saying to one another about the show.

Afterward, usually over a meal far too heavy, given the hour, Billy, Des, Billy's manager, David Steinberg, and I went over our notes. What worked, what needed help, what we could add, subtract, rearrange. We looked closely at the material that had already appeared in his stand-up act—did it fit the arc of the story? Des and I kept stressing that this was a play—so the stand-up material was subject to reevaluation. If those first-person routines could be incorporated and made contextual within the story we were telling, they would be included. "But unless your dad actually played in the Negro baseball leagues," I joked, "that piece where the old player tells what it was like to bat against Satchel Paige, as brilliant as it is, can't be in the show." Of course Billy laughed and agreed wholeheartedly.

Mornings were when I worked alone. In the business center at the hotel I was staying in. Writing what I had taken note of the night before. Trying to figure out how to use the printer. Then giving the pages to Billy. Some of the material found its way into that day's rehearsal and then into that night's show, where five hundred people let us know if they enjoyed it. The immediate feedback was thrilling for me. The indescribable energy in that theater evoked a sense memory that I'd longed for, as my daily routine became reminiscent of show day at *SNL*. It was like live television but with a bunch of chances to do it over to get it right.

By the end of our two-week stay in La Jolla, what had begun as four pages of Billy's anecdotes was now a 105-page, fully fleshed-out script that we would take to New York. Most plays would have been taken on the road at this point for out-of-town tryouts. However, given the audiences' overwhelming response to what we'd created over the course of fourteen shows, we went straight to New York.

This time the rehearsal space was in a building called the Duke on Forty-Second Street. Two floors above us, our old friends Eric Idle and Mike Nichols were prepping *Spamalot* for its Broadway run at the Shubert Theatre. We would go up the alley to the Broadhurst. *The Producers* was across the street at the St. James Theatre. Angus McIndoe was the restaurant next door to it. Suddenly we were a part of a vibrant theatrical community. Our gypsy run-through brought the casts and crews of the other shows to see us on a Monday afternoon when their own theaters were dark. That was followed by previews that were all sold out, thanks to Billy's popularity and the word that was circulating that the show was something special. In fact, the advance was, at the time, the highest grossing non-musical in Broadway history. And then came opening night, when, sitting with Robin, our three children, and Adam's fiancée, Cori, I watched my friend conquer still another domain.

As for me, though I had gotten a taste of the Broadway scene years before when I was one of many writers who contributed to *Gilda Live*, which ran at the Winter Garden Theatre in the summer of 1979 (*Bunny Bunny* was off-Broadway at the Lucille Lortel Theatre), this was different. While Gilda's show offered a wonderful variety of her *SNL* characters and great songs written by her and Paul Shaffer, Billy's story had a compelling emotionality that drew me to the theater every night, where I got lost in the resurrected images of bygone eras that I felt so comfortable revisiting time and again like an old favorite song.

I kept on tweaking the script long after the show was a bona fide hit and doing my very best to resist jumping to my feet and shouting

"Author" every time a new line I'd written got a big laugh. Still, I continued to write new material (oftentimes e-mailing it to Billy from whatever city I was visiting during a book tour) to maintain topicality in those areas of the script that allowed for it or to simply furnish new material so Billy could look forward to saying something different. Adding what I could to Billy's story—conveyed by monologue, mime, song, and impersonation—culminated in a poker game with God in which Billy, playing the hand he was dealt, comes to the conclusion that, despite the early loss of his dad and his tongue-in-cheek lament about not being a couple of inches taller, the rest of his cards—which included having his mom in his life up until her death in her eighties, having the beautiful family he and his wife, Janice, created, and fulfilling his childhood dream of enjoying a wonderful life by making people laugh—were more than enough to make God fold his hand.

⚡⚡⚡

AT FIRST SOME PEOPLE WONDERED whether Billy's story was particular only to Jewish people who grew up on Long Island. But that thought was proven wrong when 700 Sundays went on the road and had the same effect on audiences in Boston, San Francisco, Atlanta, Toronto, etc. Even in Australia, where it is not customary to give standing ovations, audiences made an exception by rising to their feet to show their appreciation after every performance. So, no, the only common denominator you needed to enjoy and relate to this story was to have a family.

Rave reviews and box office records followed. As did a Tony Award that I allowed myself to get a little sentimental about. It represented the culmination of years of an amazing relationship that began when Billy drove me to and from the New York City comedy clubs when we were both starting out.

"What was special about 700 Sundays," says Mike Birbiglia, whose own one-man shows, Sleepwalk with Me and The New One, were hits a few years later, "was that its specificity of word choice combined with its conversational tone had a way of transporting me into another time and place and into an experience that was nothing like my own, but executed the magic trick of feeling entirely familiar. Plus, it was hilarious. Hundreds of jokes—if you're counting."

As a result of this Broadway experience, the national tour, and shows in Australia, I found the writing process so exhilarating that I wanted to do more theater.

It also encouraged Robin and me to move back east. Being back in New York all of those months with *700 Sundays* reminded me of what I had been missing. The energy that was imbedded in the very fabric of the city, coupled with the fact that when Adam and Lindsay finished college, they had opted to settle in New Jersey. So, very much because we didn't want to be absentee parents and (eventually) grandparents, we sold our home in Brentwood and followed our kids. We enrolled Sari in the same high school that Robin had gone to, and though Short Hills, New Jersey, could hardly be considered a hotbed of show business, I exaggerated the definition a little by allowing the town's proximity to the Hudson River to define me as what I'd always wanted to be—a New York writer.

⚡⚡⚡

"MARTIN SHORT IS THE FUNNIEST person in the world."

The speaker was Gilda Radner, and she told me this in 1975, when we first started *SNL*. I hadn't heard of him at this point and thought she may have been exaggerating just a bit about her old boyfriend in Toronto. Here we were, working on a show that featured John Belushi, Dan Aykroyd, Lorraine Newman and Gilda herself, but she just wouldn't shut up about this guy.

"I'm telling you, Zweibel, he'll make you laugh until you bend over and vomit."

And then I became familiar with Marty. As Ed Grimley. In *The Three Amigos*. Later as Franck Eggelhoffer in the *Father of the Bride* movies. As Jiminy Glick. And when he danced, I saw his body move in ways that made me laugh until I bent over and almost vomited. Gilda was 100 percent right, and I told her that I didn't know of anyone else who could do so many things as well as Martin Short did.

"I knew you'd like him."

She then added—and said this on a number of occasions—that she wanted Marty and me to be friends.

"Okay," I answered.

"No, I'm serious, Zweibel. It's important."

She was right about that, too, though I wouldn't realize it for a number of years. Though we had seen each other a number of times at parties, my first real interaction with Marty was when I returned to *Saturday Night Live* as a guest writer in the 1980s. Dick Ebersol was now the show's producer, and if a host had a certain writer that he or she felt comfortable with, that writer joined the staff for that show. All told, I did that three times. Once when Eddie Murphy hosted. A few years later, when Lorne Michaels returned, I rejoined the writing staff for the week that Garry Shandling hosted. And, for reasons I still don't fully understand, in the 1984–85 season, when Reverend Jesse Jackson hosted, Dick requested that I help out. This was the season that the cast included Billy Crystal, Christopher Guest, Julia Louis-Dreyfus, and Marty —with whom I wrote a parody of an old *Twilight Zone* episode, in which Ed Grimley was a passenger on a plane, looked out the window, and saw a gremlin. We got along great, the sketch played quite well, and it really stoked my interest to work with Marty again.

Still, almost two decades passed before that would come to pass.

✦✦✦

AFTER THE SUCCESS OF *700 Sundays* and my association with it, a number of people asked me if I wanted to write one-person shows for them. While flattered, I was no longer interested in writing anyone else's autobiography. I didn't have the desire to learn the details about someone's personal life to the extent necessary to have them speak honestly and effectively onstage. But in 2005, when Bernie told me that Martin Short was planning on doing a one-man show that *had a cast of five other actors*, with music by Marc Shaiman and lyrics by Scott Wittman, that was essentially a parody of one-person shows, I was intrigued. And after I spent an afternoon (along with the great comedy writer Andy Breckman) at Marc and Scott's apartment listening to the songs they'd written and offering jokes and suggestions for pieces in the show, I knew that this was something I wanted to be a part of.

But the calendar was unkind. I had written a novel titled *The Other Shulman* and was about to embark on a national book tour. The book had taken close to two years to write, so I was excited by its impending publication and all of the speaking engagements as well as radio and late-night television talk show appearances that I would be doing to promote it. Unfortunately, however, that schedule pretty much conflicted with the one that Marty's show had for its writing and workshop process, so I was disappointed that I was not going to be able to write the show.

The book tour took me all over the country. With audiences as large as seven hundred in St. Louis and as small as, well, as small as the six people who showed up at a Barnes & Noble in a New Jersey mall on a Friday night that a Ben Stiller movie was opening at a theater at the other end of the same mall. Try as I did to make the room look less sparse by having the attendees move to the front row of the 250 chairs that were set up, I only succeeded in making it look like a crowd when I squeezed the entire "audience" into a booth at the Legal Sea Foods restaurant next door and signed their books over the dinner I treated them to.

Years later, this dubious record was broken when Adam Mansbach and I were flown into Chicago and then driven to a church in Naperville, Illinois, where our publicist had booked us to promote our middle grades book *Benjamin Franklin: Huge Pain In My* . . . and six people showed up. Sure, I know that sounds like it tied the amount of people who showed up at that Jersey mall, but I maintain it was a smaller audience since Adam and I had invited four of those people.

"When you play to an almost empty audience, you're not mad at the people who didn't show up," says David Steinberg. "But you really hate the people who did, because now you have to go onstage and perform to such a small crowd."

The greatest thrill for me, though, was when David Letterman invited me to come on his show and read from *The Other Shulman*. I chose a passage in which my main character, named Shulman, was in college and failing a poetry-writing class. So, in a last-ditch effort to pass, he submitted the lyrics to Paul Simon's "The Boxer," figuring that his ninety-two-year-old professor wouldn't recognize the song. She didn't. But she was so impressed with it that she asked Shulman to come up and read it to the rest of the class. Though he resisted, the professor prevailed, Shulman read "his poem," and when he got to the chorus, Letterman's entire studio audience started singing, "Lie lie lie, lie lie lie lie lie lie la la lie lie lie" along with me. Everyone was happy. In particular, my publisher, who was ecstatic, as the book climbed from something like 195,000 on Amazon's ranking to 57 after the show aired. (And then within a few short days, it plummeted to its former depths.) The next day I got a very funny e-mail from Paul Simon telling me how sales of "The Boxer" had soared because of my reading. To which I wrote back, "Paul, the fact that the studio audience sang along when I recited your lyrics is testimony to the enduring effect your poetry has had on our culture. That said, can I trouble you to write another song that I can plagiarize the next time I'm a guest on the Letterman show? Thank you in advance."

Still, I enjoy book tours, as they give me a chance to get out from behind my laptop, actually interact with other human beings, and develop new material that I can hone and use on talk shows and future speaking engagements. And when this particular one ended, I returned home to New Jersey exhausted and looking forward to some downtime with Robin and the family when the phone rang.

"Hey, kid!"

"Hi, Bernie!"

"You home?"

"Yeah, the tour went great. Twelve cities in sixteen days. So happy to be home and relax . . ."

"Great. Now get your fat ass on a plane to San Francisco."

"San Francisco?"

Marty's show had started its out-of-town runs on its way to an eventual Broadway opening, and it needed a fresh pair of eyes. Another writer had been hired to write the book for the musical, and I was sympathetic to him when we were introduced at the Curran Theatre before one of the performances. We've all been through it—pouring your guts into something, only to have it go unappreciated.

After seeing the show, which I absolutely loved despite the audience's tepid reception, I called Bernie and told him that I thought I could be of help. The songs were hilarious, and the supporting cast of Brooks Ashmanskas, Nicole Parker, Mary Birdsong, Capathia Jenkins, and Mark Shaiman was fantastic. That, plus the fact that this was parody, was going to be a lot of fun for me. The familiar formula of the one-person show—in which a celebrity like Elaine Stritch told about the obstacles and vices they struggled to overcome to achieve success—was primed to be lampooned.

Given that the show already had great songs like "Step Brother to Jesus," "The Strumpet of Samaria," and a sendup of the predictable staple of musicals in general, Capathia Jenkins singing "A Big Black Lady Stops the Show," my job was to help fix the book and punch things up with new dialogue and jokes.

With pals David Steinberg, Larry David, and Marty Short.

So, just as it was with *700 Sundays*, my live-television background was invaluable when it came to going back to my hotel room after watching that night's show, rewriting, e-mailing the new material to Marty, and then staying on the phone with him (sometimes for hours) tweaking what I'd done so it could get put into the next day's performance.

Writing for Marty, given all of his characters, was tantamount to furnishing material for a one-man variety show. Jackie Rogers Jr., Irving Cohen, Ed Grimley, and, my personal favorite, Jiminy Glick, who would interview a celebrity or a daring audience member onstage every night and grill them with such pressing questions I'd written such as, "If Lincoln were alive today, do you think he'd be happy with his tunnel?" and "Self-flushing toilets—do they actually know when you're finished, or is it just a good guess?"

The real test, however, came when the show moved from San Francisco to Toronto. Because of the new material I was writing and the blocking changes that were now being proposed by the new choreographer, Kathleen Marshall, the show had gone back to being a work in progress. Since the Toronto performances would start the following evening, the cast ended up rehearsing the "new show" in the lobby of the Canon Theatre during the day while performing the show that had been staged in San Francisco at night.

As a result, the Toronto run was rocky, which was frustrating, as those audiences were seeing a production that would soon no longer exist. I remember standing in the back of the theater, resisting the urge to run up and down the aisles, shouting that they should disregard certain scenes, and reciting the changes I'd already made to the show they were watching.

A poignant moment came at the opening-night party at the Toronto home of Eugene and Deborah Levy, when Eugene raised a glass, offered a warm toast wishing the show good luck, cited how great it was that so many of the old Second City people who had started out together were there, and referred to Gilda, whose spirit he said was in the room with us. During which Marty and I looked at each other and nodded—as if the request Gilda had made so many years before had finally come true. We were friends. And our collaboration was proving to be successful as well, because by the time *Martin Short: Fame Becomes Me* had moved to its next stop at the LaSalle Bank Theatre in Chicago, the show that had been rehearsed in the Canon Theatre's lobby was now performed in front of enthusiastic audiences and critics who encouraged us to take the show to New York, where we would join *Spring Awakening*, *High Fidelity*, and a revival of *Les Miserables* already on Broadway.

♪♪♪

ON AUGUST 17, 2006, *Fame Becomes Me* opened on Broadway at the Bernard B. Jacobs Theatre. That night was great fun, with so many of our friends and family members in attendance. Of course I sat with Robin and the kids, and, of course, I poked Robin in her arm every time anyone said any of the dialogue that I'd written. One awkward moment ensued, however, when our director, Scott Wittman, was kind enough to thank me for my contributions from the stage during the curtain call. I took a bow, then spotted the original writer seated with his family, embarrassed that his name went unmentioned, even though he still shared credit with Marty as co-author, while my credit was for "additional material by."

In the weeks afterward, as I had done with *700 Sundays*, I went to as many performances as I could. I wrote new jokes for Marty in an attempt to keep things fresh as well as to provide myself with an effective diversion from the TV pilot script I should have been working on. While the audiences were wildly enthusiastic, there was always one person who seemed to enjoy the shows more than anyone: Marty's wife, Nancy.

For the most part, unless there happened to be an empty seat in the theater, I would watch the show from the back of the house. With pen and pad in hand, I'd take my notes. On most nights, Nancy stood nearby watching her husband tell jokes, sing, dance, fly, and send the audience into hysterics. Nancy laughed harder than everyone. I was so taken by her appreciation of Marty's antics that I often watched her watch the show. The pure joy on her face. The laughs as if she was seeing and hearing things for the very first time. Counting out-of-town performances, previews, and the Broadway run, it would be safe to say that I stood next to Nancy well over a hundred times and always saw her react the same way.

"Why can't you look at me with the same wonderment?" I asked Robin.

"Do something wonderful and I will."

"Boy, you Jewish women are so demanding."

CHAPTER 11

UNFINISHED BUSINESS

(Saying Goodbye to Garry)

IRONICALLY ENOUGH, the call came to me at the Friars Club, where Bernie Brillstein had first phoned me about Garry Shandling some thirty years earlier. This time it was my daughter Sari, who wanted me to learn about it from her first instead of being shocked by hearing about it elsewhere.

Garry had died? I googled him. There it was. *Garry Shandling Dead at Age 66.* No, not possible. Maybe it was one of those internet hoaxes where a famous person is reported dead but it's proven to be false? Like Harrison Ford? And didn't that happen to Miley Cyrus? And Adam Sandler? I googled Garry again. All the news outlets had stories. There was also a report from the Los Angeles coroner.

I left the club, stunned, and met my friend Carol Leifer, who had just arrived in New York, for drinks at the bar in the Peninsula Hotel. Few words were said. In fact, the virtual silence was not broken until that evening, when I started crying in a Japanese restaurant and Robin reached across the table to hold my hand.

A death in the family. Calls to and from Judd Apatow. Larry David. Bob Saget. Kevin Nealon. Sarah Silverman. Condolences. Commiseration. Despite the nature of some of our individual histories with Garry, we all reached out in sadness. I even heard from Brad Grey. That one surprised me, given how things had wound up between him and Garry. Maybe he merely wanted to see how I was doing, or perhaps he was harkening back to a fun, simpler time when they were both starting out. When they were sleeping on each other's couches. Well before things got really ugly with accusations of financial malfeasance by Brad that resulted in a highly publicized $100 million lawsuit. A far less complicated time.

♪♪♪

THE DAZE LINGERED. As did the incongruity. It seemed unnatural to think about Garry and feel sad. To give interviews during which television personalities showed clips of our co-creation before asking me questions using words like "was" and "did." A tribute I was asked to write for *Variety* was somewhat cathartic but hardly enough. I'd been through this before; still, this was different. Gilda's death had taken a wider turn. There had been time to prepare. And sum up. The phone calls. That late-night walk on that Santa Monica beach. Garry left without warning. There were loose ends. Words still waiting to be said.

We had been making progress. After Robin brokered the peace in Atlantic City, slowly we'd been reestablishing our friendship—or were we establishing a real friendship for the first time?—but it was not easy. After *It's Garry Shandling's Show* ended, we both went to work on different projects, so our seeing each other had to be voluntary as opposed to working together in the same offices and studio every day. I discovered that I had to be the pursuer—and if Garry returned one out of every three calls or e-mails, I had to be happy about that one as opposed to unhappy about the two that went ignored.

We did see each other intermittently but usually at an occasion instigated by someone else. We were once both invited to Rob and Michele Reiner's house to watch the Academy Awards in their screening room. While Garry and I sat next to each other, Warren Beatty, whom Garry was friends with, sat on his other side. When the show was over, Garry and I went for a walk and I asked him if he was okay and why he kept rubbing his thigh. Garry said that before the show, Warren told him that he'd tap him on the leg whenever a woman he'd slept with appeared on the screen and now, three hours later, his leg was black and blue.

The basketball games allowed us to see each other more regularly. Those now-legendary Sunday afternoons when anyone who was in town went to Garry's house in Brentwood to play on his court. In that setting Garry and I were fine playing among Ben Stiller, Judd Apatow, Al Franken, David Duchovny, Adam McKay, Kevin Nealon, Jay Roach, Adam Sandler, Bob Odenkirk, Wayne Federman, Jay Kogen, Bob Costas, Sasha Baron Cohen, et al. I'm a big jock, but basketball was never my sport. For some reason when I'm on a basketball court, my arms and legs behave as if they were never introduced to each other. So I do remember getting upset with Garry right before one game when he pointed to a player on the other team and said, "Guard her." What an insult, I thought. "Yeah, I'm not a great player, but, Jesus, Garry." It was only when the girl, Sarah Silverman, started popping baskets from the outside and ran me ragged driving to the hoop and grabbing rebounds like they were going out of style that I looked at Garry and we both started laughing again. "There was no class system at Garry's game," says Sarah. "The PA or writers' assistant was the same as the movie star. We were all just playing basketball and trading stories. Is there anything better in the whole world?"

The games were fun and competitive and a welcome break from the mental stress that we'd all experienced during our workweeks. For a couple of hours we were athletes again, our diminished skills inflated by overcompensation—I didn't mean to break Al Franken's thumb, I swear.

"You broke my thumb," Franken says today. "You were guarding me, and I was passing the ball to my left. You took a very fast, hard swipe. The moment I got the pass off cleanly, you caught my thumb with the full force of your swipe and broke it. I think you drove me to the hospital. The doctor was supposedly a specialist (it's a Sunday) on this sort of thing. My thumb was very swollen by this point, and he gave me a plastic thumb cast that fit over the swollen thumb. Then he wondered aloud what size to give me for when the swelling went down and my thumb was back to its normal size. I looked at him and then slowly raised my left hand and showed him my other thumb."

I swear I don't remember this. Just like I don't remember dislocating Judd Apatow's shoulder. "To this day, my right arm goes a little lower than my left," says Judd. "Every time I put on a shirt, I think about you."

But it was the people, in particular the younger writers, who got to Garry's house well before the games started and stayed after I left who intrigued me. The ones who felt a kinship with one another because, as *Ibiza* director Alex Richanbach said, "We all had the same comedy dad."

Judd says, "I really didn't know why Garry let me hang out with him. I was thrilled, mind you, but I was a kid and didn't have that much to offer. He was living with Linda Doucette at the time, and the three of us would go to dinner or just sit around and watch TV in his house. It was like I was their experimental kid."

I remember Garry taking such pride in Judd's success. And Ed Solomon's. And the messages he left for me when he read the book and then saw the staged version of *Bunny Bunny*.

There are a number of people who have surpassed the role of mentor to writers. Those who not only gave them their initial breaks, for which they were eternally grateful and loyal, but who also taught them the craft of writing—usually by the osmosis of being in their company. Producers Garry Marshall, Jim Brooks, Norman Lear, and Lorne Michaels to name a few.

But I also learned that Garry took personal care of his progeny. Assuming their medical bills. Imparting advice about finances. And when we had a home invasion, during which Robin was held at gunpoint, Garry immediately dispatched security specialist Gavin de Becker to psychologically counsel us in the aftermath.

Judd told me a story that Norman Lear related to him about Frank Sinatra. How Sinatra would look in the newspaper and, if he saw a story about someone who was in need, he'd send that person a check. Norman did that, too. Lorne Michaels is exceedingly generous in many ways. And I remember Penny Marshall telling me that her brother, Garry, would sit with his staff and, aware of his power to do so, refer to a stack of resumes and say, "Whose life are we going to change today?" Tangible gifts in addition to the joys their talents gave to people.

Kelly Carlin told me, "The day after my dad died, Garry called me. I didn't know Garry. We'd never met. But he wanted to reach out to me. I remember being on the phone with him sitting on my bathroom floor while we both wept. It was very surreal. You see, before my dad died, I knew not a single comedian. And now I was on the phone with one of my favorites, and we were consoling each other. Garry says he would not have been who he was without my dad's words. I know I would not be who I am today without Garry's."

Was Garry always like this? I wondered. Did I somehow miss these traits our first time around, while we were so preoccupied with our work? Or was it because we had been locking horns? Sure, I knew of Garry's spirituality all along. The loss of an older brother, Barry, at a young age that filled him with questions. The revelations after his own near-fatal auto accident. The cabin in Big Bear where he went to meditate. The crystals he collected way before they were in vogue. His choosing to go to a certain West Hollywood restaurant because it had "good energy." The books he gave me that had "God" in the title.

Or did that spirituality take stronger root after we parted? Is that when he underwent his otherworldly growth spurt? The first year of *It's Garry Shandling's Show* for my birthday he gave me more than twenty store-bought VHS cassettes of every one of Woody Allen's movies. But for my fiftieth he sent me the book *Letters to a Young Poet* by Rainer Maria Rilke and circled the paragraph that read, "Embrace your solitude and love it. Endure the pain it causes, and try to sing out with it. For those near to you are distant."

I remember speaking with Judd after he'd sent me a cut of his brilliant HBO documentary *The Zen Diaries of Garry Shandling* and telling him that it was reminiscent, in form, to HBO's two-part documentary about George Harrison called *Living in the Material World*. "Part One" was about the early years and the Beatles, whereas "Part Two" was concentrated on George as a solo performer and, even more so, his spirituality. I appear in "Part One" of *The Zen Diaries of Garry Shandling*. Somehow I missed the "Part Two" of Garry's life, the part where it seems he was getting closer to what he had always been looking for.

For example, when Garry took up boxing, it was more than a sport.
It took on religious overtones. At one of our last dinners he drew analo-
gies between boxing and life. Speaking metaphorically about picking
oneself up off of the mat after a knockdown while bobbing and weaving
in his chair across the table from me. "Are you davening?" I half joked.
Because in a way, he was. It was a part of his next step in the search for
the peace he so desperately sought. A step that was somehow at odds
with his comedy, which was born from angst—the wellspring of his
humor in a world where he was never quite comfortable. His version of
Gilda wanting to return as a ballerina?

If these were the new rules, if this was the evolved Garry, I was
more than willing to follow an intangible beyond the "material world."
I opted to have Garry in my life because, in a way that I found both baf-
fling and soothing, we were still connected. Whatever it was that drew
us toward each other to begin with—as much as it was clouded by a
bevy of irritants, as happens in so many long-term relationships—still
existed, and all else was subject to redefinition.

Our e-mails were superficial, mundane exchanges that remained
guardedly above the waterline. I knew he had been sick, but I honestly
didn't know the extent and gravity of things. So when I would send a
friendly e-mail asking, "How you doing?" as a way of reviving dialogue,
I didn't know that his response of "Getting better every day" was, at
times, literal.

But at least we were communicating, and I was happy about, it
so when I took my next trip to Los Angeles, we made a point of trying
to see each other. The pretext was to talk about the next steps in sell-
ing *It's Garry Shandling's Show* to HBO or a streaming network like
Netflix or Amazon. To catch up. Mostly just to be talking again. But
when e-mails back and forth proved frustrating—"Dinner Sunday
night?" he suggested, but I couldn't—"I go back to New York Sunday
morning, because we start rehearsals Monday"—we looked at the
week ahead and made a date to speak Thursday night. Garry died
Thursday morning.

⟋⟋⟋

BECAUSE I WAS HOME IN New Jersey, I wasn't able to participate in a last basketball game at Garry's house. I spoke to Kevin Nealon, saw the picture of everyone on that familiar court, and wished I had been there. So when Judd asked if I wanted to speak at Garry's memorial, Robin and I flew to Los Angeles. It was a pilgrimage of sorts, as people came from all over to the Wilshire Ebell Theatre to pay tribute to a man who, as Bill Maher put it, "Changed television twice."

"I have physical and emotional pieces of him all over my apartment," says Sarah Silverman. "From advice he's given that resonates daily, to old furniture of his he gave me for my first roommate-less apartment that I still have today. From his jar of weed to his Bar Mitzvah yarmulke to photos of us playing ball. It's not a shrine; it's not all in one place or even in plain view. Just pieces of him here and there."

Just like that *Variety* article was a form of therapy, as it forced me to revisit our relationship, just as I had done when I found refuge in *Bunny Bunny*, writing a eulogy for Garry gave me another shot at being in touch. Sitting there listening to the speakers before me describing different versions of the same Garry. Anecdotes about events that all of us either experienced or that, at the very least, sounded typical. Everyone getting laughs reciting Garry's jokes. Funny people interspersed with footage of Garry dressed in robes philosophizing about writing from the core; that the jokes will come later. Me ending my tribute telling Garry's "fingers in the ass" joke, not realizing that I would be followed by a Buddhist priest, who, to my great relief, was laughing when he replaced me at the podium. The reception afterward, where a few hundred people who knew one another because they either worked or played basketball with Garry gathered and became reacquainted. And the collective feeling that if there is indeed a place we go after our body's life is over, Garry was ready for it. It was also where Norman Lear, the consummate producer, who was then ninety-four years old, approached and started giving me notes on my eulogy. I listened politely and thanked him. But when he continued, I said, "Norman, I appreciate what you're saying, but the memorial's over. It's not like Garry's going to die again and I'll have another shot at it."

It was a memorable night, and thoughts of it lingered for weeks. Months. As for me, it had taken many years filled with many changes to finally reconnect with my old writing partner. And, like so many others who are better at their craft because of Garry, he is still writing with me to this day.

CHAPTER **12**

ANOTHER KIND OF COLLABORATION

(Dave Barry and Others Who Spend Their Days Alone)

ONE OF THE GREAT PERKS of doing what I do is that you get to meet the people whose work you admire. And have been inspired by. And, if you're lucky, somewhere down the line you get to work with them. And, if you're extremely lucky, they also become your friends. Yes, that last sentence probably sounds a little naïve. And a little awestruck, given that it stands to reason that with success and longevity you eventually get to cross paths with everyone and opportunities naturally present themselves. True, but there is a subtle difference between starting out as friends on the same footing who are struggling and rising through the ranks together, and the satisfaction of achievement you feel when someone whose body of work influenced the very reason you entered your chosen field in the first place suddenly becomes a peer.

I remember having this discussion with Tina Fey on the set of *30 Rock* when she appeared on an episode of *Inside Comedy* hosted by David Steinberg. I was a producer on this series where David, a supreme interviewer who guest hosted *The Tonight Show* a record number of times when Johnny Carson went on vacation, spoke with prominent people in all walks of comedy. During a break, I wondered aloud who had the bigger thrill when it came to *SNL*. Those of us who helped launch this new show and played a role in its growth into the institution it was to become? Or a kid who grew up watching that show, dreaming of someday being on it, and who eventually stepped onto that stage in that very studio as a cast member? Though we envied each other's experiences, I still hold firm that there's something more special about the latter. Seeing the actual incarnation of all you wanted to do and attaining your goal by actually becoming a part of it. As Rachel Dratch says, "I started watching *SNL* in the very first season, when I was in third grade, because I was sleeping over at a friend's house and her older brother was watching it and I was immediately fascinated by it and would try to watch it every time I had a sleepover or could finagle staying up that late. And then, after Second City, auditioning and getting THE CALL from Lorne that I got the job, it still seems like a dream sometimes! Hearing Don Pardo say your name and being up on THAT STAGE!"

✦✦✦

I MET DAVE BARRY ON October 23, 2005. I remember because it was the date Steve Martin was given the Mark Twain Prize for American Humor. Steve was a fan of Larry David's and wanted him to be one of the speakers at the Kennedy Center but didn't know him at that point, so I told one of the show's producers, Mark Krantz, that I would speak to my buddy on their behalf.

"This would be a great thing for you," I told Larry.

"I have to give a speech?" he asked.

"Yeah. If you want, I can help you with it. It could be fun."

"It's in Washington?"

"Yep. Washington, D.C. The place with the big monuments that they light up at night. If you want, I'll also go there so I can help with any last-minute changes in your speech and pick up a few souvenirs for my kids."

Other speakers included old friends like Carl Reiner, Tom Hanks, Eric Idle, Lorne Michaels, Lily Tomlin, Mike Nichols, Marty Short, Paul Simon—as well as the Pulitzer Prize–winning humorist Dave Barry, whom I introduced myself to at the after-party. Although he is only two years older I had long been a fan of Dave's syndicated columns and books but thought that would be a rather trite thing to say—so as I approached him, I opted for another opener.

"You're a big fan of mine, aren't you?" I said.

"Huge," he answered in a tone that could best be described as profoundly sarcastic.

"That's what I figured," I said. "So perhaps I'll allow you to be my friend."

"You do this a lot? Approach people you don't know and beg them to be your friend?"

"Would it hurt your feelings if I said there were others before you?"

"Not in the least."

"You're my twelfth."

And we became friends. E-mails. Phone calls. Late-night dinners when we ran into each other on our respective book tours. Plus Robin and Dave's wife, Michelle Kaufman, a sportswriter for the *Miami Herald*, immediately liked each other a lot. It was easy. To the point that when I suggested we write a novel together, he felt comfortable enough to respond by saying, "How the hell are we going to do that?" Most likely in deference to the fact that, according to Waze, it was approximately 1,094.2 miles from my driveway in Short Hills, New Jersey, to his in Coral Gables, Florida.

Okay. Good point. Still, we explored the possibility, because everything else we were both working on were solitary endeavors, and the thought of a collaboration of any kind was an attractive diversion. It would be social. There'd be immediate feedback. Built-in editing. And something to look forward to being e-mailed other than ads for penis enlargers that don't work—or so I'm told.

The premise we came up with was simple and made sense considering our geographic challenges. Dave's then eleven-year-old daughter, Sophie, played soccer in a local AYSO league. Because my and Robin's children had done the same years before, I was quite familiar with all the goings-on, especially among parents, and called Dave.

"Okay, here's the situation. It's a tie score in the championship game of a local soccer league. In the waning seconds, a girl kicks a goal that would make her team the winner, but, just as the celebration is about to begin, the ref calls her offsides, thus nullifying the goal. The girl's father, an über soccer dad and a supreme asshole, goes ballistic, and a feud ensues between him and the referee. It starts off as a local contention between two suburban New Jersey neighbors but escalates to the point that it has international implications, and, who knows, maybe there's a new pope as a result."

We were both excited about the idea. He wanted to be the soccer dad, me the ref, and we would alternate chapters. A tag team. I went first and chose to make my character a timid man named Philip Horkman who owned a pet store that was struggling due, in no small part, to the fact that it was called The Wine Shop, because his wife's parents (Mr. and Mrs. Wine) gave him the money to open the place on the condition that it be named after them. He was a tightly wound good citizen who played by the rules and more than likely never had a bowel movement larger than a nickel.

I e-mailed the pages to Dave with no knowledge whatsoever what his character would be like and how he would advance the story, as we had no outline. We were, in effect, going to improv a novel by simply reacting to what the other person presented and building upon it.

What Dave sent back was shocking. He fashioned his character to be an ill-mannered lout named Jeffrey Peckerman who was certain he was the only sane person on the planet and who, to avenge the nullification of his daughter's goal, stole a prized lemur from The Wine Shop. And Dave was absolutely right. If my guy was going to be a straightlaced person, his had to be the polar opposite, as it would enhance the conflict between them.

And so our back-and-forth process began. For me it was like corresponding with a deranged pen pal, as my character Horkman's attempt to retrieve the lemur segued into a car chase, there was an encounter with a terrorist dressed as Chuck E. Cheese, and when the two of them were ultimately pursued by authorities, these strange bedfellows stowed away on an ocean liner and had to depend on each other during their ensuing adventures, which brought democracy to Cuba, much-needed food to the starving citizens of Somalia, and peace to the Middle East. Their journey, in the spirit of Steve Martin and John Candy in *Planes, Trains and Automobiles* or Peter Falk and Alan Arkin in *The In-Laws* was fun. At the suggestion of our editor, Neil Nyren, we titled the book *Lunatics*, and, once again, I learned a few things from the person I was collaborating with.

First, the speed with which Dave wrote. I like to think that my background in live television prepared me to write quickly (from the core, as Garry used to put it) and not regard anything as too precious. That is, getting it down on paper fast is important, given the expectation that the words will be edited a number of times before they're either spoken by an actor or read by those who still read.

However, Dave, more than likely tapping into the muscle that allowed him to bang out newspaper columns for over thirty years, wrote and sent me his chapters, for the most part, the next day. While it sometimes took me close to a week to conceive of and then write my installments, Dave not only did his with incredible dispatch, but in the end his chapters were the ones that needed the least tweaking. I say "in the end" because we'd decided at the outset that we wouldn't edit each other until we finished the manuscript. With no outline or detailed blueprint to follow, we figured that the details would be addressed after we concluded our story and were certain that it tracked. The lone exception to this plan, however, was when . . . Well, I'll let Dave explain it:

> *Before I met Alan, the only writing collaborator I'd had was Ridley Pearson, with whom I wrote the Starcatchers series of young-adult books for Disney. Alan and Ridley have very different approaches to writing. Ridley is very focused and organized. He pays close attention to plot details; he knows exactly what he's going to write, and why. So I always knew exactly what I was going to get from Ridley.*

Not so with Alan. He was fine with winging it; he did not feel a compelling need to know exactly where our book was going. For example, when we were writing Lunatics, *Alan sent me a chapter that ended with a major surprise plot development. Specifically, Alan had killed off the major characters. I wrote him an e-mail pointing out that we were only about a third of the way through the book, which seemed a tad early to be whacking the people whose actions had, until then, been the entire point of the book. To his credit, Alan did not become defensive. He agreed that he was an idiot, and redid the chapter in such a way that the main characters were still alive at the end.*

This is one of his better qualities: He always readily admits when he has done something idiotic. Which—and I say this as a friend—happens often.

Lesson learned. But Dave, like so many others, also found it necessary to call attention to the size of my head. And while I agree that God was not stingy when he presented me with this skull and these facial features when I was born, to listen to them you'd think that my head was big enough to affect tides. "When Alan and I appear together in public, I like to bring up the subject of his head size right away," says Dave, "because I realize it is making the audience members uneasy, and I want to reassure them that there's nothing to worry about. 'You may feel the gravity field around Alan's head,' I say reassuringly, 'but it will be just a gentle tug, nothing to worry about, although you should keep a firm grip on your jewelry or small children.'" Rob Reiner also notes, in what in football terms would be called "piling on": "In the movie *North*, Alan played a Little League coach, but we couldn't find a baseball cap big enough for him. Even the adjustable ones were too small. So we had to call the hatmaker, who put on an extension like they do with seat belts for overweight people on airplanes."

ƒƒƒ

LUNATICS SOLD WELL, BUT, MORE important, Dave and I went on a book tour together, where I had the rare opportunity, after we both went onstage and made audiences laugh with our respective presentations, to sit behind a table and watch long lines of fans wait to meet and take selfies with Dave and even hand me their phones so I could snap those pictures for them. In literary circles Dave Barry is a big star, who introduced me to other bestselling authors when he asked if I wanted to become a member of the Rock Bottom Remainders—a band whose members have included Stephen King, Amy Tan, Scott Turow, Mitch Albom, Ridley Pearson, Carl Hiaasen, Frank McCourt, James McBride, Greg Isles, Roy Blount Jr., Mary Karr, and guest singer Adam Mansbach (*Go the Fuck to Sleep*), with whom Dave and I co-wrote a parody of the Passover Haggadah and *A Field Guide to the Jewish People*.

Founded in 1991 by Kathi Goldmark, a media publicist based in San Francisco who later married band member Sam Barry (Dave's brother), the Remainders have played at book festivals across the country and even appeared at the opening of the Rock & Roll Hall of Fame. While they describe themselves as mediocre—an adjective that may, in fact, be a slight exaggeration—their performances are enhanced by legitimate musicians like saxophonist Erasmo Paulo and drummer Josh Kelly and have attracted the likes of actual rock stars Warren Zevon, Bruce Springsteen, Judy Collins, and Roger McGuinn, who's been a band member for over ten years.

"Would you like to be a Remainder?" Dave asked me on the phone.

"I'd love to, but I can't sing and I don't play an instrument."

"Sounds like you're going to fit in just fine," he answered.

So I "perform" with them. I don't have a solo. They don't even trust me with a tambourine. In fact, I wouldn't be surprised if I found out that my mic was not attached to any power source as I unabashedly wail away as a backup singing, "Da doo run run run, da doo run run," in a voice that sounds more like the plaintive cries of a wounded animal than anything even remotely musical. I usually stand between Mary Karr and Scott Turow, who take turns tapping me on the back to signal when I should start and stop singing. As Dave so poetically describes it, "Sometimes when we're playing, I will glance over to where the non-instrument-holders hang out, and there will be Alan, engaging in bizarre bodily gyrations and emitting unnatural noises that have nothing remotely to do with the song we are playing, or any song ever performed on the planet Earth. This reassures me. I think, I may not be playing the exact right chord here, but at least I'm not doing that."

The songs are, by and large, oldies, and so are the band's audiences. Sometimes as many as 1,200 middle-aged book-lovers are singing, dancing, and clapping along to "Midnight Hour" and "La Bamba," and hopefully laughing when the band throws me out there to tell jokes while they set up for their next song. I would write some of those jokes here, but you've already read most of them on the preceding pages, so I'm loath to waste your time.

In a sense, I regard the Remainders as a different form of the Sunday basketball games at Garry Shandling's house. Or those late-night dinners at Elaine's. Writers who spend their working hours alone getting together to do something other than writing. I remember meeting Stephen King for the first time when the Remainders performed in Minneapolis in 2019. He was a great, surprisingly funny guy with whom Robin and I became instant friends. Being a fan of his incredible body of work, beginning with the novel and motion picture *Carrie*, I just silently prayed that he wouldn't telekinetically seal the doors of the venue we were playing in and set the place on fire.

Another great diversion that gets me out of the house and among fellow human beings is *Celebrity Autobiography*. Susie Essman is a terrific comedienne and close friend who, after Larry David saw her be particularly hilarious on a Comedy Central roast of Jerry Stiller, called her the next day and offered her the role of Susie Greene on *Curb Your Enthusiasm*. After we moved back to New York, it was Susie who recommended me to Eugene Pack and Dayle Reyfel, who cocreated this show where actors get on a stage and read passages from celebrities' autobiographies. While you're not allowed to change any of the words, readers can use dialect, editorialize with facial gestures, and, trust me, it's extremely funny when the likes of Matthew Broderick, Kristen Wiig, Rachel Dratch,

Mario Cantone, Nathan Lane, Laraine Newman, Rob Reiner, etc., read aloud the indulgences of people like Joan Lunden who seemed to think it was important for people to know what order she put her clothes on in the morning. Or to hear Dick Cavett portray one of the Jonas Brothers. One show I was doing a mash up with Florence Henderson where I was to read from Tommy Lee's book and she from Pamela Anderson's. There was a passage in Tommy's book where he wrote that when he had written that he was smitten with Pamela's good looks when he first met her, he couldn't stop himself from licking her face from her chin up to her forehead. So I said to Florence beforehand, "When we get to this part, I'll pretend to lick your face," but she replied, "No, lick it." To make sure I heard her correctly, I said, "Really? Lick it?" and she insisted, "Yes, really lick my face!" in a tone that almost sounded like a command. So when

Me licking Christie Brinkley's face. Easily the 3rd, 4th, 9th, and 14th best night of my life. Credit: Thomas Kochie

we got to that part onstage, I looked to the audience and said, "Okay, here comes the part where I lick Mrs. Brady's face," and proceeded to do so to their enjoyment. Little did they know that it took a few days to remove all of Florence's makeup from my tongue and that I had a much better time months later when I read the same piece with supermodel Christie Brinkley who also insisted that I lick *her* face.

Most of the readers who partake in *Celebrity Autobiography* are terrific actors. And while I am able to hold my own just being me, I find myself marveling at their talents while at the same time they ask me questions about writing.

It's often the people who do what we can't who are a source of intrigue. Not unlike when Robin threw me a surprise fortieth birthday party in a gym in Santa Monica and invited a number of athletes like Olympian Mark Spitz and New York Mets ballplayers like Rusty Staub and Keith Hernandez, who kept staring at funny people like Garry Shandling, Buck Henry, Laraine Newman, and Martin Mull, who were on the other side of the gym staring back at them.

But even when it comes to people in the comedy field, there are certain folks I am simply in awe of. People whose minds operate on a different (higher?) plane than the one I inhabit. Like how comedian John Mulaney does a brilliant routine about how out of place Donald Trump is in the White House without ever mentioning his name but by using the metaphor of a horse in a hospital.

I remember as early as when I was with *Saturday Night Live*, sitting at the table during a read-through, secretly feeling a slight degree of competition when a fellow writer had written a sketch I felt I could have thought of. Because while I loved how they executed them, those sketches were within the realm of my sensibility; we were playing on the same field. However, there are also ideas that I simply appreciate as being otherworldly—ideas that were born from a place that I didn't know existed, let alone be able to access. So when Michael O'Donoghue wrote a commercial parody for a product called Shimmer, which was both a floor wax and a dessert topping, or when Dan Aykroyd wrote Bass-O-Matic, which was a blender that could be used by anyone who wanted to drink a fish, I just sat back and let them take me wherever they wanted us to go.

Just like I had no other choice than to marvel when I was once at Carl Reiner's house and he pointed into his living room and asked, "Did I ever tell you what happened behind those curtains?" When I said that I hadn't, Carl proceeded to tell me that one Saturday night many years before, he and his wife, Estelle, had returned home after seeing a movie and were greeted by their then sixteen-year-old son, Rob, and his friend Albert Brooks. After exchanging pleasantries about their respective evenings, Carl and Estelle started upstairs, when Rob called them back down and said, "Mom, Dad, Albert has something he wants to show you."

They came back downstairs, where Albert took a doily off of a coffee table, draped it loosely over his held-together wrists, and declared, "I'm an escape artist. I can get out of anything. Now, I'm going to go behind those curtains, and when I come out, I will have extricated myself from this doily." Remember, this was a plain, regular doily, and it was not tied around Albert's wrists but simply resting on top of them. And then, he disappeared behind the curtains, and Carl and Estelle began laughing their asses off when the curtains started billowing this way and that as if there was a struggle going on behind them. And they laughed even more when they heard a body drop to the floor and watched the curtains flail outward again as the body rolled to the left and then to the right and back and forth again before a befuddled Albert emerged with the doily still lying upon his outstretched hands and sheepishly said, "I don't know what happened—it usually works."

Again, Albert was sixteen years old when he thought of this! Some months later, when I ran into Albert in Los Angeles and asked him about this, he paused for a moment and then reached back as if connecting with a distant memory and said, "Oh, yeah, I remember when I did that." Huh? Trust me, if I had the ability to think of a bit like that, I would've gone door-to-door performing it for anyone who wouldn't call the police on me.

CHAPTER **13**

GIANT SHADOWS

(Lessons from Heroes)

I WAS ONCE in an elevator talking with Mel Brooks when it stopped on a floor, its doors opened, and an Indian woman, dressed in a sari, stepped in. Mel indicated the red dot in the middle of her forehead and whispered to me, "Her coffee's ready."

I debated just where in this book I should tell this story. I knew I wanted to include it because it was funny, though in today's world quite politically incorrect. I suspect I've decided to mention it here because, no matter how old you are, certain people continue to be inspirations, no matter how old *they* are.

While consulting on David Steinberg's Showtime series *Inside Comedy*, I was on the set when David spoke with Carl Reiner and Mel Brooks—separately, but they were edited into the same episode. At this point in their lives, the two of them, who were well into their nineties, watched movies at Carl's house four to five nights a week. It was such a sweet image: two old friends who had contributed so much to the comedy culture spending this kind of quiet time together. Yet they were as sharp as ever, because when David asked Carl which movies they watched, he said, "Any one that has the phrase 'Secure the perimeter,'" while Mel, when asked the same question, replied, "Mostly *The Bourne Ultimatum*." When David pressed him for an elaboration, asking, "What do you mean, mostly *The Bourne Ultimatum*?" Mel explained, "We're at that age where we forget who the bad guy is, so every night we sit there saying, "I think it's him. No, I think it's *him*. Maybe it's that one. Or maybe *that* one."

Again, I truly believe funny is innate. It's a mind-set of how you look at the world. From what angle you view it. It's about one's inner wiring. And the battle scars accumulated during one's trek from one end of life to the other.

Like the story I heard about Phillip Roth, who is probably my favorite author ever. The year was 2016, when Roth was quite sick and there was talk that he could very well be given the Nobel Prize in Literature for his tremendous body of work. But when his close friend Mary Karr learned that the award was given, instead, to Bob Dylan, she went to the hospital to gently break the news to the eighty-four-year-old Roth, who spoke first by telling Mary that he had just received good and bad news. The bad news being, "I didn't win the Nobel Prize." The good news? "I'm going to be inducted into the Rock and Roll Hall of Fame."

It's also Larry Gelbart that night when I was seated next to him at a table in a New York nightclub. The wife of a mutual friend had decided that she wanted to jump-start a singing career she had abandoned many years before. A number of us went to see her perform. She was beyond terrible. High notes, low notes, and all the notes in between sounded like a car's engine grinding to its final halt. It was so uncomfortable to all at our front table by the stage that diplomatically averting our eyes became the priority on everyone's agenda. Except for the husband of this singer, who sat in the chair closest to the stage looking adoringly at his wife of fifty-some-odd years. This did not go unnoticed by Larry, who softly elbowed me, gestured in the direction of the enamored husband, who was visibly swooning, and whispered, "Apparently love is also deaf."

As a writer I marveled that I didn't (and couldn't have) come up with that line. So simple. Yet that's the way Larry Gelbart was. Even within the group of Sid Caesar's writers, arguably the greatest gathering of comedic talent in any writers' room in any era, Larry was the acknowledged master.

"My dad always said that Mel was the funniest," says Carl Reiner, "but Larry was the fastest with the best quips."

Larry, like my estimable mentor Herb Sargent, loved words. Funny words, the greater part of the time. Yet his words could be poetic as well. When the legendary Broadway lyricist and playwright Adolph Green passed away, Larry sent a condolence note to Adolph's widow, Phyllis Newman, that read, "That sound you hear is God breaking the mold."

f f f

THE NEXT TIME I WAS with Larry Gelbart was an evening I will never forget. None of us will.

Rob Reiner and his wife, Michele, have a screening room on the property of their Los Angeles home, and on Sunday nights they liked to screen old films for their friends. And because Rob Reiner was, well, Rob Reiner, he was able to invite a guest who had been involved in the making of the movie to watch it with us. A perfect example of this was the time Rob invited us to a screening of *Raging Bull* and brought along its director, Martin Scorsese, to watch it with us. After the lights came up, we all then had the opportunity to ask Marty a million questions about how he shot the fight scenes, how he came to the decision to make it black-and-white, did Robert De Niro gain all that weight for the end of the movie first and then lose it for the beginning or was he thin at the beginning and then ate like a slob to look like a fat pig at the end? These evenings were fun and amazingly informative.

One night we were invited to Rob's house for a screening of restored footage of classic sketches from *Your Show of Shows* and *Caesar's Hour*. His guests of honor that evening were his father, Carl, Mel Brooks, Larry Gelbart, and Sid Caesar—collectively the greatest comedy minds of their or any generation. Also present—at the kids' table, if you will—were Robin and I, Tom Hanks and Rita Wilson, Billy and Janice Crystal, Larry David and his then wife Laurie, and Jon Lovitz.

While Carl, Mel, Larry, Sid, and their wives sat in the last row of the screening room, Robin and I purposely took seats in the row directly in front of Mel, Carl, Larry, and Sid so I could eavesdrop on whatever comments they might make while watching clips they had written and performed in some forty-five years earlier. While everyone was laughing at sketches like "The Bavarian Clock" and "Dressing the General" and "This Is Your Life, Al Dunty," I was able to hear such observations as:

"Woody wrote that piece."

"Yeah, but I think Doc (Neil Simon) gave him that joke about her bonnet."

I was stunned. Despite the vast bodies of work that these luminaries who sat behind me had created—all of the television series, movies, Broadway shows, record albums, and books they'd contributed to the shaping of our culture over the past forty-five years—each one of them was still able to recall who had written which line, joke, or setup nearly a half century later. I'm well aware that whenever I see an *SNL* rerun from the years I was there, I, too, have a pretty good idea about how those sketches came to be. But to sit there in that screening room and listen to those legendary writers in the back row call out the names of those Hall of Fame writers was the equivalent of a baseball player listening to an old-timer tell tales of the greats he played alongside of and against.

When the lights came up, we walked down the steps to the front of the screening room, where we all sat cross-legged on the floor around a large low table filled with food not just from the legendary Beverly Hills restaurant Spago, but, because Rob Reiner is, well, Rob Reiner, the food was prepared by Wolfgang Puck himself. The atmosphere was like a master class where the younger comedy kids (us) were able to ask the legends everything we'd wanted to ask them about themselves ("Sid, is it true you once held Mel upside down by the ankles out of a window?") and about the process of producing those shows ("On *SNL* the entire show is written on Tuesday because we had read-through on Wednesday. Was it the same for you?"), and we even got them to talk about the early days of television, when there were only seven cameras in all of New York City that were divided up among news remotes, televised baseball games, and live TV shows. We were so enthralled that at one point, Carl, who had just seen *Forrest Gump*, asked Tom Hanks to explain how the filmmakers were able to get that feather to float down and land on his shoulder. Tom quickly cut him off, said that the night was about them, and that he would be happy to discuss the feather trick another time. (Which reminds me that I still don't know the answer to that one.)

But the most touching part of the evening was seeing how Carl, Mel, and Larry honored the now-frail Sid Caesar, whose brilliant career, quite arguably, had peaked during the time those shows originally aired. Anytime a question was asked by one of us, the three of them would defer directly to Sid, and either he would answer it, and, if not, Carl, Mel, and Larry made sure to refer to Sid in their response. It was dutiful homage to the man who had given each of them their start, and the rest of us quickly caught on and asked Sid our questions directly.

The next day, Robin and I took our kids to the birthday party of one of Rob and Michele's children. When I saw that Carl and his wife, Estelle, had pulled into the driveway behind us, I asked Carl, "How was last night for you guys? Because as far as we were concerned, we died and went to heaven." In response, Carl put an arm around me and said, "Zweibel, what you kids did for Sid last night added ten years to his life. Thank you."

Since then, I've thought about that night a lot. Compared to those older, bitter writers I'd overheard at that coffee shop in the Brentwood Country Mart in Los Angeles, these men had been able to sustain long careers, weather the challenges of the ever-changing comedy world, and have long, successful marriages and close families while they continued to navigate the rough patches of their crazy career choice of being comedy writers. They are my idols and role models. And I am still impressed by how each one of them remembered how they got started in the business and paid their respects to the man who first took a chance on them. I feel the same way about Lorne Michaels. Not only did he give me my break, but he has been there for me whenever I've needed him since.

"Carl Reiner is the best person ever to have at a dinner party," says Paul Reiser. "He is amazingly skilled at keeping everyone in a conversation, and if conversation falters, he will recharge it himself. One time, there were about twelve of us—men and women—at dinner, and when whatever we were talking about had run its course, and there was a slight lull. Carl, cheerfully, and in the most elegant, non-offensive manner, announced to the group, 'I think we need to come up with a new word for the vagina. I don't think what we have is working.' And of course we went around the table, and it was just ridiculously silly and funny."

≨≨≨

THE LAST TIME I SAW Larry Gelbart was about ten years after that dinner party at the Reiners' home. I was sensitive to the fact that I really didn't know him well enough to ask him for a blurb for one of my books, *Clothing Optional*, which was a collection of my short stories and essays. But after I sent him an e-mail making that exact request, he asked to read about six of the pieces and, after doing so, sent me a blurb for the book jacket along with a personal note that read, "Herb would be proud."

Flattered and grateful, I offered to take him to lunch the next time I went to Los Angeles. He accepted my invitation, and when that day came, he got to the Beverly Hills restaurant a few minutes after I did. His wife drove him, because he was no longer able to. He was wearing black thick-framed eyeglasses and walking slowly with the aid of a cane; his health had markedly worsened since I last saw him that night at Rob and Michele's house. Still, his mind was sharp, and I hung on every word as he answered my questions (most of which I'd scribbled on a crib sheet, so there wouldn't be any dead air) about the writers' room on *Caesar's Hour* and how many drafts of *Tootsie* he'd written. But what started out as an interview soon became a dialogue with, you know, each of us taking turns speaking in what is generally known as a conversation. He even referred to *Clothing Optional* and expressed regret that it hadn't sold better. It had been released the exact same day that the stock market collapsed in 2008, so it happened that people were more concerned about their financial ruin than my essays and short stories.

"So selfish of them," he said, shaking his head.

After about two hours, he then had a question for me.

"Do you sit while you're writing?"

And while this question may sound like an obvious bit of nonsense unworthy of the ink my publisher has used to print it, please bear with me, because some writers write standing up with their computers on a lectern or high table in front of them. There's a writer in Los Angeles who's been known to lie on his stomach with his arms outstretched while pecking away on the laptop lying on the floor in front of him. And in the movie *Trumbo*, Bryan Cranston portrayed Dalton Trumbo—the black-listed screenwriter of such landmark films as *Exodus*, *Roman Holiday*, *Spartacus*, and *Johnny Got His Gun*, which he adapted from his book—as someone who wrote while in his bathtub. Naked. Submerged from the waist down. Cigarette in mouth. With a wooden board perpendicularly extending from one edge of the tub to the other, upon which sat his typewriter. How did Trumbo figure out this was the most productive way for him to write? I wondered. What preliminary steps did he take before he settled on the bathtub? Did he first try writing in the shower, but the pages got wet unless he held an umbrella, but that only slowed down his typing? To me this line of thought is reminiscent of that classic *New Yorker* piece written by Woody Allen that he included in his book *Getting Even*, where he chronicled the Earl of Sandwich's early attempts to perfect the culinary creation named after him. "1741: His first completed work—a slice of bread, a slice of bread on top of that, and a slice of turkey on top of both—fails miserably." Later, in that same diary, the Earl puts two slices of turkey on either side of a single piece of bread. No, still doesn't work. A few years later, the Earl is destitute and can no longer afford turkey or roast beef, so he switches to ham before finally getting it right in 1758.

"Yes, I sit while I'm writing," I said to Larry Gelbart.

"Good, because anyone who does it one of those other ways is fucking crazy," answered the man I'd always regarded as a poet.

"Alan . . . ?"

"Yes?"

"Can you give me a ride home?"

"Sure."

And I did. Then we shook hands. Both said that we had a great time. And that we'd keep in touch. Then he got out. And I sat there and watched as he slowly made his way up the walk before disappearing into his house before I drove away.

CHAPTER **14**

IN PROGRESS

(Here Today)

A FEW YEARS AGO Eric Idle told me that George Harrison's wife, Olivia, had shown him a video of the Traveling Wilburys playing their song "Congratulations" in their kitchen, still trying to figure out how it should go. Experimenting with different chords, different lyrics. And Eric mentioned that strange feeling, even a little frustration, of the viewer, knowing how the song will eventually end up, while those composing it still didn't.

That story is not terribly dissimilar to what once occurred when I was at the Coral Gables, Florida, home of Dave Barry and his wife, Michelle. During halftime of the NBA finals between the Miami Heat and San Antonio Spurs, which we were watching on their TV, Michelle showed me a column she had written some ten years earlier for the *Miami Herald* about a high school basketball sensation from Akron, Ohio, named LeBron James. While extolling his otherworldly heroics, she had been left with the question about what his future would be, whether his talents would prove effective at a higher level of play. Again, with the benefit of hindsight, we knew the eventual fate of that young man; that night we watched him dominate the game on his way to receiving his second consecutive MVP award.

I cite these incidences for an analogous reason. Because as I write these very words, dear reader, you know the ending of this chapter, whereas I don't. I'm referring to a movie that will be called *Here Today*, and though I will be offering this information in real time by giving a running, diary-like account of how this project unfolds, the amount of lag time between when I submit this book's final corrections and the actual date of its publication means that the fate of this movie may still not be determined for another six months. Nonetheless, since my mission on these pages has as much to do with process as it does about results, I will proceed somewhat blindly.

This project started with an article I had written for the now defunct Sunday magazine section of the *Los Angeles Times*. Titled "The Prize," in it, I recounted a true incident about a young woman who had won a lunch with me in a silent auction to raise money for a local charity. The meal proved to be a spectacular disaster. The winner revealed that she only bid $22 to win the auction, had no idea who I was, and had only entered these sweepstakes to get back at her ex-boyfriend, who had bid $21.50. Then she had an allergic reaction to the shellfish salad she was eating, which left her gasping for breath, her face contorted into a Diane Arbus photograph.

I wondered what my obligations to this contest winner were—insult to my pride aside, I couldn't abandon her—so I decided to accompany her to Lenox Hill Hospital, where I signed a bunch of papers, because she didn't have health insurance; purchased an EpiPen at a nearby pharmacy; injected her in her tattooed butt; and ultimately spent upward of $900 for lunch with someone who'd paid only $22 to be with me.

I told this story on one of my appearances on the Letterman show, and the day after it aired, Billy Crystal called and suggested that we write a script, a May-December love story, where the two characters meet as I'd described in that article. I hadn't written with Billy (who wanted to play the older writer) since *700 Sundays*, and while neither of us had any idea how the tale would unfold beyond this eccentric meet cute, we started mapping out a story—long-distance via e-mails and phone calls. Though we'd both worked at *SNL* during different eras, Herb Sargent was still at the show when Billy got there, and he had the same affection for Herb that I did. So we initially decided that Billy's character would be modeled after Herb—a legendary older writer with an illustrious past who consulted on a live television show in New York City.

We called the character Charlie and then searched for another dimension to him so this would be more than your standard older man–younger woman love story that plays the age differences for comedy. And more than the younger woman's (Emma) being a comparative free spirit who shakes the world of the predictably staid Charlie, who's been on automatic pilot since the passing of his wife many years before.

We turned to our personal lives. My dad, eighty-nine at the time, was starting to experience the onset of dementia. It was heartbreaking to see a once so vital man slip into and out of alternating states of disorientation and lucidity. This subject also hit home for Billy when the wife of his dear uncle was also diagnosed and he witnessed firsthand her slow retreat from our reality.

So we discussed the idea that Charlie, suffering the beginnings of this affliction, would be in a race to finish writing an elegy to his deceased wife, before he lost his words. And that Emma ultimately would have to make a decision whether to put her own life and career on hold to be something of a caregiver to a man who's estranged from his children and needs the company of someone who cares.

We worked on the script for three years, dividing scenes that we sent to each other via e-mail and rewriting the other's work while we both worked on other projects as well. Since Billy was going to play Charlie, it was relatively easy for me to write for that character. I say "relatively," because, unlike 700 *Sundays*, which used Billy's specific voice that I'd known for so many years, this would be a role that he'd play, a man with a different voice, past, and point of view. But still, since Billy and I were collaborating, I tended to follow his lead when he had a strong feeling about how he wanted Charlie to behave.

As for Emma, I remember a conversation in which we discussed who would be the prototypical actress to play her, so we could both be writing for the same person. I immediately said "Gilda!" Billy agreed. A cute, quirky woman with her own offbeat philosophy that, in some convoluted way, made perfect sense. Like what Gilda once said after a girlfriend dumped me and I lamented that it hurt so much, I didn't want to ever fall in love again. "You're an idiot, Zweibel. You don't not get a dog because it's going to die someday."

When the first draft (actually our eleventh draft, but one we finally felt good enough about to call the first draft) was finished, it got a positive yet tepid reception from the small circle of people we showed it to. Managers, agents, and spouses agreed about the story's potential but said it wasn't landing the way we were hoping. Emma's character was without defined purpose. She should be more dynamic. Charlie and Emma should not sleep together. We rewrote the script and then had an informal read-through that was more successful than anticipated. Laughs and pathos. Still, when we sent it out, we got no nibbles from Scarlett Johannsen, Kate McKinnon, or Amy Schumer. Emma Stone's manager wouldn't even give it to her to read.

We did more drafts. Made Emma a street singer with recording contract aspirations. And funnier. And took out the scene where they slept with each other. The script became more about love as opposed to romance. And when we were happier with the script, Billy had a great idea. "How about Tiffany Haddish?" he asked me.

I wasn't familiar with Tiffany until she hosted *SNL*, and I thought she was great. Then I watched *Girls Trip* and agreed she would give Emma a hilarious vibrancy that could deepen into something more dramatic if Billy got the chance to direct her to reach a softer, more compassionate place as Charlie's condition worsened. It would be a more challenging acting role than what she had been asked to do up to that point.

Billy's CAA agent, Jimmy Darmody, sent the script to Tiffany's managers, who saw the potential of this movie's providing a career-defining role for their client. In a sense, it had the potential to do for her what *Ghost* had done for Whoopi Goldberg so many years before. They also felt she might have an affinity for the role because her grandmother, with whom she was very close, had dementia. Tiffany read to her. Sang to her. Did all she could to keep her from drifting away to somewhere else.

Tiffany liked the script and immediately attached herself to it. The next step was to find a studio that would be excited to finance the movie. Jimmy and Tiffany's managers made a list, and after Paramount, Universal, and New Line passed—saying they liked the script, but the movie was too small for them—FOX Searchlight responded enthusiastically and asked to meet with Billy as soon as possible. Billy called afterward and said he was heartened by the reception and respect he was afforded by the much-younger people in that room—an occurrence that bears further discussion.

When you start your career, you appeal to others for validation. Quite often it's elders to represent or hire you and contemporaries who want to work with you. When you're on the back nine, age-wise, it's often younger people who can give you work. And while your name and resume may be impressive to those who grew up watching your shows and reading your books and who are respectful in deference to your body of work, whether they feel you're right for their projects is another story. I've experienced that a number of times as someone in a position to hire.

Before the third season of the Shandling show, when Garry and I were really starting to have our differences, Bernie Brillstein and Brad Grey felt that the show needed an adult to help keep us in line. The adult they suggested was Sam Denoff—a legendary television writer whose credits (along with his partner, Bill Persky) we'd grown up seeing on *The Dick Van Dyke Show*, *That Girl*, and countless other shows. Sam was funny and engaging, and the very thought that a writer with such a pedigree might want to join our team was indeed flattering. In fact, the romantic in me secretly hoped that perhaps he could be my consigliere. A trusted advisor. To be to me what Herb Sargent was to Lorne.

So we hired Sam, and the staff was armed with dozens of questions about what it was like to work with Carl Reiner and how the writers' rooms in his era compared with ours, and Sam held everyone spellbound with a story of how he first heard about JFK's assassination while he was on the set of *McHale's Navy*. Sam was charming and highly entertaining, and I could not have felt worse that there wasn't a single word he wrote that we used in any script that season.

I liked Sam a lot. We remained friends after he left the show, and I have often told his son, the Broadway producer Doug Denoff, how much I admired his father. Our differences came down to a matter of sensibility. Sam's was an older style that, as classic as it was, we were parodying. Hiring Sam had been simply a well-intentioned idea that turned out to be a miscalculation for the show and for Sam himself.

I am now ten years older than Sam Denoff was at that time. At the beginning of this book, I was twenty-one years old and writing for Catskill comics. Now, as I write these words, I'm sixty-nine, and by the time this book is published, unless something dreadful happens, I will be alarmingly close to seventy. And I completely understand if anyone is hesitant to have someone twice his or her age on their team. First of all, just as I had my own group of contemporaries that I worked with, younger stars have their own peers who can capture their voices, make one another laugh, and socially feel comfortable with them. No matter how much I appreciate what they're doing, I speak a different language. So while I've always prided myself on acclimating my ear to other people's syntax, inflections, and nuances of character, my reference points and life experiences are different. As a result, just as I had trouble relating to the language of those older comics when I started out, in many cases it would sound just as fraudulent to do so for younger voices. An exaggerated example of this was the middle-grade book I co-wrote with Adam Mansbach titled *Benjamin Franklin: Huge Pain in My* . . . In it, by virtue of vintage postage stamps that magically send letters back and forth through time, a thirteen-year-old boy living in the present starts corresponding with Benjamin Franklin, who's still living in the eighteenth century. As I'd done with Dave Barry in *Lunatics*, Adam and I alternated chapters. Since Adam was in his thirties, it was easier for him to assume the attitude and jargon of the sarcastic teenager, while I am now at an advanced age where it made sense that I would be Benjamin Franklin.

For that same reason, I don't believe I could effectively write for *Saturday Night Live* today. I watch the show every week and cheer for its ongoing success the same way I root for my alma mater to win football games. But just as I can no longer play ball for my old school, I'd sound like an old man trying to figure out what would make younger people laugh if I tried to write for *SNL* some thirty-nine years later. Similarly, while I'm a big fan of Judd Apatow's movies and television shows, I'm not so sure that I could write for his younger characters with the same credibility that he and his writers so effectively have.

I first remember meeting Amy Poehler, Seth Meyers, and Colin Jost on the picket line during a Writers Guild strike. Like so many *SNL* cast members and writers who came to the show after me, their intrigue with the early days of *SNL* was similar to that of children of my generation begging, "Grandpa, tell us what it was like before Thomas Edison invented the light bulb." Their questions were not unlike the ones we had asked Carl Reiner and Mel Brooks and Larry Gelbart and Sid Caesar that night at Rob and Michele Reiners' house. Years afterward, when the Writers Guild gave me an award, I asked Seth to introduce me at the ceremony. He agreed, and it was then, after I did the math, that I realized that Seth was just one year old when *SNL* began. Today most of the current cast and writing staff are younger than my children. This is all a credit to Lorne Michaels for creating and sustaining an institution that remains relevant to this day.

Marty Short always says that it's hard to get a comedy career going but even harder to sustain it. For a writer, sustaining a career can be daunting. "Do I still have something to say?" Or, even worse, "I still have a lot to say, but nobody wants to hear it."

Mickey Mantle, a boyhood hero who was possibly the most popular New York Yankee ever, used to talk about a recurring nightmare he'd had long after he retired from baseball. He would dream that he was standing outside Yankee Stadium and could hear the sounds of the crowd cheering the game inside. He wanted to be a part of it again, but the stadium doors were locked, and the ticket takers at the gate didn't recognize him, so he unsuccessfully tried to tunnel his way into the stadium.

Will I ever feel that way? That I'm no longer a part of a world I've contributed to, even though my mind insists that it's as vital as it always has been? As scary as those thoughts of detachment can get, an inner voice that sounds remarkably like Garry Shandling keeps repeating that if you are a writer, as long as you write from your core, you will connect with your audience. The audience will respond to the validity of your voice and find your words meaningful because of their honesty. The comedy and the jokes will come later.

I've come to believe that a writer should embrace his age and write from the place he is at that moment. I witnessed the sad desperation of those writers from the generation before me who started dyeing their hair, didn't let on that they were grandparents, and didn't dare utter the word "prostate" in any context to someone who could give them work. And in those bygone days before IMDb, I saw them leave their earliest credits off of their resumes to give the impression they were not as old as they actually were. And now, well, so many of my own peers are doing the same.

Writers write. We have to. Or else we explode. Today, I still wake up at 5:30 every morning and write words to be put into the mouths of other people. I follow the examples of heroes like Buck Henry, who, after a bout with bladder cancer followed by a stroke, uses a program on his computer to transcribe the words he speaks that will fill his autobiography. Or Carl Reiner, who, at the age of ninety-seven, not only churns out one book after another but also speaks his mind by tweeting many times a day.

All of which brings us back to *Here Today*. A script whose theme, plot, and overall sensibility were foreign to me years ago. When my life experiences did not include what they do now. But these days they are in my world and seem as natural to write about as it was to write "Samurai Night Fever" back in the third season of *SNL*.

The film was produced by a man named Fred Bernstein. His company is called Astute Films, and his mandate is to make the kind of movies that no one else will. We certainly fall into that category, as *Here Today*, despite the star power of Billy Crystal and Tiffany Haddish, is a smaller, more intimate movie than most, not a broad comedy that would require a huge opening weekend at the box office to be considered successful. By today's standards, its $14 million budget is modest, and care should be taken as to how it is presented and marketed. Billy was the director. There was a lot of goodwill shown to Billy and I when it came to this movie. Fine actors consented to work for a fee lower than their normal quotes, and when we wanted to shoot a scene in the American Museum of Natural History, it was an appeal to Lorne Michaels on their board who helped make it happen. Pre-production took place in WeWork offices in New York City. It's there that all departments like wardrobe, location scouting, etc., set up shop. Casting, which took place in a mid-town studio, brought us a terrific cast that included Anna Deavere Smith, Laura Benanti, Penn Badgely, Alex Brightman, and Louisa Krause. The film also has appearances by Kevin Kline, Sharon Stone, Bob Costas, and Barry Levinson.

Not unlike how we worked when we were doing *700 Sundays*, Billy and I rewrote scenes daily—after incorporating what we learned from casting, and almost every night or early morning once we began

Billy and I the first day of shooting *Here Today*.

production on October 2, 2019, and ended November 14. The shoot was arduous but a lot of fun. Most of the film was shot in and around New York City and Brooklyn, with the exception of a scene that takes place at a lake house we found upstate.

I was now working differently—not so much with Billy my cowriter as I was with Billy the director. Listening to how he envisioned scenes and adapting accordingly. Again I marveled as to how multifaceted his talents were as he brought what we wrote to life. How he choreographed movement, huddled with the director of photography about camera angles and lighting, and his talks with Tiffany, reminding her that she was not playing a comedian but rather a character named Emma who was funny, but also had to react and emote to the demands of the situations she was in. In brief, she had to act. And from everything I've seen and from the reports from Billy who is now editing, Tiffany is quite fantastic in this movie.

To say the least, everyone involved worked very hard and did their best to make our film funny and touching and something that will resonate for all of you who see it. I pray it does, though I'm a little nervous, because, although Roger Ebert is still quite dead, I do fear those snarky reviews that could very well say, *"Here Today* will be gone tomorrow."

While, on the other hand, I already know the gist of my Oscar acceptance speech. Its theme that writers, no matter their age, still have something to say. Plus, the joke I want to tell about my cummerbund. And whom I'm going to thank. Robin. The kids. The grandkids. My parents. Lorne. Gilda. Herb. Garry. Buck. Anyone in my life who ever did or said anything that I could make fun of.

And of course my dear sister Franny—the very first person I ever made laugh. And am still trying to do at 5:30 every morning while I write sitting down.

ACKNOWLEDGMENTS

The English have an expression that, when someone asks, "How're you doing?" the answer is, "Not bad considering the odds." My life has been, for the most part, a charmed one where I've beaten the odds. Where I've been allowed to have an existence where the main objective is laughter—making people laugh and seeking out those voices that help make other people laugh.

Where I've been lucky enough to have found a beautiful wife named Robin who, after forty years of marriage, still makes me laugh more than anyone I know. Robin has been my life partner in so many ways, with the greatest production being the family we've coproduced, consisting of our three children, Adam, Lindsay, and Sari, as well as our five grandchildren, Zachary, Lexi, Jordan, Kylie, and Sydney. And lucky enough, through no doing of my own, to have had parents who encouraged me to enter the world of laughter and who had, at times in those early days, more confidence in me than I did.

There have been so many others that helped immeasurably along the way. Those who were and still remain inspirations. Those with whom I've creatively thrived through the collective energy of our sensibilities. And those who went to bat for me by helping revive a career those times it took a downturn. Not to mention all of my writer and comedian friends who took time out of their very busy schedules to answer the questions I sent them and whose answers provided substance in so many of the sections of *Laugh Lines*. Since these dozens of people's names already fill the pages of this book, after giving it serious thought, I came to the conclusion that to list them and their contributions to my wonderful life

Sari, Lindsay, and Adam—three kids who would've
starved if I didn't stay funny.

in these acknowledgments would necessitate writing this same book again, and you would also have to read it again, which would seem to be, unless I'm very wrong, a waste of everybody's time.

So let's turn our attention to those who made this book happen. First, to my agent Laura Nolan, who not only insisted that I put my story down on paper but who took the time and care to read and meticulously edit each draft of my proposal until she felt it was ready to send it to Jamison Stoltz—my astute, funny, and eternally patient editor, who I hope is still talking to me after everything I've put him through. Jamison is a throwback to a bygone era when book editors were literary giants in their own right, and he is a gift to any author who has the chance to work with him.

A most heartfelt thanks to my friend and fellow Rockbottom Remainders backup singer, the great poet and memoirist Mary Karr who read an early draft of this book and gave me invaluable notes.

And, once again, Robin and for all the hard work she put into gathering photos and memorabilia for this book. The personal nature of this project has truly been a family affair

My late manager Bernie Brillstein deserves a thank-you as big as he was, and I hope he somehow knows that there isn't a day that goes by that I don't think about him. Same with Herb Sargent. And my grandparents Dora and Joseph Bram, who came to this country in the 1920s and showed me by example that laughing is the only way to endure whatever tricks life chooses to play on you.

And before I sign off so you can put this down and turn your attention to whatever it is you do when you're not reading acknowledgments, I would be remiss if I didn't give a hardy shout out to the first face I saw when I was born. Dr. Isaac Nelson, the obstetrician who delivered me on May 20, 1950, in Crown Heights Hospital in Brooklyn, NY. It's been quite a while. Just wanted you to know that I'm generally happy and I've become what I've always wanted to be. So a much belated thank-you, Dr. Nelson. I've been having a great time in this world you brought me into.